WOMEN AND POWER
Perspectives for Family Therapy

Edited by
Thelma Jean Goodrich

W.W. Norton & Company • New York • London

Chapters 1, 4–8, 11–17, 19–24 also appear in *Journal of Feminist Family Therapy*, 3, 1&2, 1991.

A Norton Professional Book

Library of Congress Cataloging-in-Publication Data

Women and power : perspectives for family therapy / edited by Thelma
    Jean Goodrich.
        p.   cm.
    "A Norton professional book."
    Includes index.
    ISBN 0-393-70117-4
    1. Family psychotherapy.   2. Patriarchy – Psychological aspects.
3. Women – Mental health.   4. Power (Social Sciences)   I. Goodrich,
Thelma Jean, 1940–
    [DNLM: 1. Family.   2. Power (Psychology)   3. Women – psychology.
WM 430.5.F2 W8722]
RC488.5.W652   1991
616.89'156 – dc20
DNLM/DLC   91-2554

W. W. Norton & Company, Inc., 500 Fifth Avenue, New York, N.Y. 10110
W. W. Norton & Company, Ltd., 10 Coptic Street, London WC1A 1PU

1 2 3 4 5 6 7 8 9 0

To Mary,
old acquaintance

POWER

Living   in the earth-deposits   of our history

Today a backhoe divulged   out of a crumbling flank of earth
one bottle   amber   perfect   a hundred-year-old
cure for fever   or melancholy   a tonic
for living on this earth   in the winters of this climate

Today I was reading about Marie Curie:
she must have known she suffered   from radiation sickness
her body bombarded for years   by the element
she had purified
It seems she denied to the end
the source of the cataracts on her eyes
the cracked and suppurating skin   of her finger-ends
till she could no longer hold   a test-tube or a pencil

She died   a famous woman   denying
her wounds
denying
her wounds   came   from the same source as her power

1974

Adrienne Rich —
The Dream of a Common Language

THE LIONESS

The scent of her beauty draws me to her place.
The desert stretches, edge from edge.
Rock. Silver grasses. Drinking-hole.
The starry sky.
The lioness pauses
in her back-and-forth pacing of three yards square
and looks at me. Her eyes
are truthful. They mirror rivers,
seacoasts, volcanoes, the warmth
of moon-bathed promontories.
Under her haunches' golden hide
flows an innate, half-abnegated power.
Her walk
is bounded. Three square yards
encompass where she goes.

In country like this, I say, *the problem is always
one of straying too far, not of staying
within bounds. There are caves,
high rocks, you don't explore. Yet you know
they exist*. Her proud, vulnerable head
sniffs toward them. It is her country, she
knows they exist.

I come towards her in the starlight.
I look into her eyes
as one who loves can look,
entering the space behind her eyeballs,
leaving myself outside.
So, at last, through her pupils,

I see what she is seeing:
between her and the river's flood,
the volcano veiled in rainbow,
a pen that measures three yards square.
Lashed bars.
The cage.
The penance.

1975

Adrienne Rich—
The Dream of a Common Language

Contents

III. STORY AND RITUAL

IV. FAMILY THERAPY

V. CLINICAL PRACTICE

Preface

WOMEN AND POWER COMPRISE a worrisome subject — unsettling to discuss and complicated to analyze. For family therapists, it has become an unavoidable subject, raised for us more and more frequently by our clients or our culture, if not by our theory. In hopes of moving it from worrisome to workable, I have called on some of the foremost thinkers and clinicians in our field to write of their efforts to understand and change women's position in the power structure of the family. To that end, the first three sections of the book address the shape, meaning, and impact of power in patriarchy and in the family under patriarchy. The shape, meaning, and impact are different for men and women, and these differences are sharply drawn for us. The fourth section presents issues and approaches for our clinical work. The fifth section contains brief presentations by 14 therapists concerning women and power in their own clinical practice. Some describe ideas that puzzle or challenge; some describe a case; some describe a method.

Women's position in the power structure of the society limits our success as therapists. These limitations are readily apparent and readily acknowledged in all the chapters. Still, there is always the "nevertheless": We must do the work, even so. The limitations give us no excuse. As Jimmy Durante put it, "Them's the conditions that pervail."

Acknowledgments

THANKS BE TO:

Loyce Baker for helping me with my manuscript, my nerves, and my spirit; Lois Braverman for nursing the book along from the beginning; Susan Barrows for giving me her ideas and her support; the contributors for letting all of us in on their work.

Contributors

Judith Myers Avis, Ph. D.
Associate Professor
College of Family and Consumer
    Studies
University of Guelph
Guelph, Ontario, Canada

Michele Bograd, Ph. D.
Private Practice
Cambridge, Massachusetts

Lois Braverman, M. S. W.
Director
Des Moines Family Therapy
    Institute
Des Moines, Iowa

Alice S. Carter, Ph. D.
Assistant Professor
Department of Psychology
Yale University
New Haven, Connecticut

Betty Carter, M. S. W.
Director
Family Institute of Westchester
Mt. Vernon, New York

William J. Doherty, Ph. D.
Department of Family Social
    Science
University of Minnesota
St. Paul, Minnesota

Barbara Ellman, M. S. W.
Private Practice
Houston, Texas

Virginia Goldner, Ph. D.
Senior Faculty
Ackerman Institute for Family
    Therapy
New York, New York

Thelma Jean Goodrich, Ph. D.
Faculty
Family Institute of Westchester
Mt. Vernon, New York

Kris Halstead, M. S. Ed.
Private Practice
Washington, DC

Rachel T. Hare-Mustin, Ph. D.
Professor of Counseling and
    Human Relations
Villanova University
Villanova, Pennsylvania

Nadine Kaslow, Ph. D.
Associate Professor and Chief
    Psychologist
Emory University School of
    Medicine
Atlanta, Georgia

Jo-Ann Krestan, M. A.
Co-Director
Family Therapy Associates
Brunswick, Maine

Joan Laird, M. S.
Professor
Smith College School for Social
    Work
Northampton, Massachusetts

Deborah Anna Luepnitz, Ph. D.
Philadelphia Child Guidance Clinic
Philadelphia, Pennsylvania

Monica McGoldrick, M. S. W.,
    M. A.
Associate Professor and Director of
    Family Training
Psychiatry Department and
    CMHC
UMDNJ–Robert Wood Johnson
    Medical School
Piscataway, New Jersey

Jean Baker Miller, M. D.
Director of Education
The Stone Center for Develop-
    mental Services and Studies
Wellesley College
Wellesley, Massachusetts

Lucy Papillon, Ph. D.
Private Practice
Laguna Beach, California

Peggy Papp, M. S. W.
Senior Faculty
Ackerman Institute for Family
    Therapy
New York, New York

Cheryl Rampage, Ph. D.
Faculty
Family Institute of Chicago
Chicago, Illinois

Ronald Taffel, Ph. D.
Director, Family and Couples
    Treatment Services
Institute for Contemporary
    Psychotherapy
New York, New York

Marianne Walters, M. S. W.
Director
The Family Therapy Practice
   Center
Washington, DC

Linda Webb-Watson, Ed. D.
Brief Therapy Institute
Dallas, Texas

Daniel J. Wiener, Ph. D.
Co-Director
PeopleSystems Training Institute
New York, New York

Donald S. Williamson, Ph. D.
Associate Professor and Director,
   Family Psychology Section
Department of Family Medicine
Baylor College of Medicine
Houston, Texas

I
THE SOCIAL AND PSYCHOLOGICAL CONTEXT

1

THELMA JEAN GOODRICH

Women, Power, and Family Therapy: What's Wrong With This Picture?

IS POWER WHAT WOMEN WANT? This is not an innocent question, for it reflects back on the context that produces it, highlighting features ordinarily unmentionable in polite conversation. Talk in mixed company and in public speech always describes a free society, open access, and abundant resources for any hard worker. Then this embarrassing question intrudes, which exposes a hierarchical ordering of the sexes with men in the dominant position, women in the subordinate. The question not only embarrasses, it requires consideration of possible yearnings among subordinates for power and thus engenders fear and consternation for men, fear and confusion for women.

WOMEN'S REACTION TO POWER

Boys pride themselves on their drab clothing, their drooping socks, their smeared and inky skin; dirt, for them, is almost as good as wounds. They work at acting like boys. They call each other by their last names, draw attention to any extra departures from cleanliness. "Hey, Robertson! Wipe off the snot!" "Who farted?" They punch one another on the arm, saying, "Got you!" "Got you back!" There always seem to be more of them in the room than there actually are.

—Margaret Atwood, Cat's Eye

Women's response to the idea of power cannot be separated from what women have known about power, not only from being powerless but from watching the powerful. We watch the violence men use or threaten to use in order to maintain their position, the damage that comes to their own body and soul, and we wonder if we really want to partake. We want the gains, but what might we lose? As we explore the issue of power, we necessarily use language and concepts which contain the assumptions of a destructively power-using, power-seeking culture, and these are re-flected in the choices we see for ourselves. The assumptions and the ambivalence they engender are illustrated in the following remarks made at a recent discussion on power held by professional women:

How can women move into positions of power and not end up the same way men are? We have to play their game to even get there, and then if we act different, the system will chew us up.

Women want power-over, too. I wish I could shout and have my kids mind.

I realized the other day that, on automatic, I have been telling my little boy to beat up monsters and my little girl to make friends with them. Which way should I change it?

Don't men and women really want the same things? Both the man and the woman want more time for self and for creative work. The values are the same, but one consistently gets it.

Money may mean power, but as far as I can tell, rich men have a lot more power than rich women.

Does the one who has the most options have the most power in a relationship— options like the most money or the most lovers or the richest lovers? Is that it?

If she makes no money and he makes some money and she has no relation to a workplace to earn her own, she can't control her destiny. He says, "Write any check you want." But he can moan or fuss or change his mind. So regardless of what he says, she still feels unentitled—and is.

The danger for women in trying to do power differently is that separate but equal doesn't last long. It's always separate but unequal.

First I was married to a macho pig, then I was single, then I became a macho pigette. I love this position—in this new marriage, I make more money and I manage the money. It's a terrible burden in a way, but I won't let it go. There's no question that who has the money has the power, and that feels great!

My father is afraid for me to leave my job and go into private practice because then I wouldn't have a paternal element in my life, a protector. He has a point.

Womanhood. Our problems about power have to do not only with how we have seen it used, and not only with the barriers to our gaining access. There is also the reigning image of womanhood which leaves out power or, rather, makes it explicit that powerlessness is appealing, submission is erotic, and helplessness is feminine. Well-socialized into identification with that image, women find it extremely difficult to integrate woman and power in a way that appeals to them and therefore can instruct them.

The sex-linked and sexuality-linked aspects of power were underscored recently by Vivian Gornick in an article in *The New York Times Magazine*. Gornick described a discussion among her friends regarding the different atmosphere at parties now as compared with parties in the early '70s.

"You know why, don't you," said Ann. "Because these days the most interesting people in the room are likely to be the women."

"That's right," said Debra, "and can you picture sexual charge at a party where the women are powerful, and the men hover around them?" (1990, p. 53).

The shock of absurdity that strikes us upon considering these reversed positions lets us know how thoroughly we have taken the usual order to be the natural order, the naturally sexy order.

Too long told that we do not really care about power and participation in public affairs, too long told that we are "completed" by serving men and children, too long told that ambition and mothering are actually opposing drives, women frequently do not admit a desire for power even over our own lives. As Goldner put it, women have been "deprived of their subjectivity by a culture that expected them to be sexual objects for men and facilitating environments for everybody" (1989, p. 42).

"Deprived of their subjectivity" means, among other things, that expectations women have for themselves have matched the culture's. Love of men becomes our vocation, our way of entering the stream of life. Persuaded that love can only be had in exchange for self-sacrifice, we set about to make life run smoothly for husband and children, and also to make sure that the latter do not interfere with the former. So begins our career of protectiveness—i.e., guarding and supporting another's personhood. Although a virtuous skill in principle, the form it actually takes is to honor a man's personhood at the expense of our own and to feel ashamed at ever putting ourselves ahead. Thus, what first developed as a fine sensibility eventually becomes an instrument of self-abuse: It is not possible to defer and hold one's own at the same time.

We do our part, make our sacrifices, give ourselves away, renounce any strivings for power, and wait for the reward, the "completion" so bewitchingly described in story and song. Time after time, its failure to come has been understood to be evidence of our own failure, or sometimes his, but not the contract's. Until feminism, neither the culture nor family therapy provided any ground from which a woman could formulate such an analysis.

Before we examine more closely how family therapy has traditionally positioned itself with respect to the issue of women and power—and then propose a repositioning—it is important to take a hard look at the context in which any discussion of women and power takes place. It is the same context in which family therapy takes place. Discussions as well as therapy are necessarily shaped by that context: the overarching fact of women's oppression.

WOMAN'S PLACE

The peculiar thing about the women in the history of the world is that there have been more women than there have been men, but when you go to look for clues of them they're hard to find.

— *Marianne Wiggins,* Separate Checks

In a society predicated on male authority and male privilege, what is woman's place?

Women walk the streets of our cities in danger of attack by men.

Women, along with their children, live vulnerable to rape or blows from their husbands.

Women, along with their children, make up the majority of the poor and homeless.

Women are exploited by a pornography industry which makes an enormous profit by doing so.

Women who hold themselves apart from men suffer dubious status and discrimination.

Women receive underpayment or nonpayment for their labor.

Women are given drugs and surgeries without medical necessity.

Women cannot find themselves in history.

Women have no place like home.

Home. Regardless of economic necessity, personal desire, natural talent, or acquired skills, a woman is expected to find her true place and true joy in the home, in marriage, in motherhood. Her much-touted reign in this "private" sphere is, however, illusory. The gifts and labors she provides there are discounted by very reason of their being expected and considered natural. Further, they have no collectable value in the marketplace and grant her no usable credentials in the "public" sphere. More to the point, her authority in the home, in the marriage, and with the children is only delegated; her husband is the recognized authority, however minimal his participation might be. Her manner of performing her duties is thus directed not by her own lights but by his wishes and by the moral and social customs of a culture oriented to his privilege.

Motherhood. Wives typically have less power in their marriage than their husbands, but it is when wives becomes mothers that their inequality and oppression are most clearly revealed—and sealed. This process occurs because, on the one hand, motherhood is a relationship, but, on the other hand, it is a political institution. As Adrienne Rich describes,

This institution . . . is visible in the male dispensation of birth control and abortion; the guardianship of men over children in the courts and the educational system; the subservience, through most of history, of women and children to the patriarchal father; the economic dominance of the father over the family; the usurpation of the birth process by a male medical establishment. The subjectivity of the father . . . has prescribed how, when, and even where women should conceive, bear, nourish, and indoctrinate their children. (1979, p. 196)

As further evidence of our oppression, we must socialize our children to fit into this culture, and we must not notice the terrible irony of so doing—of training our daughters to laud and magnify, our sons to conquer and acquire. To complete our subjugation, we are then blamed when our children do not "turn out right," as if no fault belongs to this social order which studies war, rewards competitiveness, restricts resources, promotes isolation, and punishes those who are colored, female, or poor.

Economic exploitation, patriarchal motherhood, nuclear family, compulsory heterosexuality—these institutions control women and are supported by law, religion, media, and the full weight of (managed) public opinion. These institutions, as long as they remain as they are, limit the possible response to the question "Is power what women want?" Indeed, the way power is understood and used in our culture shapes the question itself.

THE NATURE OF POWER

"Why doesn't [God] care about people?" The spring air dried Julie's tears. "Why all the diseases and earthquakes?"

With a final twist of the knob, [the devil's] body became a gaseous haze . . . "Actually, the answer's quite simple." Two red eyes floated in the mist.

"Really? Tell me. Why does God allow evil?"

The red eyes vanished, leaving only the lantern and the night. "Because power corrupts," said [the devil's] disembodied voice. "And absolute power corrupts absolutely."

—James Morrow, Only Begotten Daughter

Efforts to explicate the nature of power usually begin by drawing a distinction between *power-to* and *power-over*. Power-to refers to the ability to perform or produce and implies also the freedom and resources to do so. Power-over refers to domination and control. Those who dominate have much more power-to than do their subordinates, and thereby they have the means to increase their domination. Key for that purpose is the power to name and define things—to give something a name and have it stick and to define the nature of something and have it felt as reality. In patriarchy, men have this power-to and have used it in theology, law, education, psychiatry, and history to justify their domination of women. Men have used their domination to limit and monitor closely the realms where subordinates are allowed to exercise any power-to.

Power-over may be used with benevolent intent, but whatever good may come, it also always has destructive consequences because of its self-serving and restricting nature. Power-to sounds benign, minimal, and respectful in its aims compared with power-over, but, as I mentioned, in the hands of the oppressor, it may be used to increase power-over. In the hands of the oppressed, it represents a danger to the oppressor regardless of intent not to use it to obtain power-over. Consider, for example, how disruptive to the regime are these possibilities for women despite the fact that no element of domination is inherent or need result:

The power to define ourselves, our nature, our place in human affairs.

The power to choose our position vis-à-vis others, how and whom we will love, how and if we will mother.

The power to say no in business or personal relationships.

The power to comment, to construe, to shape, to influence.

The power to act on behalf of self and to concentrate on acting on behalf of self.

Were women to have these powers, this personal authority, in any legitimate way, men's power-over position would be severely threatened. For women to tend to their own business would shake the foundations. Thus, we are as dangerous to patriarchy with our desire for power-to as if we wanted power-over; for if men could not have control of women, what would become of their definition of manhood? What would become of patriarchy?

Shaky ground. As solidly in place as power seems to those who do not have it, those who have it know it to be ephemeral and costly. Constant effort and vigilance are required to keep subordinates subordinate—on the corporate ladder, in the Old West, among nations, between men and women. Men feel compelled to demonstrate themselves as being superior in order to establish themselves as men, but " . . . they can do so only by cheating, stacking the deck, by imposing on women deprivations which imprison them in a condition seen as inferior by the male culture" (French, 1985, p. 535). On a societal scale, this method works well in achieving its aim. On a personal scale, it precludes from men any sense of rest and safety. The practiced display made of bluff and bravado leaves men feeling out of control, never enough in control. As a result, men are anxious and fearful around women, anxious about potential rebellion, fearful about possible exposure.

To counter its tenuous nature, power-over carries with it the necessity for violence against subordinates, both physical and sexual. More in their bones than in their minds, women live with this threat and, one way or another, act accordingly. Even in the presence of a man who is not threatening violence, there stalks the knowledge that he could change his mind. The influence of this dynamic on heterosexual relationships is underestimated in the theories of family therapy, largely because neither men nor women want to acknowledge it openly.

Conundrums of Power

> At first I do not win these fights, because of love. Or so I say to myself. If I were to win them, the order of the world would be changed, and I am not ready for that. So instead I lose the fights, and master different arts. I shrug, tighten my mouth in silent rebuke, turn my back in bed, leave questions unanswered. I say, "Do it however you like," provoking sullen fury from Jon. He does not want just capitulation, but admiration, enthusiasm, for himself and his ideas, and when he doesn't get it he feels cheated.
>
> —*Margaret Atwood*, Cat's Eye

If women are powerless, how is that they sometimes seem so powerful? Confusion about this issue arises from at least two sources. One is a mystification accomplished by word-play and aimed at keeping women satisfied with their lot. Instructed that we do not really want power, we are then told that what we have actually is power. I think of such sops as the "power" of weakness, the "power" of love, the "power" of sexual surrender. The mystification, combined with the taboo on the subject of power which I mentioned earlier, makes a clear discussion of power virtually impossible.

A second source of confusion arises from transposing some private experience with social reality. A woman may be able to "get her way" with those to whom she matters through her wits, charm, or stubborn will. (Men, of course, also have this ability.) As welcome as this capacity may be to a woman, it is not the same as power. It is not power to have to have a headache to avoid sex. It is not power to have to nag to get heard. It is not power to have to use feminine wiles to get access to adult decision-making. What women have is personal influence akin to what a backseat driver has who can bribe, wheedle, irritate, or flirt the driver into following her instructions. This situation differs sharply from being the driver and thus controlling the car. It also differs sharply from sitting in the backseat to be chauffeured, such that the right to command is overtly recognized and favor overtly courted.

Even when a woman manages to be in the driver's seat or the chauffeured seat and becomes the dominating figure in an interaction or a family, that interpersonal circumstance has no bearing on women's relation to power in this culture. Her emotional significance may make her seem powerful, but emotional significance is not the coin of the realm and has no currency outside the charmed circle. *Power is the capacity to gain whatever resources are necessary to remove oneself from a condition of oppression, to guarantee one's ability to perform, and to affect not only one's own circumstances, but also more general circumstances outside one's intimate surroundings*. As has been described and detailed, women as a class do not, in this sense, have power. Because of membership in this class, an individual woman cannot attain access to all the necessary resources and influence that add up to power as just defined, regardless of her wealth or wit.

Men feel powerless. What are we to understand when men say they do not feel powerful? It is not uncommon for clinicians to hear such reports from men who have just beaten up their wives, from stockbrokers working toward their second million. A man may feel powerless to think of what else to do to have his way besides bully and threaten. A man may feel powerless because there are men above him in the ranks. A man may feel powerless in the face of emotions. A man may feel powerless because of the necessity for constant vigilance, as described earlier. A man may feel so accustomed to his privileged status, or so entitled to it, that he does not count it as powerful.

It is useful and desirable for a man to address his feelings of powerlessness in therapy, but clinician and client alike must be clear that feeling powerless in individual circumstances does not cancel a man's membership in the dominant class or limit the privileges that attend that membership. It is true that the dominants take the dominant/subordinate distinction into their own group and arrange themselves hierarchically, such that some men have more power than other men. "Feeling powerless" bears no necessary relation to a man's place in this hierarchy, however, neither does "feeling powerful." Feelings, period, are irrelevant to the fact that our society is organized so that, as a class, men hold power in general, and, most particularly, over and in contrast to women.

Power in the Family

> *All fathers . . . are invisible in daytime; daytime is ruled by mothers. But fathers come out at night. Darkness brings home the fathers, with their real, unspeakable power. There is more to them than meets the eye. And so we believe the belt.*
>
> — *Margaret Atwood,* Cat's Eye

It is exactly in the family that women's oppression and men's power are enacted most plainly and personally. The reproduction of patriarchy occurs through family structure and family process, from who serves the coffee to who drives the car, from who pursues conversationally to who has the last word, from minor acts of deference to major decision-making. The lessons are lost on no one.

On Mother's Day, 1990, at a large downtown church in the Southwest—and doubtless in many others—the minister intoned his gratitude for what mothers do. The litany of gifts held up sewing, scrubbing, cooking, tending, and wiping bottoms and tears. Although he was profoundly silent regarding any gift of intellect, ambition, spirit, values, or guidance in the ways of the world, still he delivered what he had chosen to include with moist eyes. That mothers do these things brings deep and sincere gratitude, at least once a year, precisely because, if there is no money for servants, who else will do them? Which is to say, what right-thinking adult would sign up for such tasks except a servant or a mother?

See no evil. In family after family, pairing mother with low status and undesirable tasks tells the whole tale about power. So effectively and cleverly has the patriarchy done its work that, by and large, unequal privilege between husband and wife, father and mother, is rarely noticed or experienced as unfair. Rather, it becomes fixed in the minds of the children as the natural way to be—right alongside the dead-sureness about the true menu for Thanksgiving and the real name to call grandmothers.

The injustice in the set up—indeed, even its status as an arrangement of power—is hidden from and by family members through a collection of myths, subterfuges, self-delusion, and sour grapes. Some of these are spun out of the personal life and history of each family. Additionally, the society offers an array of legitimations to build on or borrow from: biological differences, psychological proclivities, separate but equal realms, anatomical destiny, God's plan. (See Hare-Mustin, Chapter 4.) Despite the work of feminist scholars to expose these social legitimations as wholesale propaganda, they continue their influence and their utility for those who stand to gain from them. Perceived benefits go not only to the powerful father/husband but to the disadvantaged mother/wife. Both of them prefer the self-image that accompanies a version of family life which obscures the true distribution of power.

Wedlock. The area of family life where power is least recognized in all its ramifications is the marital relationship. There may be many conflicts read by others or even by the partners as "power struggles," but these actually serve to obscure the fundamental inequality in the relationship by seeming to locate and thus restrict it to designated areas. Fights over garbage removal keep covert the true issue about who has the power to make the rules and win disputes.

Inequality in marriage stems from the inequality in the wider society that follows men and women into marriage. Men and women, in fact, continue to choose one another on the basis of this inequality. Women are led to want someone smarter, richer, taller—the perfect reciprocal to what men want in order to reinforce their power.

Further reinforcement of their power comes from the rights accorded to men as husbands. So legitimated are these that rights become a category husbands think in when rights should not even be the issue (Rich, 1979). For example, sex from his wife, priority attention from his wife are the things the husband thinks of as his rights rather than as behaviors she can choose to give him out of desire or even kindness. He claims the further right to experience sex and attention as freely given rather than as the rights he is demanding.

For their part, wives typically honor this "right" of access. "Wash your hair on your own time," said a client's husband. "When is that?" my client asked. "After midnight," he answered. "After I'm asleep." She had been following his directive for several years without any recognized reactions on her part. In fact, if obliging wives feel some resentment about their obliging behaviors, they are more likely to feel guilty for it than justified in it.

Listen for how women manage their friendships around husband's time.

"John doesn't like me to be on the phone when he gets home, so I'd better ring off."

"Jim isn't going out of town next week, so I guess you and I can't go to dinner."

It is not as if these are given in a complaining way, but they are also not given as:

"I have so much fun with John that I want to be sure I'm free to be with him the moment he walks in the door."

"Jim is such grand company that I don't want to miss a single meal with him."

The point here is not simply that men are demanding, but that both men and women expect that wife will make herself available for husband. This expectation is extensive in its reach and is decidedly not reciprocal.

How is it that so many women cooperate so fully in so lopsided an arrangement? Rather than list their familiar gains—economic benefits, protection from other men, social status—I will give an example:

Deborah, the mother of two young children, first came to therapy seeking help in recovering from continuing grief and guilt about an abortion she had four months prior to her coming. "Joe made me have the abortion because he didn't want any more children right now. He made me do it, but yet *I* did it. I don't believe in abortion." She did not want him to join her in therapy because, she said, "I can't talk to him. I never could. I just close up. I can't tell him how I feel about most things, especially about this, because it feels too intimate, too personal. I want to sort it out without him first and then have him come, too."

Over time, she came to understand how it was that she had felt unentitled to use her voice in the marriage about many things, while he had felt entitled to use his freely. She came to understand how her experience in her family of origin and in her family of creation fit well with cultural expectations for women's behavior. She came to understand how radical an act it would have been for her suddenly to speak a different position from her husband's about abortion when she was not doing so about much less important matters.

When she was ready, she invited Joe to join her in therapy. Although she told him what had initially brought her to therapy, she said she did not want to spend time on that topic just yet. Instead she wanted to begin with some other matters which she thought would be easier to discuss. She asked if he had any areas he wanted to discuss. He said no. With some reluctance and much nervous laughter, she began by complaining to him that he yells at her and orders her about.

"I don't know what you mean," he said. "What are you saying?"

"Like last night when you told me to turn off the light."

"No, I just said, 'Turn off the light.'"

"You said, 'TURN OFF THE LIGHT!'"

Joe let out air through his lips in a gesture of dismissal and a charge of exaggeration. With his shoulders shrugged in helpless befuddlement, he laughed in my direction as if in league with me.

"Women!" he exhaled.

Deborah pursued her case on the grounds of civility, calling his tone rude, not barbaric, and said it embarrassed her, not degraded her. I knew from our previous meetings that those deeper feelings were there. In fact, she had told me that she would not stay all her life with a man who not only speaks to her the way he does but cannot recognize or does not care about it. Yet, and this is my point here, when I asked her what was keeping her from directly saying to him how she experiences his routine treatment of her, she said softly and tearfully, "I don't want to hurt his feelings." What came to my mind was a letter I once read, a letter to God from a little girl. "Dear God, make my Daddy quit beating me, but please God, don't hurt him."

Yes, we could look at her fear of losing her voice if she pits it against his too strongly, or her fear of losing a grip on her own experience if she pits it against his too forcefully, or her fear of finding her hard-won bravery used against her if she pits it against his too directly. We could look at how frightening her own anger has been made to seem to her. We could look at how economic dependency and concern for her children affect her sense of entitlement and load her risk. As important as those considerations may be for Deborah, her feelings for Joe also are central to her bind. To dramatize the force of certain feelings and their capacity to direct us, Adrienne Rich calls on an old image: the devil.

The "devil" is always that which wants us to settle for less than we deserve, for panaceas, handouts, temporary safety; and for women, the devil has most often taken the form of love rather than of power, gold, or learning. (1979, p. 257)

For any particular woman caught in the throes of love, the knowledge that her feeling, her urge to self-sacrifice, and her misdirected compassion have been politically arranged, reduces their sway not at all.

Sex. What do we say of sex and power and family? How loath we are to link those! How long has incest been kept out of the light and then, no sooner brought in, than laid to mother! How long has law supported a husband's access to his wife's body such that marital rape was a contradiction in terms! We like to put sexual harassment safely in the workplace and deplore how men take advantage of women's economic vulnerability. Confining it to the workplace lets us avoid seeing the parallel between the conditions and actions there and the conditions and actions in the home — the parallel and the connection.

Betsy and Phil, who were the parents of one child, came to therapy because for six months Betsy had been continuously feeling gloomy and confused. Recently, she had discovered that thoughts of leaving the marriage seemed to lift both her spirits and the mental fog. She had told Phil of her discovery, and Phil had become panicked.

"I cannot live without you. I have no life without you," he wept.

"I have no life *with* you," she answered. "*You* have a life. I don't even have personal time." She listed the many ways she accommodates to him. "But the main thing is sex." She described how impossible Phil had been to live with during the three weeks of medically prescribed sexual abstinence prior to the birth of their now eight year old. Directly upon her return home from the birth, Phil had begun to push for sex.

"He was beside himself waiting for the four-week checkup. The day finally arrived. I came home from the appointment with the news that the doctor said I wasn't healed yet. Phil had a fit. I couldn't take it anymore — not another day of his pouting and meanness. I said OK. It tore some internal stitches, and I eventually ended up in the hospital. I cannot have any more children."

Phil said, "I just never heard of anybody having to wait more than four weeks after. But anyway, that was eight years ago. I'm sorry. What else can I say? I can't change the past."

"What do you mean 'the past'? That's the story of my life with you. I know I can have maybe two days to myself, two times of saying 'no thank you' to sex. On the third day, you'll be mean and grumpy. You'll yell at me and our son. It's not worth it to me to say no because I'm dealing with you one way or the other. I pay either way."

"That's just the kind of guy I am," Phil offered. "I'm just really sexual. I can't help it. And besides the sex, I need that stroking from you so I know you still love me."

Betsy remained quiet and began to look unsure of herself. After a time, she whispered, "I know that's how you are. You deserve to have a wife who matches what you need. I guess I just can't fit with that."

After another of Frank's violent outbursts, Judy initiated therapy for herself, saying that she wanted to learn how to deal better with her husband so that she "wouldn't set off his temper." A subsequent individual session with Frank led to a joint session the following week. Frank agreed to a contract of nonviolence for the present and began, along with Judy, to designate the problems in the marriage.

"The biggest thing is she's never interested in sex. She's always too tired—asleep as soon as she puts the kids to bed before I can ever even get up to the bedroom. I can't live like that."

"Frank, it's not that I'm not interested; it's just I'm so tired. I get all the kids up and dressed, fix their breakfast, pack their lunch, fix your breakfast, pack our lunches, go to work all day, fix dinner, throw in the laundry, bathe the kids, put them in bed—I'm beat. And you won't help me."

"Why should I? You won't give me what I want!"

"Maybe if you'd help me and be nice to me during the day, I'd feel more like sex at night," Judy suggested.

"We've been through that before. You always quit your part. The last therapist we saw told you to have sex with me three nights a week and not to let what happened between us during the day change the plan for the night. And you only followed the deal for one lousy week."

"Well, at least I always have sex one or two times a week," Judy murmured. "I'm just so tired."

Once we remove sex from the customary haze of romantic language and examine its conspiracy with power, we have to question how real are the differences between sexual harassment, rape, and intercourse. One accused rapist was clearly making the connection when he said that he had not used "any more force than is usual for males during the preliminaries" (MacKinnon, 1979, p. 219). In explicating the connection, MacKinnon has argued that

taking rape from the realm of "the sexual," placing it in the realm of "the violent," allows one to be against it without raising any questions about the extent to which the institution of heterosexuality has defined force as a normal part of "the preliminaries" (1979, p. 219).

Even more crucially, she says, "Never is it asked whether, under conditions of male supremacy, the notion of 'consent' has any meaning" (1979, p. 298). Given that the rights claimed by Phil and Frank are common ones, given that the pressures felt by Betsy and Judy are common ones, given that marital intercourse usually occurs between physical and economic unequals, we must, at minimum, acknowledge that our usual discussions of sexual abuse do not include the most common form.

FAMILY THERAPY AND POWER

We are all responsible for reinforcing a state of pathogenic adaptation to social conditions of oppression in women if we do not make explicit the existence of such a set of conditions and make it possible for the individual to acquire a choice about it — the choice to defy acquiescence to this order.

— Teresa Bernardez, "Women and Anger — Cultural Prohibitions and the Feminine Ideal"

Until recently, family therapy has been profoundly mute on the subject of power and its unequal distribution either in the family or in the society. Even now, the depth and breadth of women's inequality seem glossed over, for scarcely had we begun to examine the implications for therapy when we glided into "gender sensitivity" and "gender bias" instead. By creating the safe harbor of studying a seemingly two-sided phenomenon, we have been rescued from noticing how one-sided has been the damage of our traditional work. In fact, traditional work still holds sway in many quarters despite some new awareness and strong feminist critique. A brief review of this critique follows. The critique developed through discussions, readings, and presentations among kindred spirits as well as through solitary struggling individually. A reference list of books and articles related to the feminist critique is given in Avis, 1989. Here I will cite the people and works most directly influential on me: Avis, 1988; Bograd, 1986; Goldner, 1985, 1989; my colleagues for Goodrich et al., 1988; Hare-Mustin, 1978, 1987; Luepnitz, 1988; McGoldrick, Anderson, and Walsh, 1988; and Walters, Carter, Papp, and Silverstein, 1988.

Systems theory. How did family therapy manage to omit power as an organizing principle of family life? Systems theory has been the primary way of seeing and thinking, and systems theory is both too abstract and too concrete to generate any challenge to the cultural sanction against acknowledging power as central to family life. Systems theory is so abstract that it can provide a seemingly coherent account of family phenomena while leaving out significant variables, i.e., power, gender, and the link between the two. Since systems theory focuses entirely on the moves rather than the players, who has power over whom, and with what regularity, never has to be noticed.

The omission of power is all the more curious since some of the most widely used concepts in the field have power-over at their core: collusion, complementarity, hierarchy, triangles. These have been viewed as if they were intellectually entertaining puzzles for a theorist to work out, with no consequences any worse for one person than another. The concept of circularity assisted in this regard. It masked power and the consequences of power by promoting the idea that responsibility for and effect from any given interactional sequence are evenly spread over the participants.

Systems theory is also too concrete in that it maintains a narrow focus on each individual, particular family. Patterns across families reflecting large-scale oppression of women have thus been kept from troubling the field of vision. Also left untroubled have been the theoretical models used to organize observations of family life. Whether based on analogies to a biological organism or to a mechanical thermostat, the models assume a drive towards harmony, a natural fitting together of disparate parts, a general listing towards the welfare of the whole. At whose expense this progress might be happening was not a question that could arise out of such paradigms.

Models of family. It would take a different model of family to produce a question about differential benefits, a view of family as the site of conflicting interests where battles for territory, attention, resources, and influence are daily fare. These battles, then, are taken to be endemic to conventional family form rather than temporary for a family with problems. Such a model, however, runs directly counter to the romantic fantasy of family life so dear to the heart of American culture and, obviously, to family therapy.

Excellent articles and books have recently been published giving in much detail how and why the field in general and various schools of thought in particular have functioned without power as a named principle of family life (Goldner, 1989; Goodrich et al., 1988; Luepnitz, 1988; Walsh & Scheinkman, 1989). These are readily available and necessary readings. The point I want to make is that for family therapy to continue to accept as ideal the conventional model of family, with its gendered division of labor and its hierarchy of privilege and power, puts family therapy in complicity with the society to keep women oppressed. Fundamental to that oppression is the assumption that women belong in the home, so that even if we venture forth, we are still responsible for home. It is the knowledge that she is the unilateral provider of the experience of family for others—and the necessary years and years of thinking of others first and continually (because he will not)—that robs women of power.

Family therapy has gone along with the culture in regarding mother, even if she is working outside the home, as having primary responsibility for the children. Moreover, her career, as well as her personal needs, is treated as second in importance to her husband's. (Research supporting this statement is cited in Avis, 1988.) Family therapy has gone along with the culture on this version of family life, despite its unfairness to women and despite three decades of research reporting the destructive and distorting effects of this arrangement. (Much of this research is reviewed in Thorne with Yalom, 1982.) Even in the area of economic power, where the differential of wife to husband is so dramatic and its effect on interactions is so profound, family therapists, by and large, have remained silent.

Hierarchy. Just as we are drawing attention to the hierarchical relation of husband to wife ordinarily obscured in family therapy theory, let us also draw attention to a hierarchical relation regarded as perfectly acceptable: parent(s) to child. This generational ordering—let us not obscure: this arrangement of power-over—is taken for granted as right, proper, and necessary, despite research demonstrating that family can function well in an arrangement of consensus. Specifically, research regarding single-mother families describes consensual arrangements as typical and indicates that, because of this structure and in contrast to what hierarchical structure promotes, conflict is low, closeness is habitual, mothers feel competent, and children are responsible, both in tasks and in decision-making (Cashion, 1982; Brandwein, Brown, & Fox, 1974; Weiss, 1979).

If mother and children can work well as a democracy, why cannot the same be true of mother, father, and children? Why continue teaching about "protecting the parental dyad by a firm boundary to mark the hierarchy" and teaching this lesson as if that arrangement were in the best interest of *all* the members? Yet when father is not part of the household, so the teaching goes, hierarchy is not necessary (Fulmer, 1983; Minuchin, 1974). How is it that the correlation between father and hierarchy goes unmentioned? The commitment to patriarchy has kept family therapy committed to hierarchy. The "king of his castle" ideology, not family health, gives hierarchy its grip on theory.

Violence. The most devastating consequence of family therapy's commitment to patriarchy has been its failure in the areas of wife-battering and incest. Articles and conference sessions were rare until five yeas ago, and then leading approaches were wrongheaded and damaging to victims. It is feminists who have brought the subject of violence in the family to the fore, not only because feminists care about women, but because feminists, by definition, focus on power, including the power in marriage and family. From a feminist standpoint, any theory of family or therapy has to be measured against the case of violence, because if it cannot deal with the abuse of power, it cannot deal with power. If it cannot deal with power, then whatever else it may help or clarify, it works to keep inequity in place.

Short of becoming social reformers—or in addition to such action—what can family therapists do differently in our work with families? How can we use our limited access to women and men to affect their relation to power? Before we discuss how best to position ourselves, let us consider a dimension of power underemphasized as a resource—the power in connection.

Empowerment

"What are you women doing out alone?"
"We're not alone; we're with each other."

—*Lily Tomlin, "Saturday Night Live"*

Empowerment is a relational word, a relational action. Frequently heard in the women's movement, the term usually designated a benevolent but unilateral transaction in which one person enhances another's ability to feel competent and take action, that is, enhances another's power-to. The concept has lately been elaborated to designate a mutual process (Miller, 1986; Surrey, 1987). Both participants in a relationship can interact in ways that increase connection and enhance personal power for each. These interactions involve mutual attention, mutual empathy, mutual engagement, and mutual responsiveness.

To have an encounter of mutual empowerment requires a capacity to carry "the psychological reality of the other as part of an ongoing, continuous awareness beyond the momentary experience, and to 'take the other into account' in all one's activities" (Surrey, 1987, p. 6). Note how far this description is from what Bowen described as proper consciousness and behavior, despite his promotion of personal relationships among family members. It is as if there can be intimacy or action rather than intimacy as productive and undergirding of action. Bowen indicates that the ideal actor is "principle-oriented, goal-directed," "not affected by either praise or criticism from others," able to "assume total responsibility for self," and to "disengage from [intense emotional experiences] and proceed on a self-directed course at will" (1966, p. 359).

Men's development. Although Bowen offers his description to conceptualize the mature generic adult, in truth, it reflects the culture's ideal of the male adult. Neither the culture nor the mental health field wants female adults to behave in such a self-focused way. (See, for example, the studies by Broverman et al., 1972.) For men to develop the ideal character, it is thought that they must separate from their mother and from their father, and then identify with their father's way of being powerful without connecting with him emotionally (Surrey, 1987).

The prescription to disconnect distorts later experiences of intimacy for men. Intimacy, they fear, will threaten the sense of self, promote a loss of control, and drain away the capacity to act *for* oneself. Thus, men's course, as usually described and directed, militates against developing the very capacities necessary for engaging in mutually empowering relationships.

Women's development. In contrast, the culture's training and expectations for women promote the development of skills needed for nurturing relationships, responding to the feelings and opinions of others, and fostering the growth and well-being of others. The mothering of girls by women means that girls develop alongside someone like them whose qualities they are encouraged to incorporate. Differentiation is seen to be an aspect of connectedness, not an opposing force. As a result of the circumstances of their development and the culture's plan for their abilities, women are allowed to experience intimacy as life-giving rather than life-threatening, enhancing rather than depleting.

Typically, then, women have the ability to empower others, to move others to action. This ability rests on personal authenticity. Listening and responding from the heart, as they say, creates emotional connection and releases energy. For each person in a conversation to give the other this quality of attending leads each one to increased self-worth, zest, knowledge, energy for action, and desire for more connection (Miller, 1986). Power—energy to act—is thus grounded in emotional and equitable relationship rather than in imposition or intimidation or privilege.

Again, I must emphasize that, regardless of the strong sense of self and the sheer pleasure that may derive from mutually empowering relationships, the resulting urge to action comes to nothing for women without political changes in the family and in the culture. Feeling good is a value in itself *and* so also is the ability to put oneself into the world. As Carolyn Heilbrun writes:

Women need to learn how publicly to declare their right to public power. The true representation of power is not of a big man beating a smaller man or woman. Power is the ability to take one's place in whatever discourse is essential to action and the right to have one's part matter. This is true in the Pentagon, in marriage, in friendship, and in politics. (1989, p. 18)

REPOSITIONING OURSELVES

Today I believe we will not learn to live responsibly on the planet without basic changes in the ways we organize the family because the family provides metaphors for broader ethical relations.

—Mary Catherine Bateson, Composing a Life

For family therapists to address the issue of women and power requires a different vision of marriage and family than we currently use. Such change is necessary because marriage and family, as presently constituted, are not designed to support women's empowerment. But serious commitment to empowering women will push us beyond reforming traditionally acceptable structures to validating choices for what are unaffectionately referred to as "alternative life-styles," that is, choices to live as a single woman, to live in sexual or nonsexual partnership with another woman, to live as a mother with her children—in short, to live without a man.

Our attempt at revision labors under enormous burden because, in the first place, we are limited by patriarchal values and categories that permeate our language and shape our thinking. Therefore, it is very difficult for us to imagine a substantially different way of being family. Our position is similar to cartoonists who draw extraterrestrials: The creatures always look human—some eyes, a head or two, distinguishable limbs. Slight variations on the basic structure of patriarchal marriage and family will not move us far enough.

In the second place, we typically limit our focus to the psychology of experience or the mechanics of interaction or the preservation of the family. We thereby exclude from attention the economic and other material realities that help mold psychological experience, interaction, and family into the forms we then try to re-form. Perhaps because it has not been a central part of our business to affect these material realities, we have not made them integral to our theory and rarely even attend to such matters in individual cases.

A radical shift. To illustrate a contrast, let me use an idea from Betty Carter. In taking seriously the effect of economic inequality on the negotiation of marital problems, she suggests that we send our clients to legal mediation to divide family assets equitably between the partners, putting the wife's part in the wife's name and the husband's part in the husband's name. With economic parity, wife and husband return to marital therapy on very different footing.

When I have told professional audiences about Betty Carter's idea, it has been met, without fail, by a stunned silence, soon broken by claps, not applause, but claps of surprise and delight—but only from the women. Looks of deep dread seep from the shaded eyes of the men. As both reactions testify, we have made a first-time trip to the heart of the matter. That is a different place to hold a theory-building discussion than the usual abstract tower.

We cannot wait for fully developed theories in the field or for transformation in the society before instituting changes in our practice. As individual clinicians, we must explore out loud the distribution of power in each family that we see, how the beliefs in the culture support it, how different members maintain it or resist it, how it is implicated in the family's current difficulties, and how it eliminates or imposes certain solutions. Then, in order to work towards a change that matters, we must take a different position than we have routinely taken—towards women, towards men, towards "alternative life-styles," towards marriage, towards family.

The crucial clarity. Above all else, we must make clear for ourselves and our clients that *powerlessness is not fundamentally an attitude problem*. Our society is founded on the bedrock of women as powerless. There are structures—economic, social, political, religious, and then psychological—that oppress women and work hard to keep them oppressed.

In therapy with women, we do see that the external difficulties of getting power become mirrored by internal conflicts about getting it. These are created by the culture's stories of what women should want and by the culture's version of powermongering. Underscoring all else is women's economic vulnerability, which typically haunts even those women who have money.

To reduce a woman's submissiveness or a woman's ambivalence about power to a clinical category or personal problem is not only incorrect, but it also misdirects us in our search for therapeutic approaches. In the remarks that follow, I will focus on positioning ourselves most efficaciously rather than on techniques of empowerment. Clinical work is detailed in other chapters.

Women

> *I remember on the day this story is about back in September some man came up to me while I was in a hurry to cross Seventh Avenue and he said, "Hey, aren't you a model?" and I said, "No, I'm full-scale."*

— *Marianne Wiggins*, Separate Checks

If a woman comes to us who is not in a traditional family of creation, our stance has usually been to help her get one if she wants one and to help her want one if she does not. If a woman comes to us who is in a traditional family of creation, our stance has usually been to help her tone down her expectations, to help her adjust, to help her accommodate to her husband's suggestions for concrete, behavioral changes, to help her leave her less definable goals of intimacy and empathy as epiphenomena of "better negotiation and communication." (See, for example, Wynne as quoted in *Family Therapy News*, 1987. Also, see Sprenkle & Fisher, 1980 regarding family therapists' goals for treatment.) With this guidance, a wife finishes therapy with no more power in the family than when she began and no different perspective on herself.

We would position ourselves very differently if we helped a woman, in or out of family, make commitments to work for change, to monitor the erosion of her energy and self-esteem in the process, to keep alternatives alive for herself, to do regular cost/benefit analyses, to find relationships where she can act with authenticity. These latter relationships are virtually certain to be friendships with women—the prime resource of empowerment for women whether they are living in traditional family or not. This resource is generally devalued as girlish, because our field, like our culture, is focused on supporting and maintaining women's relationships with men. Additionally, our field, like our culture, holds up a male ethos of self-sufficiency so that the strength derived from connection is discounted as ill-gotten gains from too much dependency. In fact, women become "dis-empowered when connections with men are fragmenting, that is, maintained at the expense of the deepest connections to self and other women" (Surrey, 1987, p. 19).

Connection to self. To position ourselves differently entails our promoting these deepest connections to self and to other women for our women clients. Many women urgently seek a man not primarily to have a companion, a lover, a helper, but to have a center for their lives. For a woman to change her relation to power, she must become the center of her life. If we are to promote deeper connections for her with herself, we must foster woman-identification, largely through urging her to seek out the hidden, forbidden knowledge of women's history. "Enforced ignorance has been a crucial key to our powerlessness," teaches Adrienne Rich (1986, p. 2). We also foster women-identification by helping a woman understand her position in an oppressive, misogynist society and how she has been shaped by it. Equally important is helping her name the ways she has resisted so that she may know her strength.

Connection to women. Promoting deeper connection with women means that we challenge our client to be responsibly interactive in forming or honoring relationships with women. The importance of this resource for power cannot be emphasized too strongly. Heilbrun writes that "power consists to a large extent in deciding what stories will be told" (1989, p. 44). Men have used their power to allow only stories that suit them and work for their benefit. Other stories—what are or might be women's stories—are made unthinkable. Therefore, in Heilbrun's words, "Women must turn to one another for stories; they must share the stories of their lives and their hopes and their unacceptable fantasies" (1989, p. 44). To urge our women clients to engage in such truth-telling is to urge radical action. But we must go even further. We must help to counter the prevailing instruction to trivialize the talk of women. We must help our clients begin to privilege it over talk with men.

Men

> *They both looked at the sea. Why, thought Mr. Ramsay, should she look at the sea when I am here?*
>
> — *Virginia Woolf,* To The Lighthouse

Since it is relatively rare for men to enter family therapy at their own instigation or by themselves, we are much more accustomed to having women as customers, men as reluctant presences. Often, we, as well as family members, are so eager to keep men coming that none of us asks much more of them. A compromise here and there, a bit more help around the house, a touch more involvement with the children—these spread gratitude. A shift in levels of participation in the household, however, bears no necessary relation to a shift in the balance of power; everyone's relative place in the hierarchies of privilege and decision-making can remain quite familiar. To alter the balance there, we will have to position ourselves differently with the husband: in addition to offerings of empathy and understanding, we will have to create discomfort, institute losses, and entice him to work for changes in himself that he does not even see as desirable in principle, let alone want for himself.

Dependency. Chief among these necessary changes for a man is his very view of himself, in particular, his ideas of his neediness and what to do about it. The cultural idea that Real Men are self-sufficient forces actual men to feel helpless in the face of their inevitable and human dependency needs. The feeling of helplessness comes because they are so inexperienced in acknowledging, expressing, or managing such needs in any adult manner. As a result, men's fear of women's power is not so much that women will take over the fun of running the world but that, as Adrienne Rich puts it, women will become "whole human beings." At that point, women will "cease to mother men, to provide the breast, the lullaby, the continuous attention associated by the infant with the mother." Rich advises that we recognize these needs as "arrested development" and "re-examine the ideal of preservation of the family within which those needs are allowed free rein even to the point of violence" (1979, p. 221).

Mutuality. As family therapists, are we ready to act as if we expect men to grow up, as if we expect men to understand the potential for family to be a *mutually* empowering and *mutually* caretaking relationship? Are we ready to act as if we expect men to look beyond the family and move past "male bonding" into real connection with one another? Are we ready to side with the idea that the self gains power by joining a web of relationships rather than by beating out other people or keeping them away?

For us to promote connection for men puts us in a challenging stance to the notion that independence is the mark of power—both for acquiring it and for using it. Even though such a position would be radically different, we have in our favor the fact that men do say, just as women do, that they feel more "enlivened, appreciated, safe, and 'heard'" in "horizontal exchanges" (Surrey, 1987, p. 22). As was discussed earlier, the one-up,

power-over position is always unsafe, always tenuous, and so always engenders vigilant defensiveness. Not every man, but some men, will think
the potential gains we can hold up are worth some sacrifice of privilege
and self-image.

"Alternative Life-Styles"

*I feel safe with women. No woman has ever beaten me up. No woman has ever
made me afraid on the street. I think that the culture that women put out into the
world is safer for everyone.*

— Alice Walker

The annoying quotation marks around "alternative life-styles" are there
in an effort to discredit the phrase on two counts. First of all, the phrase
implies and enforces marginal status despite the fact that these ways of
living outnumber marriage. They are alternatives not to some large majority of households but to the injunction from the patriarchy that women
must make themselves available to men. To choose to live in single bliss,
to pair with another woman sexually or nonsexually, to mother alone, to
lead a woman-centered life with only intermittent attachments with men—
when these are chosen, they are choices *for*, but also choices *against* what
one is expected to provide in traditional marriage and family. Because of
the esteem in which these latter forms are held, and because, to date, they
embody and promote patriarchal values and structures, choices by women
not to participate are taken as acts of rebellion in a culture that does not
tolerate rebellion well in its women.

This last is the second reason for the attempt to discredit with quotation
marks; the phrase serves as a gloss that keeps family therapy from addressing the full implications for women of choosing to live without a man.
Disadvantaged even when swimming with what is defined as mainstream,
women who swim against it are pushed to precarious depths. Yet, it is
from those for whom the prevailing culture does not work that reformers
can best learn.

To position ourselves differently and become such students, family therapists must look where we are not accustomed to looking. Single women
and women who choose women have little visibility, let alone stature, in
our professional theory, despite the fact that they also hold membership
in the traditional families we focus on. Unmarried women have mothers,

fathers, sisters, brothers, nieces, nephews, aunts, uncles. In adulthood, these relationships are frequently seen as mere leftovers. Our task is to help them be reciprocally valued, enriched, and honored as primary or potentially primary.

Marriage

> *It sometimes entered Mr. Pontellier's mind to wonder if his wife were not growing a little unbalanced mentally. He could see plainly that she was not herself. That is, he could not see that she was becoming herself. . . .*

> —*Kate Chopin*, The Awakening

Positioning ourselves differently towards marriage may be the most difficult change to imagine, for marriage is the least examined and most honored lynchpin in the entire structure of patriarchy. Consistently protected from radical critique—even the one implicit in divorce statistics—marriage still enjoys a good reputation in our theory, while in our sessions, we focus on two people at a time who seem to be doing poorly in theirs. The people are questioned, the institution is not. The people are searched for failures and flaws, the institution is not. For us, as family therapists, to challenge our clients and ourselves with critical examination of marriage and the formulation of new models starts to position us differently.

Pleasure. Any fundamental change in marriage requires that it be moved from the realm of power into the realm of pleasure where mutuality and reciprocity replace hierarchy and control. Such a shift is constrained, however, by the unequal power in the world for men and women. The constraint is there even when the shift is fervently desired by both partners—a desire which is itself constrained by unequal power in the world. It is important that we acknowledge this limitation so that we do not mystify ourselves or our clients. Even so, it is important that we proceed because the potential rewards may appeal enough to some for them to take extreme measures to obtain them.

To give a brief example, suppose we measured marriage against the standard of a relationship that *is* designed and taken up purely for pleasure: women's friendships. At the outset, we note that people often pick as mate someone they would never choose as friend. We note also that because friendships are governed by the pleasure principle rather than the power principle, the assumptions, agreements, and expectations in friendship are radically different from those in marriage. As a result, the rules so relevant to marriage have no place in friendship, rules such as "might makes right" or "money talks." Problems so difficult in marriage do not appear in friendship, problems such as how to find something enjoyable to do together or how to fill the silence at dinner. (See Chapter 4 in Heilbrun, 1989, for discussion of the possibilities and problems in construing marriage as friendship.)

Balancing. What would it mean to challenge *clients* to position marriage differently in their lives in the service of empowering women? In studies comparing different types of households—men alone, women alone, men living with their children, women living with their children, husbands and wives living together with and without children—the person who does the most housework is the woman in a household with a husband present. In fact, the presence of a husband creates more housework for a woman than the presence of a child under ten, even in cases where he reports himself an equal partner in the chores. This additional housework does not arise because men are messier or less helpful than children, but because husbands expect more of their wives, and wives expect more of themselves, in the presence of one another (Hartmann, 1980).

A variety of functions may be served for husband and wife by all this extra, make-work activity. Perhaps the point is to enact or enforce difference in status. Perhaps it is to match standards their mothers met and thus feel approved and at home. Perhaps it is to exhibit how intertwined are their lives and how necessary their ties (Bateson, 1989). Regardless, the result is to keep the woman in her place and limit other possibilities for her. For us to help a husband and wife position the marriage differently would be to challenge them to enact an equality in status, to seek other ways of feeling approved of and at home, and to be more creative about exhibiting their importance to one another.

The repositioning described above involves helping both husband and wife to value more highly than is usual her work and activities that are not in direct service of the house or the husband. Read how Mary Catherine Bateson describes this problem:

As a young woman, I never questioned the assumption that when I married what I could do would take second place to what my husband could do. Twenty-five years later, I have slighted my own value so often that it is hard to learn to take it seriously. . . . For at least twenty years, whenever I interrupted my husband when he was busy, he finished what he was doing before he responded. When he interrupted me, I would drop what I was doing to respond to him, automatically giving his concerns priority. (1989, p. 40)

Can the marriage organize itself to support the wife's so-called "outside" activities as it does the husband's? The wife must be encouraged by therapists and by her husband to acquire any skills she needs in order to pursue these interests more fully. For the husband to position his marriage differently would usually mean that he needs to make it more central, thus moving in the reverse direction from his wife's. To increase what he gives to the marriage would typically require that he become more accomplished at the ways of relating that empower another and empower a relationship. As long as marriage remains unequal, mutually empowering interactions cannot occur. Promoting one another's power to act and power to be are obviously not compatible with interactions aimed at keeping control and resisting control.

Sex and violence. We are thus led once more to the most difficult linkage — sex and power and violence. How prepared is family therapy to move into this territory? (See Chapter 4 by Hare-Mustin and Chapter 5 by Goldner in this volume.) Luepnitz has set the proper perspective for us:

The question of why a woman "needs" an abusive relationship with a man is more fruitfully posed, "Why do women need to be in relationships with men so much that they will stay even if abused, and even if financially able to go?" And conversely, "Why are so many men willing to take the risk of losing their intimate relationships with women?" (1988, p. 163)

We must add another question: Why do family therapists typically work so hard to "save" a woman's relationship with a man who abuses power, even if he manages to control its physical manifestations? The answer to these questions does not lie solely or primarily in individual psyches or particular couples. Or, rather, it lies there but does not begin there and is not validated and sustained there. All I have detailed, and more, about the patriarchal order structured the answers to these questions before we or any men or women we see were born.

Family

David tried to imagine himself returning to this house, supervising the children, helping them with homework, insisting on chores. Abruptly he recalled a time, years earlier, when he was telling Liddie what to do in what he thought of as a calm, businesslike way — a way he congratulated himself on for being so different from Lainey's way. Liddie had turned to him in fury and said, "Why do you always have to preside *over us? Why can't you just* live *with us, like* Mother does?"

                    — *Sue Miller*, Family Pictures

Because of the way it is presently structured, validated, and valued, the family is indeed threatened by the movement women make towards greater autonomy and power. That is to say, family life as traditionally understood necessarily undergoes profound changes even with only moderate changes in the woman's role there. Those changes, even if specifically and consciously sought by a woman, still produce fear in her. Pressures to conform, to not go so far as to disrupt the family, come from all around her and from within her. Family therapists join that cautioning chorus by our very label, aligning us as it does with the view that family — heterosexual, perpetual, and, so far, inherently oppressive to women — is better than no family. To continue to call ourselves *family* therapists and to be taken as aligned some other way requires intentionality, and some measure of neon.

To position ourselves differently means that we stop using our sessions to fix up the people so the system works better and start fixing up the system so the people work better. Focus must go towards not simply the system in the room but also the system all carry in their heads and hearts depicting how families should work and for whose benefit and on whose back. In the usual case, all the warm and nourishing things happening in that picture are produced by women, but the idea is not for women to quit doing the close discernment of others' needs or to quit trying to satisfy those needs. Rather, the idea is to make those skills bisexual, multigenerational, and highly valued. Jean Baker Miller warns us, however, that

women will remain in second-class roles, and the areas of life which have been relegated to women will remain unintegrated into the mainstream of society, unless the status of all women *qua* as women is altered (1977, p. 25).

In the meantime, our goal as therapists may include helping a wife/mother feel the right to say "no" to requests for accommodation that burden her and helping the family acknowledge that right. Even more central may be our challenge to a husband/father to make accommodations for her. The children as well, both sons and daughters, should experience this reciprocity among themselves and with their parents. Again, if we apply the ideas about relational empowerment to family life, our position shifts from its usual interest in making sure everyone leaves every-

one alone enough to examining whether everyone has sufficient involvement in mutually empowering relationships both inside the family and
outside it. Our attention goes to helping the family create and support this
kind of context, including holding the men in the family responsible for
developing the necessary competencies to contribute to such a context.

Dilemmas

Assimilation in an unworthy society is an unworthy goal.

— *Marilyn French,* Beyond Power

Those of us who are committed to women's rights demand power for
women even as we challenge what is meant by "power." We demand full
citizenship for women in the public arena even as we challenge the ways
and means that constitute the public arena. We demand full citizenship in
the family even as we challenge the structure and functions that constitute
the family. We demand *and* challenge simultaneously, because if we challenge only and shun participation, we find ourselves on the outside where
those in power want us and where we have been all along. This squeeze
play serves as the setting for our professional work and gives rise to *personal*
problems.

1. We see family after family, hour after hour, in the certain knowledge
that we will rarely change the inherent and oppressive inequality in more
than minor ways. The deeply held beliefs of our clients that structure their
relationship unequally, the commitments that hold that unequal structure
in place, the cultural ratification and rewards that accompany it, the material realities that limit alternatives—these will usually win out over our
one hour a week. Most often, we will continue to find ourselves using the
time-honored approach of helping clients aim for what will make them a
little less miserable. So, we will continue to find ourselves helping a woman
make the best of a situation that seems to be the best situation among the
possibilities that she will imagine. How, then, will we satisfy ourselves
that she is not hearing from us, "If rape is inevitable, relax and enjoy it"?
How will we satisfy ourselves that we are saying something different?

2. In our work with families to address distribution of power and its
consequences, we will be pointing to trouble, not creating it. Nonetheless,
we will foment trouble more than peace, most of all for the woman we
seek to empower, but also for the other family members. The more
empowered she becomes, the more altered will be the emotional and

logistical routines that have defined for a family its particular ethos. The loss and turmoil experienced by all members of the family may well be of an intensity we are not accustomed to stoking. How do we learn to tolerate not being seen as helpful and healing? What can build our tolerance so that we do not dampen the fire in order to soothe ourselves?

3. To increase our abilities to empower women in therapy, we consider using resources and methods perhaps not previously familiar to us—men's groups, couples' groups, women's groups, study groups, individual therapy, and our own therapy. This extending of ourselves is necessary, but narrow in focus. How much can we expect the psychology of the oppressed to change until the condition of the oppressed is changed? Is there any integrity to our working in therapy to empower women if we are not also engaged in social activism?

These dilemmas manifest the limits of therapy. Sometimes, recognizing limits can be comforting by offering us a gauge, a mantra: "I've done all I can do here." However, in this instance, in this project to take on women and power and family therapy, knowledge of the limits grants us no solace; nor does it let us resign. Too many come to us and nowhere else. We cannot be victorious, yet we dare not be defeatist. We commit not to oversimplify, not to mystify, not to temporize, not to back away. We ready ourselves for the squeeze play.

The project is not for the faint of heart.

REFERENCES

Avis, J. M. (1988). Deepening awareness: A private study guide to feminism and family therapy. In L. Braverman (Ed.), *Women, feminism, and family therapy* (pp. 15–46). New York: Haworth.

Avis, J. M. (1989). Reference guide to feminism and family therapy. *Journal of Feminist Family Therapy, 1*(1), 94–100.

Atwood, M. (1988). *Cat's eye*. New York: Bantam.

Bateson, M. C. (1989). *Composing a life*. New York: Atlantic Monthly Press.

Bernardez, T. (1988). Women and anger—Cultural prohibitions and the feminine ideal. *Work in Progress, 31*. Wellesley, MA: Stone Center Working Papers Series.

Bograd, M. (1988). Enmeshment, fusion or relatedness? A conceptual analysis. In L. Braverman (Ed.), *Women, feminism, and family therapy* (pp. 65–80). New York: Haworth.

Bowen, M. (1966). The use of family therapy theory in clinical practice. *Comprehensive Psychiatry, 7*(5), 345–374.

Brandwein, R. A., Brown, C. A., & Fox, E. M. (1974). Women and children last: The social situation of divorced mothers and their families. *Journal of Marriage and the Family, 36*, 498–514.

Broverman, I., Vogel, S. R., Broverman, D. M., Clarkson, F. E., & Rosenkrantz, P. W. (1972). Sex role stereotypes: A current appraisal. *Journal of Social Issues, 28*, 59–78.

Cashion, B. G. (1982). Female-headed families: Effects on children and clinical implications. *Journal of Marital and Family Therapy, 8*(2), 77–86.

Chopin, K. (1972). *The awakening.* New York: Avon. (Original work published 1899.)

Family Therapy News. (1987). Context of intimacy, not pursuit, emphasized by AAMFT presenters. January–February, p. 5.

French, M. (1985). *Beyond power: On women, men, and morals.* New York: Summit.

Fulmer, R. H. (1983). A structural approach to unresolved mourning in single parent family systems. *Journal of Marital and Family Therapy, 9*(3), 259–269.

Goldner, V. (1985). Feminism and family therapy. *Family Process, 24*, 31–47.

Goldner, V. (1989). Generation and gender. Normative and covert hierarchies. In M. McGoldrick, C. M. Anderson, & F. Walsh (Eds.), *Women in families: A framework for family therapy* (pp. 42–60). New York: Norton.

Goodrich, T. J., Rampage, C., Ellman, B., & Halstead, K. (1988). *Feminist family therapy: A casebook.* New York: Norton.

Gornick, V. (1990, April 15). Who says we haven't made a revolution? *The New York Times Magazine,* 14, 27, 52, 53.

Hare-Mustin, R. T. (1978). A feminist approach to family therapy. *Family Process, 17*, 181–194.

Hare-Mustin, R. T. (1987). The problem of gender in family therapy theory. *Family Process, 26*, 15–27.

Hartmann, H. I. (1980). The family as the focus of gender, class, and political struggle: The example of housework. *Signs: Journal of Women in Culture and Society, 6*(3), 366–394.

Heilbrun, C. G. (1989). *Writing a woman's life.* New York: Norton.

Luepnitz, D. A. (1988). *The family interpreted: Feminist theory in clinical practice.* New York: Basic Books.

MacKinnon, C. A. (1979). *Sexual harassment of working women: A case of sex discrimination.* New Haven: Yale University Press.

McGoldrick, M., Anderson, C., & Walsh, F. (Eds.). (1988). *Women in families: A framework for family therapy.* New York: Norton.

Miller, J. B. (1977). Psychoanalysis, patriarchy, and power: One viewpoint on women's goals and needs. *Chrysalis, 2,* 19–25.

Miller, J. B. (1986). What do we mean by relationships? *Work in Progress, 22.* Wellesley, MA: Stone Center Working Papers Series.

Miller, S. (1990). *Family pictures.* New York: Harper & Row.

Minuchin, S. (1974). *Families and family therapy.* Cambridge, MA: Harvard University Press.

Morrow, J. (1990). *Only begotten daughter.* New York: Morrow.

Rich, A. (1979). *On lies, secrets, and silence: Selected prose 1966–1978.* New York: Norton.

Rich, A. (1986). *Blood, bread, and poetry: Selected prose 1979–1985.* New York: Norton.

Sprenkle, D. H., & Fisher, B. L. (1980). An empirical assessment of the goals of family therapy. *Journal of Marital and Family Therapy, 6,* 131–139.

Surrey, J. (1987). Relationship and empowerment. *Work in Progress, 30.* Wellesley, MA: Stone Center Working Papers Series.

Thorne, B., with Yalom, M. (Eds.). (1982). *Rethinking the family: Some feminist questions.* White Plains, NY: Longman.

Walker, A. (1989). In B. Lanker (Photographer and Interviewer), *I dream a world* (pp. 24–25). New York: Stewart, Tabori & Chang, Inc.

Walsh, F., & Scheinkman, M. (1989). (Fe)male: The hidden gender dimension in models of family therapy. In M. McGoldrick, C. M. Anderson, & F. Walsh (Eds.), *Women in families: A framework for family therapy* (pp. 16–41). New York: Norton.

Walters, M., Carter, B., Papp, P., & Silverstein, O. (1988). *The invisible web: Gender patterns in family relationships*. New York: Guilford.

Weiss, R. S. (1979). Growing up a little faster: The experience of growing up in a single-parent household. *Journal of Social Issues, 35*, 97–111.

Wiggins, M. (1983). *Separate checks*. New York: Harper & Row.

Woolf, V. (1927). *To the lighthouse*. New York: Harcourt, Brace.

2

JEAN BAKER MILLER

Women and Power: Reflections Ten Years Later

I N RECENT CONVERSATIONS people have told me stories that raise inter-esting questions:

For example, a woman came up to me after a meeting and told me that she was supervisor of a large number of sales workers. She asked, "Can you tell me what to do with these women?" Then she went on to say that her company has a big meeting once a month in which all the leading sales workers are recognized individually and asked to say a few words. In the past year or so, quite a few women have been among the sales people who are recognized. The women get up and say things like, "Well, I really don't know how it happened. I guess I was just lucky this time," or "This must have been a good month." By contrast, the men say, "Well, first I analyzed the national sales situation; I broke that down into regional components and figured out the trends in buying. Then I analyzed the consumer groups, and . . . I worked very hard—overtime three-fourths of the nights this month—and. . . . " The point is, of course, that the women

Editor's Note: Jean Baker Miller delivered her lecture, "Women and Power," on November 18, 1981, at Wellesley College. Her lecture was subsequently published in 1982 as part of the Work in Progress series from the Stone Center for Developmental Services and Studies at Wellesley. Because of its early and lasting value, I asked Dr. Miller to permit its publication in this volume and to add her comments, a decade later, on this key issue for therapy and for our life together.

were doing something like that, too—or something in their own style which was just as effective.

Another kind of example came my way when a woman was describing a project she initiated. She said as she starts to work, she thinks (and colleagues and friends have told her) this work might be genuinely significant and good. "Maybe I'm really onto something here," she tells herself. And immediately, almost in the same second, she says, "This is nothing," or "Everybody knows this anyhow."

Those two examples, I think, point to the question of women and power. In recent years there have emerged some writings about women and power (see, for example, Janeway, 1980), and some meetings to consider it from several viewpoints and disciplines. But if we are really going to build the kinds of institutions and personal lives that allow women to grow and flourish, I believe that we must invest much more conscious, concerted, direct attention to women and power. At the same time I believe that most of us women still have a great deal of trouble with the whole area. The only hope, it seems to me, is to keep trying to examine it together.

I am not implying that men *don't* have trouble with power (just look around the world!), but their troubles are different from those of women at this point in history. As with other major topics, I believe women's examination of power not only can illuminate issues which are important to ourselves, but also can bring new understanding to the whole concept of power. It can shed light on the traps and problems of men, perhaps illuminating those things most difficult for men themselves to discover.

I shall begin this initial consideration by reviewing some fairly common occurrences for women—analyzing them from a psychological perspective derived from clinical work.

DEFINING POWER

There have been many definitions of power, each reflecting the historical tradition out of which it comes; also, various disciplines of study have devised their own definitions (see, for example, McClelland, 1979). An example given in one dictionary says power is "the faculty of doing or performing anything: force; strength; energy; ability; influence . . ." and then a long string of words leading to "dominion, authority, a ruler . . ." then more words culminating in " . . . military force." I think the list reflects accurately the idea that most of us automatically have about power.

We probably have linked the concept with the ability to augment one's own force, authority, or influence, and also to control and limit others—that is, to exercise dominion or to dominate.

My own working definition of power is *the capacity to produce a change*—that is, to move anything from point A or state A to point B or state B. This can include even moving one's own thoughts or emotions, sometimes a very powerful act. It also can include acting to create movement in an interpersonal field as well as acting in large realms such as economic, social, or political arenas.

Obviously, that broad definition has to be further differentiated. For example, one may be somewhat powerful psychologically or personally but have virtually no legitimate socially granted power to determine one's own fate economically, socially, or politically. Also there's the question, "Power for what?" One may think in terms of gaining power for oneself, or one may seek influence for some general good or some collective entity.

WOMEN'S VIEW OF POWER

While more precise delineations are necessary, I think it is probably accurate to say that generally in our culture and in several others, we have maintained the myth that women do not and should not have power on any dimension. Further, we hold the notion that women do not need power. Usually, without openly talking about it, we women have been most comfortable using our powers if we believe we are using them in the service of others. Acting under those general beliefs, and typically not making any of this explicit, women have been effective in many ways. One instance is in women's traditional role, where they have used their powers to foster the growth of others—certainly children, but also many other people. This might be called using one's power to empower another—increasing the other's resources, capabilities, effectiveness, and ability to act. For example, in "caretaking" or "nurturing," one major component is acting and interacting to foster the growth of another on many levels—emotionally, psychologically, and intellectually. I believe this is a very powerful thing to do, and women have been doing it all the time, but no one is accustomed to including such effective action within the notions of power. It's certainly not the kind of power we tend to think of; it involves a different content, mode of action, and goal. The one who exerts such power recognizes that she or he cannot possibly have total influence or control but has to find ways to interact with the other person's constantly changing forces or powers. And all must be done with appropriate timing, phasing, and shifting of skills so that one helps to advance the movement of the less powerful person in a positive, stronger direction.

As a result of this vast body of experience within the family as well as in the workplace and other organizations, I think most women would be most comfortable in a world in which we feel we are not limiting, but are enhancing the power of other people while simultaneously increasing our own power. Consider that statement more closely: The part about enhancing other people's power is difficult for the world to comprehend, for it is not how the "real world" has defined power. Nonetheless, I contend that women would function much more comfortably within such a context. The part about enhancing one's own powers is extremely difficult for women. When women even contemplate acting powerful, they fear the possibility of limiting or putting down another person. They also fear recognizing or admitting the need, and especially the desire, to increase their own powers.

Frankly, I think women are absolutely right to fear the use of power as it has been generally conceptualized and used. The very fact that this is often said to be a defensive or neurotic fear is, I believe, a more telling commentary on the state of our culture than it is on women. For example, in current times, one can read that women are not being strong enough or tough enough. Such statements overlook the incredible strengths that women have demonstrated all through history, and they usually refer to some comparison with men's operations in our institutions. I believe they tend to overlook a valid tendency in women—that is, the desire to enhance others' resources—and to know, from actual practice and real experience, that it is an extremely valuable and gratifying life activity. On the other side of the picture, however, such statements reflect part of a truth—that women do fear admitting that they want or need power. Yet without power or something like it (which may eventually be described by another term) on both the personal and political level, women cannot effectively bring about anything.

WHEN WOMEN CONFRONT POWER

Now I'd like to focus on women's fears in confronting power, using individual examples which will further illustrate what may have been going on in the women I described briefly at the beginning of my remarks. I will highlight some women's inner, or intrapsychic, experiences.

Power and Selfishness

Abby was a low-paid worker in the health field who sought therapy primarily because of her depression. She had spent much of her adult life enhancing her husband's and her two children's development—using her powers to increase their powers. She then started work and did an excellent job, largely because she approached her patients with the basic attitude of helping them to increase their own comfort and abilities and to use their own powers.

After much exploration, Abby recognized that she tended to become depressed not when things were clearly bad, but when she realized that she could *do* something more—for example, better understand and effectively act on a situation. She felt this especially when she wanted to act for herself. For example, she knew that she was actually better at some procedures than the doctors were—not just technically better, but *totally* better, for she helped patients to feel more relaxed, more in control, and more powerful. She began to feel that she should get to do more of the interesting work, get higher pay, recognition, etc. She also realized that almost at the same moment she felt this way she became blocked by fear, then self-criticism and self-blame. This seemed to be a complex internal replica of the external conditions. The external conditions clearly blocked her advancement; she was a woman who worked in the lowest ranks of the health care hierarchy. But the internalized forces created even more complex bondage. Initially, for Abby, as for many women, there was the big fear of being seen as wanting to be powerful. This provoked notions of disapproval, but more than that, at a deeper level, evoked fears of attack and ultimate abandonment by all women and men.

Further exploration unearthed several more sticking points: One was that the prospect of acting on her own interest and motivation kept leading to the notion that she would be selfish. While she could not bear the thought that others would see her as selfish, it was even more critical that she could not bear this conception of herself. I find this theme to be extraordinarily common in women—often women in surprisingly high positions and places—and, by contrast, a rare theme in men. With this theme for Abby there usually would come the notion that she was inadequate anyhow. She felt she should be grateful that anyone would put up with her at all, and she should best forget about the whole thing.

Eventually, this inadequacy theme gave way to yet another stage in which she felt that she indeed did have powers and could use them, but doing so meant, inescapably, that she was being destructive. For Abby, this stage was illustrated by thoughts, fantasies, and dreams indicating destructiveness.

Power and Destructiveness

Another woman, Ellen, was at a different point in dealing with the same problem. She felt able to work and to think well so long as she worked on her ideas and plans in her own house. She could not bring them into the work setting. As she used to put it, "If only I could bring my inside self outside." Eventually, she said that this fear seemed to stem from the experience that as she went into the outside world or to work, immediately she became attuned to the new context, readily picking up its structures and demands. She felt she couldn't help but respond to that context and those demands.

Again, this kind of feeling is common in women, and again it reflects a very valuable quality. Historically, a woman's being attuned to and responding to her context and to the needs of everybody in it has been part and parcel of helping other people to grow and helping a family to function. Women can bring a special set of abilities to many situations because they *are* able to attune themselves to the complex realities that are operating. (This perhaps is the essence of what mental health researchers have tried to describe in characterizing mothers' contributions to infant development. See Winnicott, 1971.)

But consider the other side: Ellen felt that she could not get her own perceptions, evaluations, and judgments moving from inside her to the outside, although she had important contributions to make. To bring her ideas and action into the outside context she had to overcome her ready tendency to be only responsive.

But that wasn't all. She felt to do so would disrupt the whole scene. In other words, she would be destructive—and that was not a way she felt she should operate.

In each person such a theme forges its specific expression from the individual's history, but the basic theme occurs regularly in many women: To act out of one's own interest and motivation is experienced as the psychic equivalent of being a destructively aggressive person. This is a self-image which few women can bear. In other words, for many women it is more comfortable to feel inadequate. Terrible as that can be, it is still better than to feel powerful, if power makes you feel destructive.

Let me emphasize this thesis: Any person can entertain the prospect of using her or his own life forces and power—individually motivated, in a self-determined direction. In theories about mental health, this is said to bring satisfaction and effectiveness. But for many women it is perceived as the equivalent of being destructive. On the one hand, this sets up a life-destroying, controlling psychological condition. On the other hand, it makes sense if one sees that women have lived as subordinates, and, as subordinates, have been led by the culture to believe that their own, self-determined action is wrong and evil. Many women have incorporated deeply the inner notion that such action must be destructive. The fact that women have survived at all, I believe, is explained by the fact that women do use power all the time but generally must see it as used for the benefit of others.

Don't misunderstand me: Using one's abilities and powers for others is not bad by any means. It does become problematic for women and for men, however, when such activity is prescribed for one sex only, along with the mandate that one must not act on one's own motivation and according to one's own determinations. In most institutions, it is still true that if women do act from their own perceptions and motivations, directly and honestly, they indeed may be disrupting a context which has not been built out of women's experience. Thus, one is confronted with feeling like one must do something very powerful that also feels destructive.

Power and Abandonment

Another woman illustrated this dramatically. Connie had difficulty finishing her work, but she discovered that she would become "blocked" not when she was really stuck, but when she was working well, streaming ahead, getting her thoughts in order, and making something happen. At those times she would get up from her desk, start walking around, become involved in some diversion, talk to someone, and generally get off the productive trajectory. Further exploration of why this happened eventually led to her saying that if she let herself go on when she was working well, "I'd be too powerful and then where would I be . . . I wouldn't need anyone else." For Connie, the prospect was that she would be out in some scary place. She said she would feel like some unrecognizable creature, some non-woman. She spoke of the prospect as if it signified the loss of a central sense of identity. Her sense of identity, like that of so many

women, was so bound up with being a person who *needs* that the prospect of *not needing* felt like, first of all, a loss of the known and familiar
self.

On the one hand, it was an unnecessary fear. On the other hand,
Connie touched on a sense that is present in many women – namely, that
the use of our powers with some efficacy and, even worse, with freedom,
zest, and joy, feels as if it will destroy a core sense of identity. One feature
of that identity, as reflected by Connie's statement, demonstrates how
deeply women have incorporated the notion, "I exist only as I need."
Again, I think women are reflecting a truth which men have been encouraged to deny – that is, all of us exist only as we need others for that
existence – but cultural conditions have led women to incorporate this in
an extreme form. Along with it we women have incorporated the troubling notion that, as much as we need others, we also have powers and
the motivation to use those powers, but, if we use them, we will destroy
the relationships we need for our existence.

THE TROUBLESOME EQUATIONS

With these examples I have outlined some of the inner experiences women
have related to me as they confronted the issue of power. They include:

A woman's using self-determined power for herself is equivalent to
selfishness, for she is not enhancing the power of others.

A woman's using self-determined power for herself is equivalent to
destructiveness, for such power inevitably will be excessive and will totally
disrupt an entire surrounding context.

The equation of power with destructiveness and selfishness seems impossible to reconcile with a sense of feminine identity.

A woman's use of power may precipitate attack and *abandonment*; consequently, a woman's use of power threatens a central part of her identity,
which is a feeling that she needs others.

It is important to emphasize again the many sides of all of this: On the
one hand, most women are keenly aware of an essential truth that we all
need others, need to live in the framework of relationships, and also need
to increase the powers of others through our activities. On the other
hand, most women have been encouraged to experience these needs as a
predominant, central, almost total definition of their personalities. And
their experience tells them that change can occur only at the cost of
destroying one's place in the world and one's chance for living within a

context of relationships. I believe this reflects accurately the historic and cultural place, and the definition, of women.

The Challenges Ahead

The examples I have cited not only tell about individual neuroses but also reflect characteristics of many women. Right now I think it is important for women to recognize that we do need to use our powers. Many times, I think, women have done things which eventually proved to be destructive, often without being fully aware, because we actually felt so much pain and reluctance even to think about the topic.

Also, we need to help each other in several important ways: First, we can give sympathetic understanding to ourselves if we recognize the weight of the historic conditions which have made power such a difficult concept for most of us. Second, we can consider seriously the proposition that there is enormous validity in women's *not* wanting to use power as it is presently conceived and used. Rather, women may want to be powerful in ways that simultaneously enhance, rather than diminish, the power of others. This is a radical turn – a very different motivation than the concept of power upon which this world has operated.

Out of this, we can see that women already may have a strong motivation to approach the concept of power with a different, critical, and creative stance. Once admitting a desire and a need for power, women can seek new ways of negotiating power with others in personal life, work, and other institutions. Certainly this is a large and difficult prospect. It can appear naive or unreal even to talk this way. But the fact that it sounds unreal must not stop us! Once we recognize the undeniable truth that the world has been explained so far without the close observation of women's experience, it is easier to consider that seemingly "unreal" possibilities can become real.

Bear in mind these truths that have not been taken into account:

- Women's experience is usually not what it has been said to be.
- It is not men's experience. It does not necessarily operate on the same bases, same motivations, or the same organization of personality.
- What we find when we study women are parts of the total human potential that have not been fully seen, recognized, or valued. These are parts that have not therefore flourished, and perhaps they are precisely the ingredients that we must bring into action in the conduct of all human affairs.

- Certainly these emerging notions must be used for the benefit of women, which is reason enough to pursue them, but they must be used also for the ultimate benefit of everyone.

*   *   *

WOMEN AND POWER – TEN YEARS LATER

I believe it is very important that women continue their exploration of power in all aspects of life. This book examines power in a very important area, and I am grateful to be a small part of it. First, a word about the word "power" itself. Some women have suggested that we should not use this word when trying to talk about concepts of power different from prior concepts. Many people do not like the word "power" because it has so many associations with power *over* others, power to act *on* others, power to control and limit others, and, most important, power to violate and abuse others. Perhaps we shall find a better word. For the present, I think it may be wise to continue to use the term. One reason to continue using this word is to not diminish or water down the "powerfulness" of the force we are trying to discuss.

In looking back at this paper, written in 1982, I see myself struggling with the whole topic. I am still struggling. However, I have moved to another focus in thinking about power, at least in the realm of psychological development and growth within families – the notion of mutual empowerment (Surrey, 1984; Miller, 1986).

In the 1982 paper, I emphasized the idea that traditionally women have used their powers to empower others, i.e., to increase other people's resources and abilities in many ways. Women certainly did so in relation to children, but also in relation to husbands and others. Indeed, we could say that this is one way of describing women's traditional main activity in life. Empowerment is participating in the development of another in a way that increases the other's strengths. This activity has usually gone under names such as nurturing, mothering, being a good wife, and the like. However, those words do not describe the very complex activity of interacting with others in such a manner as to foster their psychological development and increase their powers.

This activity of participating in the empowerment of others is essential in all societies, although we do not usually think of it in this way. Almost all theorists agree that people develop only in interaction with other people. No one develops in isolation. In these interactions, if women or men are not acting in ways that foster other's development or empower others, they inevitably are doing the reverse, i.e., participating in interactions in ways that do not further other people's development.

In general, this essential activity has been assigned to women. From a continuing examination of this activity, I believe that we can begin to propose a form of development in which everyone would interact in ways that foster the psychological development of all the people involved, something we might call mutual psychological development. This form of development would rest on interactions that are mutually empowering.

Thus, I believe that the study of the possibilities of mutually empowering interactions may be a most productive step. Our notions about the goals of development can be reframed in this light. For example, we can recognize that, historically, our central, formative relationships have not been founded on the basis of mutuality. That is, growth-fostering interactions have gone mainly in one direction: Women have been fostering other people's growth. This is a societal situation, but our major theories reflect the societal situation. Criteria for maturity, for example, have not included characteristics such as the ability to engage in interactions that foster the development of all the people involved; nor do descriptions of development delineate how children would "learn" to engage in such relationships. Instead, psychological theories have generally focused on a line of development cast as a series of psychological separations from others.

By contrast, we might define the goal of development as the increasing ability to build mutually empowering relationships. As the quality of the relationship grows, the individuals enlarge. Each individual can develop a more complex repertoire and can contribute to and grow from more developed relationships. The goal is not an increasing sense of separation but a mutually empowering connection—and these connections, in turn, will lead to more growth.

We might learn a good deal if therapists asked of families not "How can these people become separate?" but "How can these people build mutually empowering connections?"

It would seem clear that a group that has constituted itself a dominant group in society would not develop its abilities to empower others. Indeed, such a group would tend not to recognize that such possibilities even exist. Yet they do exist. Women, and some men, have been practicing them for millenia. The task before us is to find the ways to transform this valuable ability into a mutual activity.

REFERENCES

Janeway, E. (1980). *Powers of the weak*. New York: Knopf.

McClelland, D. C. (1979). *Power: The inner experience*. New York: Irvington.

Miller, J. B. (1986). What do we mean by relationships? *Work in Progress, 22*. Wellesley, MA: Stone Center Working Papers Series.

Surrey, J. (1984). The "self-in-relation": A theory of women's development. *Work in Progress, 13*. Wellesley, MA: Stone Center Working Papers Series.

Winnicott, D. W. (1971). *Playing and reality*. New York: Basic Books.

3

LINDA WEBB-WATSON

The Sociology of Power

IT IS EASY TO BELIEVE that the sociology of power is too abstract a subject to matter much in the day-to-day practice of therapy. The view of the sociology of power developed in this chapter is intended to push the clinician to examine the relationship of power within the context of society. The questions addressed here focus on the nature of social relations that perpetuate the status of certain identifiable groups of people and that relegate these groups to nonparticipation in society. We focus primarily on the ways in which power is utilized to maintain inequality within society. From this vantage point, clinicians can examine the ways in which their own therapeutic practice perpetuates the same outcomes that are produced in the larger society.

The examination of sociology can be painful to the extent that it forces us to see our own passive (or active) participation in a society that is based, in many ways, on inequality. Certainly, if we have our hearts open we must see how, as members of the "haves," we benefit from the existence of the "have-nots."

The reader should not be lulled into thinking that the word "women" successfully unites all those of the female sex. A reference to "women" in the literature most often implies or is clearly representative of European-American* women. Therefore, the reader must be sensitive to the fact

---

*In this paper the term European-American is used to denote those people, often called white, who identify their ancestral origins in Europe. African-American is used to denote those people who identify their ancestral origins in Africa, although all human beings originated from Africa. Hispanics are those persons in the so-called New World who may identify their origins on any continent but whose primary language is Spanish. The category Hispanic is not an entirely satisfying one, but is currently being widely used. Asian-Americans and Native-Americans are

that we are addressing the issues and concerns not merely of European-American women but of all women, a stance which forces us to become more sensitive to how women from different ethnic groups define their social problems and define their relationships with men. European-American women are faring better in a sexist society than African-American and Hispanic women are faring in a racist society. Because of this difference in experience, women of color explain their problems in society in ways that designate the European-American female as part of the problem (Hood, 1978). Women of color are concerned about the fate of men of color in a racist society and do not see them as having power in this society. It would be misleading to suggest that men of color are culpable in the development of sexism in this society or to support an artificial delineation between men and women of color. Therefore, there is an implicit expectation in this chapter that the reader will examine racism (one's own and society's) as well as sexism. Only in this way can we fully understand the issues that are of concern to all women.

We begin by exploring the basic nature of power. A case example illustrates some of the problems with power we encounter in sociology, including how uses of power rob the individual of her will, how society maintains and supports poverty, and how it implicitly blames females for the actions of men. In using a case example, we run the risk of diffusing the bigger picture by giving specific details that are easily arguable on the individual case level. In part, this phenomenon keeps psychology and sociology apart (conveniently?), since we can justify our actions on an individual basis without noticing how those actions are influenced by patterns of power and how they contribute to trends that are evident at the sociological level. However, a case example humanizes the sociological perspective and allows us to examine the interaction of individual case decisions and societal patterns.

CASE EXAMPLE

Juanita* cleans the hot plate in her one-room flat and contemplates the trip to the court-ordered visitation with her six children, ages 5 months to 10 years old.

---

not identified in this paper simply because data on these groups are more difficult to obtain. This is not to imply that these groups of people do not exist or suffer under the same set of circumstances as African-Americans and Hispanics.
*This is a true case example. The names have been changed to protect the identity of the clients.

Juanita is 30 years old and finished the 8th grade in school. She has worked cleaning houses for $25 dollars a day. She has never held any other kind of job. Juanita has suffered from depression since adolescence. She has seizures and takes Dilantin to control them. She was sexually abused by her father and brother. There was no intervention to protect her. When she was 18, she married a man to get out of the house and began having her children. He was physically abusive to her. Three years ago, her husband left her. He does not pay child support.

Six months ago, Juanita had not been taking her medication and began having seizures. She left her children with a woman friend, who was sharing the rent, and went to the public hospital to get treatment. As in most public hospitals the wait was long and then it was decided to admit her. So, Juanita spent the night in the hospital thinking that her children were being cared for. She had no telephone at home so she could not let them know what was happening. Some time in the night her friend decided to leave and left the children alone. Someone reported this situation to the police and the children were picked up as abandoned. When Juanita was released from the hospital, she arrived home to find that her children were gone. After determining where they were, she went to Child Protective Services (CPS) to get them.

CPS believed that Juanita had abandoned the children; in addition, CPS had a court order granting temporary custody, so there was nothing she could do to get them back immediately. She had to wait for a ten-day hearing. It took over a week for CPS to get the information from the hospital to verify her story. The separation from her children was more than she could stand. She feared the CPS was going to keep her children. Her depression overcame her and she did not go to work. Already in financial trouble, she was unable to pay her weekly rent. She was evicted two days before the hearing. Since she had no place to stay, it was determined that the children could not be returned to her. A hearing was set for 30 days, in which time she was to find a place.

She clearly qualified for Section 8 Housing, but could not apply because she did not have her children and she could not get her children until she had housing. It was a vicious cycle and she was trapped in the middle. Panic struck; Juanita did a lot of things that people do when they lose their ability to make rational judgments. Her depression became worse and worse. It seemed to her that the more she tried, the worse her situation became. Her children were also having reactions to the separation. Two of them were suffering from severe depression; one was breaking anything she could get her hands on. The more Juanita's condition and the condition of the children worsened, the more convinced the authorities became that the mother and children should not be together. At the 30-day hearing, she did not get her children back and another hearing was set. Since that time, Juanita has been involved in a series of self-destructive behaviors, including getting drunk and attempting suicide. She is convinced that she will never get her children back—and the way that things are going, she is probably right.

Now let's examine this case briefly and ask the question, "What does this have to do with the sociology of power?" Unlike those of us who believe that we are the master of our own fate, Juanita has rarely had control over her own environment. It might be easy to think of her situation as a series of bad luck, but it is important to grasp that in a society that undervalues people of color and European-American women, there is support, by commission and omission, for the conditions that exist and affect this woman.

Sexually abused as a child, she had no one to protect her and she could not leave the situation. She quit school and no one seemed to notice. Even though she went to the 8th grade, her basic skills are approximately at the 4th grade level. Without treatment, she became depressed. She could not gain access to the mental health system that provides minimal assistance for the poor. Her options and life choices were already narrowed to a significant degree. This was the situation of her adult life. She had children that she loved very much, but she got caught up in a system that could only punish her. She was punished for being poor.

Juanita can certainly take some individual action, on a very limited scale, to address her circumstances. Most of what she needs requires money. But we are not focusing here on what this individual can do, rather on the systemic circumstances that make this situation possible. For Juanita these events occur at the individual level and might be considered a deviation from the norm of how society operates, because the situation seems extreme. However, we look to sociology to delineate the trends in the society that can show us whether or not the Juanitas of this world are meeting the same oppressive forces in all aspects of their lives. And sociology does show us that there are social redundancies that extend beyond the single case example and that we could have used on the day of Juanita's birth to predict the outcome of her life.

Many other sociological questions relating to power, women, race, and the family emerge from this case example. A few of these questions are:

What is power and how is power exerted so that it maintains inequality and injustice? Who are the poor? What are the structures in society that keep women at the lowest levels of the pay scale? How do society's attitudes support crimes of violence against females? Who goes to jail and for what crimes? How does family disruption, particularly in African-American and Hispanic families, perpetuate poverty?

WHAT IS POWER?

As in any discipline that seeks a consensus about a certain definition, agreement about the meaning of power does not come easily to sociology. It has evolved over time as sociologists seek to delimit more clearly the relationship that is observed. According to Lukes (1979), the definition of power is, "A exercises power over B when A affects B in a manner contrary to B's interests" (p. 34). Wartenberg (1990) suggests a further modification of this definition by saying that "a social agent A has power over another social agent B if and only if A strategically constrains B's action environment." Therefore, she (B) is not in the normal circumstances of human action, and as a result her responsibility for her actions is modified. This definition can be applied to both the interpersonal and the sociopersonal levels. An individual's action environment and, consequently, her actions are influenced and usually narrowed through the uses of external power.

In the example about Juanita, her action environment is constrained in several ways by outside forces, and her fate is largely determined by those same forces. She is threatened with the loss of her children if she does not cooperate with authorities, even if she cannot cooperate. Her inability to find a place to live is seen as her failure. From her vantage point, a range of choices is nonexistent. The coercive power that oppresses her is largely invisible except for the CPS worker or the judge, both of whom also feel powerless.

We can call this an examination of the sociology of racism and sexism. When one has a prejudice towards any group, it remains only that, but racism and sexism have enduring social outcomes. The pattern of racism and sexism can be traced by determining who participates in what activities, and when and how they participate. In the absence of racism and sexism, one would anticipate that people would participate in society in numbers roughly proportional to their percentage in the total population. When the impact of racism and sexism is felt, then those numbers become skewed, not only because of some immediate discriminatory act, but also because of the ways in which individuals are trained and socialized.

Racism and sexism are more than mere prejudice. For instance, during the Cold War, people in the United States had a prejudice against the Soviet Union, but the ability to put that prejudice into an active form was minimal. So, while the prejudice may have been strong, those feelings had little impact on the daily lives of the Soviet people. And with the coming of *glasnost*, many of these prejudices have disappeared. Prejudices can change relatively easily with political and economic realities.

When power is added to prejudice, then a reality is created that actualizes the prejudice and transforms it from an individual opinion to a collective policy. In this way, the notion that women are less valuable than men becomes translated into women being paid less because it is "women's work," while men in comparable jobs make more because "they are the breadwinners." And, even though it is becoming increasingly clear that many families require that the woman work outside the home, an idea persists that she is simply an ancillary partner in the financial well-being of the family and that her work is optional. Naturally, prejudices against women get translated into many forms and are more complicated than just the economic issue. So, the opinion of the lesser status of women is transformed into a national policy/mentality through the coercive use of power. In this form, substantial resiliency is created, which defies changes in attitudes and policy as it becomes institutionalized in every facet of life.

Power can be observed in various forms, including coercive, expert, legitimate, and referent. For the purposes of this discussion, coercive power is the form of power generated from the organization of the social system which, at both the covert and overt levels, serves to maintain the status quo. Expert power is what accrues from a certain level of expertise, degree, or title. Legitimate power is that given as the consequence of holding a particular office. Referent power is the power one accrues through association. Our discussion focuses on coercive power, particularly as it relates to the covert level of societal functioning. It is presumed that it is the covert level that is often most potent in prescribing and predicting our outcome in society, and that expert, legitimate, and referent forms of power can be used to achieve coercive ends.

In discussions of the sociology of power wealth is rarely, if ever, included. Yet wealth significantly influences how things get done and who gets to do them. A quick review of almost any discipline shows that the extremely wealthy in this society are not the targets of research. Perhaps, since the wealthy support so much social research, they can also influence what is researched.

THE POWER TO DEFINE

There is a fabled story about a little African boy who questioned the honesty of Tarzan's ability to defeat all the animals of the jungle, particularly the ferocious lion. The child's mother explains the honesty of the tale by telling the child, "My son, you'll get a different story when the lion learns to write."

The fable tells us that there is always another side to a story but the one who controls the pen controls the meaning and interpretation of events. The development of certain linguistic shortcuts actually supports certain views of people, which maintain power relationships as they are. Edelman (1974) offered a way of understanding cognitive structures through language. He delineated two predominant myths through which people explain everyday life and events. A "pattern one" myth involves seeing the sufferer as being responsible for her own plight while authorities try to help her and protect the rest of society from her. An alternative myth, "pattern two," views the sufferer as a victim of an elite who benefits from her low status and views the social structure as basically exploitative in nature. These myths create cognitive structures that see and interpret the world from very different positions.

According to Edelman, the predominant myth in this society is "pattern one." From this myth, social labels are derived and social problems are identified. The myth can be evoked by a single term, which implies the rest of the cognitive structure without expressly calling attention to it. For instance, to state explicitly that the cause of poverty is the laziness of the poor is not a sophisticated and acceptable statement in liberal circles. But a casual reference to the "welfare problem" implicitly reinforces the "pattern one" myth because it evokes the created image of laziness, women having babies to stay on welfare, welfare fraud, and a huge, expensive system that does not seem to be getting any better. The "pattern one" myth holds the recipient responsible for the failure of the welfare system. In addition, it is this myth that generates a solution (applied in many states) requiring job training and "workfare" for recipients rather than systemic changes that address the reasons for poverty. As Edelman notes, how we refer to people and their problems keeps our attention on so-called rehabilitation efforts, diverts attention away from the counterproductive results of public policies, and further distracts us from solutions that would correct the system rather than the victims (Ryan, 1976).

The resiliency of "pattern one" thinking is due to the way the individual must cling to his or her self-conceptions, including his or her role, status, powers, and responsibilities, which, in turn, are justified through the "pattern one" myth. Further, "pattern one" myths are reinforced by the fact that questions that should rightfully be political in nature are often turned over to professionals or experts and labeled as nonpolitical. Mental health professionals reinforce the norm that cheerful adjustment to poverty or war is healthy, while anger or despondency in the face of these sociopolitical pathologies is sick. The decision is labeled medical (evoking science), rather than political, thereby removing it from the public arena and, more often than not, placing it in the realm of incontestable fact.

The power to define through "pattern one" myth is central to the maintenance of power relationships. When one has the power to define, all aspects of society cooperate to substantiate the currently accepted definitions. Power must perpetuate itself, and it does so through the socializing institutions of the society. Goldenberg (1978) illustrates several tendencies that develop with power and facilitate the maintenance of power relationships. Of particular relevance is the tendency of power to become theology, the tendency of power to drive intelligence underground, the tendency of power to create its own language and system of communication, the tendency of power to spawn imitators, and the tendency of power to create a favorable environment for itself.

So we notice that in the United States there are certain characteristics of the social order that allow for self-perpetuation. To begin with, a system has been established in which the underlying philosophical values are money driven and antihuman. This system had to be sophisticated enough to speak in terms of concerns for humans but deliver its product and/or services in such a way that it ultimately robs people of their life force and vitality.

The system relies on a cadre of individuals who have been educated in its ways and who have an almost religious belief in the goodness of the system; they have to wear blinders to facts that emerge to the contrary. The system uses "education" to create the blinders by eliminating natural curiosity and creativity, punishing inquisitiveness, and rewarding conformity. The system uses "education" to systematically deny, distort, or falsify the contributions of some groups (African-Americans, Hispanics, European-American women) while glorifying, through falsification and distortion, its own contributions. Individuals in this cadre are taught and rewarded to place their sense of individual security on what they are not: "Thank God I'm not a woman," "At least I'm not Black," or "I may be Black, but I'm out of the ghetto." The system must make its cadre materially dependent, so that substantial change, which might bring about reconciliation of the ills of society, appears to be unfeasible, economically unsound, or too demanding of personal sacrifice.

The system uses control of the media to maintain its distortions by directing people's attention away from asking the right questions and by proffering a host of material delights. The system educates the powerless only marginally, usually just enough for them to feel obsolete and to experience themselves as being poor approximations of the images that dominate society. And finally, the system is structured in such a way that it does not matter who (of whatever gender or ethnicity) holds the title of authority. The system (as if it were a being) continues to do its thing. And by using sociological evidence, we see that the thing it does is a European-American male-dominated, male-defined thing.

WHO ARE THE ECONOMICALLY EXPLOITED?

We notice that as the federal deficit continues to climb, it is the "haves" of the society who are making more money and the poor who are being more exploited. By 1989, for every dollar that was spent on interest on the federal debt, 53 cents was paid to welfare programs. Government is now a vehicle for redistributing income to the relatively well off. It the trend continues, in 10 years the "haves" will be collecting $1.00 to every 22 cents transferred to the "have-nots."

Figure 1 shows projected 1990 population figures by sex and race. Notice that in this table, Hispanics are not identified separately and may be categorized in "Other Races".

To understand who the economically exploited are, we must have a notion of what poverty is. In 1990, the federal government established as the poverty level an annual income of $12,092 for a family of four. Of course, we know that even at several thousand dollars above this level, families are struggling to survive. Figure 2 shows the number of people living in poverty while Figure 3 shows the breakdown of this population by ethnic group.

Women and children constitute the largest group of people in the ranks of the economically exploited. The total number of children living below

FIGURE 1. Population projections, 1990.

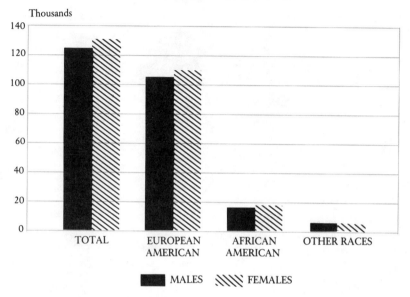

STATISTICAL ABSTRACTS OF U.S.

FIGURE 2. Persons below poverty level, 1988.

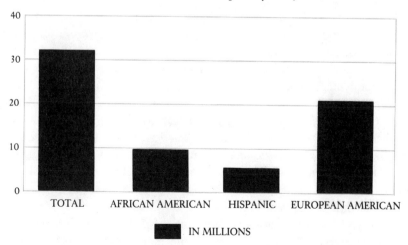

STATISTICAL ABSTRACT OF U.S. 1990

FIGURE 3. Percent below poverty level, 1988.

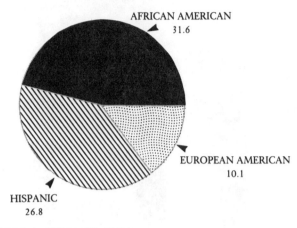

AFRICAN AMERICAN
31.6

EUROPEAN AMERICAN
10.1

HISPANIC
26.8

STATISTICAL ABSTRACTS OF U.S. 1990

the poverty level in 1987 was 12,435,000 or 20% of the population. In 1987, 33.6% of all families with no husband present were living in poverty, compared to 8.2% of all other families. The median income for female head of household is $15,419. With a male head of household, the median income is $26,157. Figure 4 shows a comparison of median income among male head of household, female head of household, and married couples.

Among African-Americans and Hispanics, even two-parent families with children have lower income levels. In 1988, the average European-American family had a median income of $33,915, the average African-American family had a median income of $19,329, and the average Hispanic family had a median income of $21,769.

Education may seem to be the answer to some of the dilemmas of the misuse of power, but compare income data for college graduates. The median income (1987) for a European-American with a bachelor's degree was $50,908, for an African-American, $36,568, and for a Hispanic, $43,382. So, even when African-Americans and Hispanics are able to obtain higher education, they are still kept at the lower levels of income. When income is equated with power, then these groups continue to be less powerful despite education. Unfortunately, we also realize that the "crisis" in education is producing more and more young people who are unable to participate in any aspect of society because they have no ability

FIGURE 4. Income: Couples and male or female head of household, 1987.

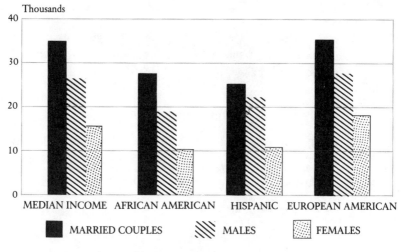

STATISTICAL ABSTRACTS OF U.S. 1990

to read, write, and compute. In 1988, the drop-out rate between the ages of 14 and 24 for Hispanics was 29.7%; for African-Americans 12.4%; and for European-Americans 10.8%. In 1988, 34.8% of Hispanic females between the ages of 18 and 21 were not high school graduates, compared with 16.5% of African-American females and 12.8% of European-American females. It is inevitable, then, that we will find more and more people of color and European-American women at the bottom end of the education and the earnings ladder.

IMPLICATIONS

It is the coercive use of power that creates the differences in income and opportunity in the society and that breeds inequality and injustice in all aspects of society. The discussion leads one to wonder about the implications. In some ways, as therapists we have power through expert, legitimate, or referent means. Simultaneously we participate, whether we are aware of it or not, in coercive, system-maintaining behavior and roles. So, whenever you think, "Well, I'm a woman, I have no power," the question must be posed, "Compared to whom?" I do not mean to imply that we forget who benefits the most from the current arrangements within the social system; rather, I suggest that, if we are to empower our clients to take new control of their lives, we must be willing to recognize the power that we have and utilize our power to create true change within the society. We may have to face supporting new arrangements in society, and therefore have to shift our own bases of identity and security. We may have sacrifices and change. Are we prepared to begin?

REFERENCES

Edelman, M. (1974). *Language and social problems*. Madison, WI: Institute for Research on Poverty, University of Wisconsin.

Goldenberg, I. I. (1978). *Oppression and social intervention*. Chicago: Nelson-Hall.

Hood, E. F. (1978). Black women, white women: Separate paths to liberation. *Black Scholar, 9*(7), 45–56.

Lukes, S. (1979). *Power: A radical view*. London: Macmillan.

Ryan, W. (1976). *Blaming the victim*. New York: Vintage Books.

U.S. Dept. of Commerce (1990). *Statistical abstracts of the United States 1990*. Washington, DC: Bureau of the Census.

Wartenberg, T. E. (1990). *The forms of power: From domination to transformation*. Philadelphia: Temple University Press.

II
ROMANCE

4

RACHEL T. HARE-MUSTIN

Sex, Lies, and Headaches: The Problem Is Power

W HEN WE THINK OF a little night music, of a little romance, we must ask, what is women's place in that romance? Was the romantic era to which we are heirs anything more than freeing of the spirit of men and asking only that women be a complement to men's needs? In *The Hearts of Men* Barbara Ehrenreich (1983) has spoken of men's flight from commitment, from family, and from responsibility. The 19th-century ideal of the husband as the "good provider" has changed and so have our social expectations of men and the economic prospects of women. The media have encouraged modern men to pursue pleasure without responsibility, while women are encouraged to read romances. How do we see this duality played out in intimate relationships? I will examine how gender is defined and redefined through male-female relationships and review some cases that show the pressures on women in traditional relationships in today's world.

Marriage has been described as a lifelong oppositional play of power masquerading as pleasure (Boone, 1986). Marriage in American society reflects the problem of how to manage inequality in a society whose ideal is equality. This is the central focus of this essay. Feminists have used the term "patriarchal" to refer to the social arrangements in which women's interests are subordinated to those of men. Although many opportunities seem to be open to women in contemporary society, all possibilities, whether in education, public life, or the labor market, have been designed to meet the needs of individual men who are unfettered by the ties of childcare and by the demands of domestic labor. Thus, patriarchal relations cannot be accounted for solely by the intentions, good or bad, of individual women or men.

As Nicola Gavey and her colleagues remind us: "All men, including those who appear to have little personal power, have the privilege of living in a world which is defined and controlled by members of their own gender (with the interests of their gender class at heart), where they exist as a version of the human norm, and where they benefit from institutionalized sexism" (Gavey, Florence, Pezaro, & Tan, 1990, p. 10). These gendered structures inhere in marriage and family life and give men a privileged position that no woman can have.

FEMINIST POSTMODERN THEORY

The ways in which gender meanings and practices come to be accepted in modern society is a focus of feminist postmodern theory and discourse analysis. By discourse, I mean a system of statements and practices that share common values (Gavey, 1989). A discourse is both the medium and the product of human activities; it is the way a certain world view is sustained. The dominant discourse in a society appears "natural" and is part of the identity of most members of that society. How natural are the ways we think! By building on the work of postmodern theorists, like Michel Foucault (1980), who has drawn attention to the way language and meaning-making are important resources held by those in power, we can examine historically specific discourses and social practices to understand how women resist, subvert, and succumb to power in a patriarchal society.

Feminist ideas converge with those of postmodernists like Foucault in several important regards (Diamond & Quinby, 1988). Both point to the intimate and immediate operations of power rather than focusing exclusively on "political" power—the supreme power of the state and state apparatuses of control such as police, army, legislatures, and judicial bodies. Power is examined as it affects daily life within the kinship system. One way feminists have attempted to draw attention to this intimate domination has been by opening up to public scrutiny what had formerly been regarded as the privacy of the family. Both feminists and postmodernists have focused on the role of the dominant discourse in producing and sustaining power and marginalizing competing discourses, such as feminist or minority ways of thinking that present a different point of view. Feminists also have shown how arguments about sexual difference conceal power by constructing difference as "natural" and thus beyond human capacity to change (Hare-Mustin & Marecek, 1990). Furthermore, both feminists and postmodernists criticize the way Western humanism has given primacy to the experiences of Western men.

The liberal/humanist tradition of our era assumes that the meanings of our lives reflect individual experience and individual subjectivity. This tradition has idealized individual identity and self-fulfillment and has shown a lack of concern about power. Liberalism masks male privilege and dominance by insisting that every (ungendered) individual is free. The individual has been regarded as responsible for his or her fate, and the basic social order has been regarded as equitable. Liberal humanism implies free choice even when individuals are not free of coercion by the social order.

Romantic individualism, the belief that one can be an unencumbered individual, has been attractive to some feminists, too, and has drawn attention away from a focus on social concerns and social contexts. Individual weakness is held accountable for failed relationships, never the institution of marriage. But the focus on the individual has unfortunate consequences, such as blaming the victim for her fate, viewing gender differences as individual deficiencies, and urging that the woman try harder to change herself. Such an approach is still characteristic of much of therapy and is the basis of popular self-help books as well (Caplan & Hall-McCorquodale, 1985; Lerner, 1990; Tavris, 1989; Worell, 1988). Furthermore, when we elevate the uniqueness of individuals, we comfortably avoid categorizing groups. Thus, we are able to deny that the social categories of gender, age, race, and class are powerful determinants of individual opportunity and individual action.

The recent poststructuralist critique holds that we are all constrained by cultural meanings (Hare-Mustin & Marecek, 1990). We construct the world around us, not from an idiosyncratic view, but from within the meaning community in which we live. The meanings we use are not simply a mirror of reality or a neutral tool, but are a shared way of viewing the world that influences our experience of it. The way we represent reality depends on these shared meanings that derive from language, history, and culture. Men have had greater influence over meaning throughout history through privileged access to education, through higher rates of literacy, and through control of the print and electronic media. These advantages constitute the power to create the world in the image of their desires (Hare-Mustin & Marecek, 1988). Feminists have deconstructed authorized meanings of what women and men are supposed to be by drawing attention to hidden meanings in discourses about gender and to meanings that have been marginalized. Let us examine a few therapy cases that reflect authorized meanings and women's subordinate position in those discourses.

Dora's Headaches

Recent research and scholarly investigation on Sigmund Freud reveals that in some of his most important cases Freud distorted the record of events to prove his theoretical points (Goleman, 1990). Such a case is that of Dora, one of the most frequently cited cases in psychoanalytic literature (Freud, 1905/1963; Hare-Mustin, 1983). Some historians now doubt its validity entirely (Goleman, 1990).

Dora, a 16-year-old girl, was brought to Freud by her father for symptoms such as a cough and repugnance at sex. Dora's father told Freud to "bring her to her senses." Freud described Dora as a young woman of very independent judgment who occupied herself with more or less serious studies and who attended lectures for women. Her father often took her along to the K household, where he was having an affair with Frau K. The husband, Herr K, had been making sexual advances to Dora, apparently encouraged by Dora's father. Dora's mother maintained the standards of housekeeping expected of a Viennese *hausfrau* of her day, and although Freud never met Dora's mother, he labeled her as having a "housewife's psychosis."

Freud, reflecting the patriarchal view of his era, assumed that any young woman would seek the attentions of a man like Herr K and be flattered by them. Furthermore, not only Freud but Dora's father and the K family claimed that Dora's allegations of her father's affair with Frau K and Herr K's sexual advances to her were not true. (Subsequently, the adults involved confirmed the accuracy of her reports, but only much later after she had long persisted in asserting that she was telling the truth.) Freud viewed all Dora's symptoms as signs of hysteria resulting from disguised sexual desire. When he tried to press his views on Dora, she quit analysis, which led to her being labeled as not only disturbed, but as "disagreeable and vengeful" (Jones, 1955, p. 33). In a follow-up written in the 1950s, Felix Deutsch (1957) described Dora as a "repulsive hysteric."

Historians have tracked down several people who knew Dora, including

a cousin who was a confidante of Dora and who was mentioned promi-
nently in the case (Goleman, 1990). The cousin reported that she had
known of the father's affair, but said the only symptoms Dora had were a
cough and what seemed to have been migraine headaches. The couple
that Deutsch drew his impressions from was found to have not really
known Dora and to have just been reporting negative gossip based on
Dora's having gone to see Freud. As Goleman points out, it is not hard to
conclude that Dora was distressed, as any young woman in such a situation
would be, but that she was not disordered.

Freud's views are often explained away as the product of the patriarchal
era in which he lived. What seems harder to explain is why, 100 years
later, his followers still cling to his ideas, especially those emphasizing that
the seduced girl is the seducer, that the seduced female is aroused and
flattered by male advances, and that the female is to be regarded as an
anatomically and psychologically defective male. Rather than focus on
determinants of behavior in the individual's "unconscious," I will examine
the discourses through which society produces the gendered identities of
men and women. But first, let us consider two, more recent cases.

The Case of the Innocent Husband and the Crazy Wife

In a more contemporary case, an author focused on the problem of im-
passes in therapy with marital affairs (Smith, 1990). In brief, a wife came
home unexpectedly from work, found the front door uncharacteristically
locked, her husband only partially dressed, a woman emerging from the
bathroom straightening her clothes, and the bed sheets rumpled and stained
with semen. The husband vehemently denied to her that anything im-
proper had taken place. The couple's relationship deteriorated, and the
couple entered therapy, but progress was limited.

After three years, the therapist invited in a consultant with a constructivist orientation. The consultant asked each member of the couple to tell his
or her story about the event. The husband's story was quite vague and not
very convincing; the wife's was vivid and detailed. The consultant pointed
out that the wife's story was better than the husband's. The consultant
asked the husband to tell the wife's story, but the husband argued that he
could not do so because her story was not true. The consultant finally
persuaded him to do so if he loved his wife. The husband told the wife's
story, she was much relieved, and they went home and subsequently
reported their relationship was much improved.

A colleague of mine said that the case should not be published because he questioned the ethics of the constructivist consultant for "manipulating" the couple. In contrast, I saw the case as one where the wife's experience had been disallowed. For three years, the wife had been told that what she saw was not "true." In effect, she had been told something was the matter with her, that her "reality" could not exist, that she was crazy.

What the consultant recognized was that this woman's experience was being denied. The emphasis on the differences between men and women, the belief that men are rational and women emotional, leads to discounting women's accounts of their experience. In the face of male authority, the wife is expected to give way to the husband's meaning, just as Dora was expected to give way to Freud's. There is a long tradition, in custom and in law, where women are not believed and where women's accounts are marginalized. In court, women's testimony has not had the authority of men's, and only recently has a woman's account of being raped been admitted as testimony in states like New York. In addition, a woman was not permitted to testify against her husband. In this case, the constructivist consultant arranged a task that confirmed rather than denied the woman's reality, that confirmed that she was not crazy.

A Simple Fantasy for a Frustrated Wife

This is another case where a therapist dealt with a woman's experience of powerlessness. In a recent article on empowerment in strategic therapy, the author (Coyne, 1987) suggested that therapists often help clients discover that they have the power to make choices. He described the case of a couple who had moved across the country so that the husband could take a better job. However, in doing so, the wife had to give up an excellent job. She had been unable to find another job and so tried to involve herself in housework. She felt frustrated and intensely angry, but felt it would be ungrateful to express these feelings.

The therapist assigned her the task of preparing dinner and then turning up the heat on the stove while imagining deliberately burning the dinner. Her fantasy was to include showing the husband the scorched mess and demanding he take her out to dinner at a nice restaurant. "With the fantasy completed, she should turn down the gas before the meal was ruined, and in order to make up for such thoughts, greet her husband particularly enthusiastically when he came home from work" (Coyne, 1987, p. 544).

The therapist regarded this as an intervention that allowed the client to engage in "absurd acts of assertion, non-compliance, or rebellion" that avoided confrontation and led to spontaneous acts of assertion. One might well ask, was the therapist doing anything other than giving the wife permission for the kind of fantasies women have had for centuries, fantasies that have not changed women's subordinate position? Moreover, when the therapist said she must make up for such thoughts, he seemed to be ascribing guilt to the wife for even allowing herself the fantasy.

As Katherine Hayles (1986) has pointed out, the only acceptable voice for women in a male world is a voice that does not directly express anger. Women's "relational" voice is distinctively shaped by the necessity to deny and disguise the anger that arises from a lack of power. Notice that the therapist stated that the woman needed to greet her husband particularly enthusiastically "in order to make up for such thoughts." What are these thoughts that she must atone for and make amends for? That she was an ungrateful wife? That she imagined burning the dinner and asking her husband to take her out to a restaurant? Why should a woman have to "make up for such thoughts?" The therapist provided no follow-up report of any acts of assertion presumed to follow from this assignment.

DIFFERENCE AND POWER

As these cases show, dealing with power has been one of the most difficult issues for therapists, perhaps because therapists often deny the power of their own position. The emphasis on different experiences of socialization and reciprocal gender differences between men and women has masked differences in power (Jacobson, 1983; Margolin, Talovic, Fernandez, & Onorato, 1983). By joining the debate on "female nature" and "women's place," some feminists have lent credence to that debate. Elsewhere I have written about *alpha bias*, the tendency to exaggerate gender differences, and *beta bias*, the tendency to ignore such differences (Hare-Mustin, 1987; Hare-Mustin & Marecek, 1990). I have concluded that alpha and beta bias have similar assumptive frameworks, both take the male as the standard of comparison, and both support the status quo of male dominance and female subordination. The underlying motive of both alpha and beta bias is the wish not to deal with inequality. The focus on gender differences has obscured inequality.

The celebration of traditional feminine qualities, as exemplified in the emphasis on gender differentiation and romantic antimodernism, has been characterized by Judith Stacey (1983) as the new conservative feminism.

Vivian Gornick (1990) has pointed out that phrases like *a different voice* and the *second stage* of feminism seem to indicate progress but they are really regressive. Iris Young (1983) has also drawn attention to the way the focus on gender differentiation has diverted feminist thinking from a focus on power.

This conservative drift is observable in theories and research that emphasize the essential nature of men and women rather than the social context that shapes them (Kahn & Yoder, 1989). Caring, which is represented as a fundamental female quality, can be better understood in relational terms as a way of negotiating from a position of low power. Thus, when a woman argues with her husband, she appeals for caring, but in dealing with her children, she emphasizes rules, while the children appeal for caring (Hare-Mustin & Marecek, 1986). Rather than a nurturing and peaceable voice, the noted feminist and legal scholar Catherine MacKinnon has suggested that the "different voice" is the voice of a victim (Toufexis, 1990).

The conservative drift is counter to what had been regarded as the most significant contribution of feminist theory, the analysis of the social processes through which individuals and social systems are gendered. In the field of family therapy, it is the emphasis on social processes that has provided the lens through which most feminists have examined the meanings that surround the family (Goodrich, Rampage, Ellman, & Halstead, 1988; James & MacKinnon, 1990; MacKinnon & Miller, 1987; McGoldrick, Anderson, & Walsh, 1989; Taggart, 1985; Walters, Carter, Papp, & Silverstein, 1988). Let us look at a case that demonstrates what this lens can reveal. Here the therapists recognized the limitations on women's choices resulting from economic inequity and cultural stereotypes.

The Peripheral Father,
The Enmeshed Mother/Daughter

This is a case of a family with a 19-year-old anorexic daughter who had had three years of unsuccessful individual and family therapy (Taffel & Masters, 1989). The father seemed to be the classic peripheral father, only occasionally entering the world of his wife, daughter, and mother-in-law to criticize them. The mother was the powerfully centralized mother of family therapy tradition. But the therapists recognized that, peripheral as the father seemed, his attitudes often became family law, and his disapproval was a powerful influence on the family. Power does not have to be obvious or based on direct force, but it is evident when one person is in a position to direct or restrain the options of another.

The therapists in this case also saw that the mother's alleged power was a hollow myth. In addition to managing the home, she worked full-time as co–manager in the family store without salary or recognition. She was merely "helping out." She believed she had no choice about doing her duty as a wife, mother, and adult daughter, although she was subject to criticism from everyone about how she handled these heavy responsibilities. The therapists recognized that what might be characterized as mother-daughter enmeshment could be a result of their shared sense of helplessness. I like to think that the progress these therapists made was due to their sensitive perception of the influence of social forces and role expectations in this family. If we are to understand how women negotiate from, sometimes resist, but often succumb to their relative lack of power, we need to examine how the prevailing social discourses influence meanings and expectations.

DISCOURSE ANALYSIS

Heterosexual relations are the primary site where the meaning of gender, of what it is to be masculine or feminine, is reproduced. At any moment, there are several different discourses concerning sexuality that define what is expected of men and women in relation to each other. Through the mutual interplay of men's and women's different positions in the discourses concerning sexuality, feminine and masculine identities are produced. These identities then become part of an individual's "nature" and constrain and impel an individual's choices. I will review in turn what Wendy Hollway (1984) describes as the male sexual drive discourse, the have/hold discourse, and the permissive discourse.

The Male Sexual Drive Discourse

The male sexual drive discourse is the dominant discourse in the production of meanings concerning sexuality and is typically regarded as common sense. Also, it is legitimized by experts. The woman is seen as the object that arouses and precipitates men's sexual urges. Men's sexual urges are assumed to be natural and compelling; thus, the male is expected to be pushy and aggressive in seeking to satisfy them.

The male sexual drive discourse of men's need and women's compliance occurs not only in the home but in the day-to-day practices of men toward women who venture into public space. In large cities in America the norm of inattention between unacquainted persons is breached by men when women venture from their homes into public life (Gardner, 1980). Feminists have drawn attention to the way women are open persons on public streets. Young women, in particular, unless accompanied by a child or a man, are subjected to free and evaluative commentary by men. In this way, women are reminded of their subordination and vulnerability.

A *"Fifty-Fifty" Marriage*

In describing a case of a family with father-daughter incest, Kerrie James and Laurie MacKinnon (1990) illustrated the male sexual drive discourse very well. They showed how lack of interest by women in sexual relationships with their husbands is portrayed as abnormal or dysfunctional, but men's "need" for sex is seen as normal and functional. In their case, the family came for therapy at the mother's request two months after the 16-year-old daughter had disclosed that her father had been entering her room at night and fondling her genitals while she appeared to be asleep. The mother confronted her husband who then moved out of the house.

The wife experienced her husband as verbally abusive and intimidating. He maintained strict control of family finances and of the children's social activities. The wife was afraid to openly disagree with her husband; the husband perceived her submission as agreement with his decisions. He regarded the decisions they made as "fifty-fifty." He experienced her as withdrawn from him and realized that she tended to side with the children. Both children were afraid of their father. The children resented that all the household work fell on their mother even though both parents had paid employment. Thus, the children discerned that their mother's situation was not a voluntary one.

In many cases of incest, therapists have focused on the mother who has withdrawn sexually from her husband, as if such withdrawal leads to his turning to his daughter. The male sexual drive discourse justifies the belief that men need a sexual outlet to feel like "real men." The implication is that it is "natural" for a father who feels inadequate to exploit sexually his younger, less powerful children. Often the failure of a mother to "protect" her children is treated as more reprehensible than the sexual abuse perpetrated by the father (Wattenberg, 1985). In this case, the therapists viewed the family in the context of a patriarchal social structure in order to understand why men attempt to control through intimidation and why women submit.

Recall that the male sexual drive discourse authorizes men to do what they need to do to satisfy their sexual desires. Often the expression of anger by men leads to submission by women. In another case, reported as prototypical in research on negative emotions in marital interaction, 78% of the husband's negative affect was anger and contempt whereas 93% of the wife's negative affect was fear, complaining, and sadness (Gottman & Levenson, 1986). The researchers regarded the wife's responding with fear to the husband's anger as revealing a clear dominance structure in the marriage. In arguing for research on sex differences, Alice Eagly has pointed out that "many of the differences in the social behavior of the sexes describe in exquisite detail the ways in which men maintain their power over women" (Eagly, 1990; see also Eagly, 1987; Maccoby, 1990). However, there are no well-designed empirical studies that support the claim that mothers collude in incest perpetrated by fathers on their children (Wattenberg, 1985).

The Have/Hold Discourse and the Docile Body

The have/hold discourse is the underpinning of the ideal family where monogamy is the rule and there is a commitment by husband and wife to have and to hold each other. However, the woman must be attractive if a man is to want to have her and be committed to her. Although men must also be attractive to women, the dominant discourse emphasizes women's need to "attract" a man. But, if a woman desires close and intimate relations, her expression of feelings, her desire, is regarded as a weakness. Thus, as part of the discourse, men are seen as necessary to support the weakness of women. The have/hold discourse is about women's neediness. Women's weakness, women's desire for closeness, in turn reinforces men's power. But the voice of caring, women's different voice, will not criticize those who devalue women's caring and feelings. In contrast to this aspect of femininity, masculinity emphasizes men's strengths and expects men to conceal their weaknesses.

How are we to understand what it is for a woman to be "attracting"? It has been argued that an unprecedented discipline directed against the body has accompanied the rise of new conceptions of political liberty in our era (Foucault, 1979). This is apparent in the postures required of such persons as students, soldiers, and prisoners. But nowhere is the "docile body" more apparent than in the forms of femininity regarded as attractive. Women's bodies are subject to disciplinary practices distinct from and more demanding than practices for men (Diamond & Quinby, 1988). These practices included corsets and bound feet in past eras, and high heels and pierced ears in current fashion.

Through education and the media, a state of conscious visibility is induced in every woman, so women are indeed preoccupied with perpetual self-surveillance (Bartky, 1988). As has often been pointed out, women's magazines with mass circulation have articles on exercise and dieting in virtually every issue. Dieting sets up the absurd condition in which a body that needs food is treated as the enemy. Further control of women is evident in the idea that a woman's face must be made-up, an idea that presupposes that a woman's face without make-up is defective. Sandra Lee Bartky (1988) points out that because no formal authorities enforce these standards, the impression is given that the creation of attractive femininity by every woman individually is voluntary and natural. Rather, this controlled body and face can be understood as part of women's need to meet the norm of attractiveness in the unequal system of sexual choice and subordination.

The Attraction of the Ice Maiden

Subordination can have various meanings. In the case of a couple I saw, I pointed out that the wife had become like the legendary Ice Maiden. After a number of years of marriage, she had become cool, remote, and sexually unresponsive to her husband's overtures. Her husband worked long hours as an extremely affable and dynamic minister of a church with active women volunteers who were devoted to him and his programs. In an interesting way, the wife's remote style of beauty – and she was beautiful – exemplified the attractiveness of the controlled body idealized in the media. He was attracted to it, but it was not a docile body in another respect. She had accepted the have/hold discourse, the primacy of being attractive in order to hold. However, in response to what she saw as his excessive involvement with his work, the warmth he spread generously to his parishioners, his workers, and his projects, she would not melt to participate in the male sexual drive discourse.

The sanctions for not conforming to the ideals of feminine appearance have extended to all classes. The importance of the woman's "attracting" in the have/hold discourse is critical. Failure to be attractive can mean loss of a male partner for heterosexual women or loss of a woman's livelihood. The meaning of acceptable femininity is centered on the appearance and sexuality of a woman's body rather than on managing a home and raising children, as in past times. For a woman to loosen the binds of the docile body, to "let herself go," is to risk censure and her very status as a woman. This potential penalty affects all women, whether prepubescent little girls or grandmothers, whether they shoplift make-up at the 5-and-10¢ store or wear designer gowns.

The Permissive Discourse

In contrast to the have/hold discourse, the permissive discourse challenges monogamy. It is essentially about masculine sexuality with no commitment or responsibility. As feminists have frequently pointed out, the permissive discourse sets a standard of compliance for women and serves further to coerce women into meeting men's needs, by labeling reluctant women either as uptight teases or frigid.

The permissive discourse and the male sexual drive discourse further the idea that women's bodies are meant to serve men's needs. This has even been enshrined in law. For example, the New York State nudity law prohibits a woman from exposing her breasts in public for any reason other than to nurse an infant or to *perform as entertainment* (Stern & Stern, 1990).

In her research, Wendy Hollway (1984) found that women often give in to a kind of interpersonal coercion, to men's pleading for free sexual activity, because it seems so important to men. Thus, women appear to consent freely even when they do not want to. The male sexual drive discourse and the permissive discourse combine to justify men in whatever they have to do to have sexual relations. This kind of sanctioned coercion, of course, renders dubious the idea that women are free to choose or to withhold consent in such relationships.

MARRIAGE BETWEEN EQUALS

I would like to suggest another discourse that influences the choices and behaviors of women and men, the ideals of femininity and masculinity—the marriage between equals discourse. Marriage is an institution that regulates relations between the sexes, including relations of power. However, the marriage between equals discourse allows marriage to conceal the extent of male domination and female subordination.

In our liberal-humanist tradition, power is only tolerable on condition that it mask a substantial part of itself (Weedon, 1987). Glance through any book or article about couples and you will find presented a balance between partners, with any inequalities related to gender viewed as unintended and argued away. Thus the husband may be "too stressed" after work to help with chores, or the wife may do most of the cleaning because she is "fussy" about the house. But Hanne Haavind (1984) has drawn attention not only to how the suppression of women is generated through marriage, but to how female subordination is concealed rather than revealed by *both* men and women. She points out that male dominance is not labeled as such because we do not regard the husband's power as stemming from a desire on his part to dominate. Acceptable masculinity is still domination, but domination that appears reasonable and not striven for.

Society does not demand that ideal femininity be completely passive, according to Hanne Haavind. Feminine and masculine identities are reciprocally confirmed within a frame of *relative* masculine domination in marriage. Femininity can involve aggression and initiative if these are not used to dominate men. Thus, women can do many things so long as they are in *relative subordination* to their men.

Often, questions about love appear to be a source of tension in the relations of men and women, obscuring the underlying questions of male dominance and female subordination. If we recall the male sexual drive discourse, the have/hold discourse, and the permissive discourse, it is apparent that these discourses relate not just to sexuality but to the differences between what men and women are supposed to do because of love. As has been emphasized in the popular press, men regard their wives' having sex with them as acts of love, women regard their husbands cuddling them or remembering their birthdays as acts of love. As the male sexual drive discourse provides, the wife is expected to meet the husband's sexual needs. Since this expectation is seen as compelling, how freely she consents is problematic. That which is required may not feel like love to her. As the have/hold discourse defines the wife's need to be cared for, cuddling and birthdays are important signs of love for her. Her husband may not see what they have to do with love.

In American society, the marital relation is supposed to have top priority for the wife, but not for the husband. Virginia Goldner (1988) has pointed out that "as long as patriarchy prevails, love will be tainted by domination, subordination will be erotized to make it tolerable . . . " (p. 30). As I observe in the case below, for many women it is important to perceive the marital relationship as equal and reciprocal and not to perceive themselves as subordinate.

The Family Myth of Upstairs/Downstairs

Do most women have a choice between having a stable marriage and an equal one? Arlie Hochschild (1989) examines this question in her study of working parents. One of her cases illustrated this problem. The wife, Nancy, arrives home from her job as a social worker and scurries between stove, sink, and washing machine, her four-year-old at her feet, while her husband is irritated if she asks him to set the table. The husband, Evan, is rather distant from their son, Joey, and it is Nancy's job to get Joey to bed. "Joey's problem" emerged as a difficulty in getting to sleep, a prolonged series of bedtime demands that left Evan tired, Nancy exhausted, and Joey in his parents' bed at 11 p.m. because his bed was "scary." Evan explained that all kids go through needing their moms and this was an oedipal phase.

The research followed Joey's family (and a number of others) over several years as the marital relationship deteriorated to bickering and bitterness. Evan did not see why he should change his life because his wife chose a demanding career. Nancy saw Evan as not doing a share that she deeply felt was "fair." She was expected to work the "second shift" at home. She felt exhausted and was no longer interested in sex with her husband, yet she was troubled about "holding out" on him. Notice here the underlying male sexual drive discourse, accepted by Nancy, that it was the man's right to have his sexual desires met.

How was this crisis in the marriage resolved? Hochschild reported a resolution that led to a dramatic lessening of tension over the issue of the second shift of work at home. Evan won. Nancy was to do it. The mythic solution was the elevating of the garage to the full moral and practical equivalent of the rest of the house. Nancy would be responsible for the "upstairs" — meals, shopping, laundry, housecleaning, childcare, and Evan would be responsible for the "downstairs" — the garage and his basement workshop, as well as the dog. Nancy cut back her career work to part-time.

Thus we have the marriage between equals discourse. To accept the arrangement as fair, the wife re–zoned the territory. Now Nancy could ignore the downstairs and be indignant only if Evan did not take care of the dog. For Evan the dog became the symbol of the entire second shift. Other men in the study also developed what the author called second shift fetishes, something that symbolized their entire share in a marriage of equals. One man reported that he made all the pies for the family. Another man grilled fish. A single act was transformed into the equivalent of the multitude of chores the wife did.

The typical therapeutic response to this family might have been to solve "Joey's problem" and get him out of the parents' bed. But this approach would have overlooked the struggle going on concerning the inequality in the family. The crisis was resolved by creating a myth that satisfied both Nancy and Evan and probably would have satisfied many therapists, too. Comparisons between Nancy's hours of leisure and Evan's were transformed into differences in their personalities. Evan noted that he was lazy while Nancy was compulsive and well-organized. To each of them this explanation was acceptable as part of their newly proclaimed view that men and women were "naturally" so different that they could not be compared. In this way, a double standard of virtue was also upheld. If the husband were to allow his relationship to his wife to be more important than other relationships, he would be seen as making a sacrifice for her. The wife is not seen as making a sacrifice. The inequity stems, in part, from the fact that marital relations are a top priority for the wife because of the have/hold discourse, but not for the husband. The inequity cannot be separated from economic conditions that make women more dependent in the larger society and that contribute to and are part of the gender discourse.

Let Me Listen to Your Headache

One way to obscure the fact that women have less power than men is to do as Nancy and Evan did, to transform inequality into personality differences or into men's and women's different essential natures. Another way to avoid recognizing women's relative lack of power is to focus on women's physical problems. In two dramatic cases of women with severe tension-vascular headaches, the women and families vehemently denied that the women were experiencing any psychological stress in their lives (Griffith, Griffith, & Slovik, 1990). The therapist, having lost his first headache patient who stormed out of the hospital against medical advice, decided to approach the second case in a different way. He asked the patient to tell her story, following the idea that therapy is a conversational process of saying and expanding on the unsaid.

In her meetings with the therapist, the wife, Dawn, and her family, gradually came to relate her pain from headaches to problems in relationships with her husband, mother, and sisters. What emerged was a series of fears centering on Dawn's father's having abandoned the family when her mother was pregnant with Dawn, on how Dawn's illness might harm her son just as her own mother's depression and hospitalization had harmed her, and on her irritation at her husband's hovering presence.

The authors speculated that "this was a family of strong women with a long history of anger toward men. Perhaps by entering as a man who eschewed power, the therapist allowed them to give him all power" (Griffith, Griffith, & Slovik, 1990, p. 26). The authors also suggested that the headaches may have served as a distance regulator between husband and wife. In addition, beneath the headaches were frightening secrets about men who left women. What I found interesting was the story of strong women angry at men who abandoned them. Were the women abandoned because they were strong, or were they strong because they had survived being abandoned? Did Dawn's headaches regulate the distance between husband and wife, or were the headaches associated with her being caught between not wanting closeness and fearing abandonment? We can see the relation of the headaches to the tension of the have/hold discourse. Regarding the question of power, I believe it could be understood not as the male therapist's seeming to give up power in order paradoxically to get the women to accord him power, but as the therapist's according power to the women to tell their story. This granting of power also happened in the Case of the Innocent Husband and the Crazy Wife.

The way the dominant group can name and control the ideas in the discourse is illustrated by another biomedical phenomenon, Premenstrual Syndrome (PMS). Mary Parlee (1989) has analyzed how the popular and scientific conception of PMS has rationalized the contradictions and suffering in women's lives. Admittedly, some women are affected by changing monthly hormonal balances. PMS, however, is a disorder for which no biological marker has been found and no biological treatment has been found, despite intensive research efforts. For women, PMS language is empowering because it accords social reality to women's experiences that have been trivialized or not understood. Its usefulness is that it provides an explanation for women's "out of role" behavior, that is, women's anger and irritability toward family members or coworkers. By individualizing and medicalizing experiences widely shared by women, PMS serves the gender discourse. The case below describes another way a woman tried to deal with her feelings of helplessness.

A Wife Runs Off With the Delivery Man

Although some women leave marriages where they feel powerless, they do not find leaving easy to do. Olga Silverstein (Walters et al., 1988) described a case where she received a frantic telephone call from a husband who complained that his wife of 12 years had run off with the delivery man. Cassie, the wife, admitted that she was increasingly unhappy in the marriage, but she had no financial resources of her own, and she felt she had no right to break up the family. How did she choose between her husband, Bill, and the lover who carried her off?

The therapist learned that Cassie had married at 20 under pressure from her parents and Bill when she had become pregnant from sexual relations with Bill. Bill was a take-charge man who alternately took care of and bullied his wife. Although a good mother to their three children, Cassie remained a child-wife. She felt powerless within the marriage; she complained that Bill did not even allow her to drive with the children in the car.

The therapist recognized that this wife's choice was not between the two men, but rather between her desire for independence and her desire to be secure in the submissive pattern in her marriage. The couple did divorce. Three years later the husband was remarried, the children were doing well, and Cassie was combining mothering responsibilities with working and studying. The lover was no longer in the picture. Cassie told Olga Silverstein that if she had understood how hard it would be, she might not have ended the marriage, but she was glad that she had. She felt that she and Bill would have gone on being miserable together. As this perceptive therapist had recognized, leaving one man for another poses less of a threat to the social structure than leaving a man because one is unhappy. The lover had served to rescue the wife from a marriage she could not leave on her own. A woman could do for "love" what she could not do for herself.

Many women see their friends and relatives divorced or abandoned and living in reduced straits with dependent children. Although some women have gained power as they have moved into the paid marketplace, whatever equality has been achieved in the economy has not been extended to the lives of most women at home. Furthermore, when men lose power by earning less than their wives, the system "balances" to allow men to maintain their dominance. One way of balancing is for men to share none of the housework (Hochschild, 1989). Women may sense that their husbands are getting discouraged and resentful so they try to restore men's power by waiting on them at home. In so doing, women exhaust themselves and are likely to feel resentful, in turn, as well as guilty, since it is the woman's job to make things right in the family. The issue of helping at home can be seen as one of maintaining an acceptable balance of power, rather than one of separate spheres of activity for men and women.

The cases I have reviewed have shown that women live under the kind of patriarchy that is represented, not by outright oppression, but by the unacknowledged preeminence of men's desires and the subordination of their own. If women have to choose between equality and marriage, they may back off in challenging male domination. What men and women do instead is create a myth of acceptance and equality, as Nancy did in the Myth of Upstairs/Downstairs. Women have been described as shrinking in marriage, as de-selfing themselves for marriage (Bernard, 1972; Miller, 1976). Family myths reflect and are part of the dominant discourses concerning gender. They disguise inequality and women's loss of self.

CONCLUSION

The possibility of reorganizing families through therapy is limited by the gender relations sanctioned by the larger society. The family is a subsystem, the pressure point for the socioeconomic and interpersonal inequities of the society. In the 19th century, it was men who had to change, more than women, in response to social and economic changes, moving from agrarian to industrial occupations. "Making money" became the mark of manhood. Those who did not make money, such as women, children, and old people, had a devalued status. In this century, women's lives are changing faster than men's, with women expected to meet the competing demands of the workplace and the family. As Ruth Schwartz Cowan (1983) has noted, many working women labor 40 hours a week on the job and 35 hours at home, a total that exceeds sweatshop conditions. Men had women to ease the occupational transition for them during the 19th century. The vast majority of working women lack such help today (Hare-Mustin, 1988).

The gender discourses that influence how men and women behave serve an important function: They disguise inequality and women's relative lack of power. Explanations based on essential differences, a focus on separate spheres for men and women, and quid pro quo solutions to family problems can be appealing to therapists and families alike because they support the ideal of marriage between equals. Also appealing is the idea of engaging in a "conversation" with clients as they tell their story. However, we need to be reminded that both the process and content of such a conversation are connected to the discourses of the society. Conversation is an interpersonal process that has relationship implications, notably dominance vs. submission (Watzlawick, Beavin, & Jackson, 1967). The therapist may fail to recognize how embedded a conversation is in the cultural belief systems and how influenced it is by the discourses that create masculine and feminine identities.

Although the subordinate person in a couple is not totally powerless, it is strange to regard her power as equal to his as some strategic therapists like Haley and Madanes do. Since the essence of contemporary femininity is to make inequalities appear as equalities (Haavind, 1984), such therapists may not recognize the influence on them of the marriage between equals discourse. What is expected of women is the appearance of volition that masks their subordination. As in the wife's fantasy of burning the dinner, the wife must be ready to disguise her anger and adapt to please her husband. Thus, men as well as women (and therapists, too) are influenced by appearances.

As the title of this essay suggests, understanding sex, lies, and headaches means understanding the question of power. The way a woman participates in satisfying male sexual desires or responds to the permissive expectations of the dominant discourse may be a source of stress. Is she permitted to acknowledge even to herself the lack of choice or pleasure? The person burdened with the ethic of care is not supposed to be so uncaring as to directly tell her partner that he is not much fun.

The options open to the therapist are limited, too, by the dominant discourses in the larger social system of which the family is a part. Theories of therapy, while not explicitly about gender, reinforce gender norms. If the therapist is to do more than encourage individuals to conform to existing norms, he or she needs to recognize how the dominant discourses influence behavior and support the power differences in the relations of women and men. A postmodern analysis does not provide specific answers, but it leads us to be self-reflective about the methods and limitations of understanding. By opening up the possibility of alternatives to the dominant discourse, we can move beyond the existing social order to its transformation.

REFERENCES

Bartky, S. L. (1988). Foucault, femininity, and the modernization of patriarchal power. In I. Diamond & L. Quinby (Eds.), *Feminism & Foucault: Reflections on resistance* (pp. 61–86). Boston: Northeastern University Press.

Bernard, J. (1972). *The future of marriage.* New York: Bantam.

Boone, J. A. (1986). Modernist maneuverings in the marriage plot: Breaking ideologies of gender and genre in James's *The golden bowl. Publications of the Modern Language Association, 101,* 374–388.

Caplan, P. J., & Hall-McCorquodale, I. (1985). Mother-blaming in major clinical journals. *American Journal of Orthopsychiatry, 55,* 345–353.

Cowan, R. S. (1983). *More work for mother: The ironies of household technology from open hearth to microwave.* New York: Basic.

Coyne, J. C. (1987). The concept of empowerment in strategic therapy. *Psychotherapy, 24,* 539–545.

Deutsch, F. (1957). A footnote to Freud's "Fragment of an analysis of a case of hysteria." *Psychoanalytic Quarterly, 26,* 159–167.

Diamond, I., & Quinby, L. (Eds.). (1988). *Feminism & Foucault: Reflections on resistance.* Boston: Northeastern University Press.

Eagly, A. H. (1987). *Sex differences in social behavior: A social-role interpretation.* Hillsdale, NJ: Erlbaum.

Eagly, A. S. (1990). On the advantages of reporting sex comparisons. *American Psychologist, 45,* 560–562.

Ehrenreich, B. (1983). *The hearts of men: American dreams and the flight from commitment.* Garden City, NJ: Doubleday.

Foucault, M. (1970). *The order of things.* New York: Random House.

Foucault, M. (1979). *Discipline and punish* (A. Sheridan, Trans.). New York: Vintage.

Foucault, M. (1980). *Power/knowledge.* (C. Gordon Ed.). New York: Pantheon.

Freud, S. (1963). *Dora: An analysis of a case of hysteria.* New York: Collier Books. (Original work published 1905.)

Gardner, C. B. (1980). Passing by: Street remarks, address rights, and the urban female. *Sociological Inquiry, 50,* 328–356.

Gavey, N. (1989). Feminist poststructuralism and discourse analysis: Contributions to feminist psychology. *Psychology of Women Quarterly, 13,* 459–475.

Gavey, N., Florence, J., Pezaro, S., & Tan, J. (1990). Mother-blaming, the perfect alibi: Family therapy and the mothers of incest survivors. *Journal of Feminist Family Therapy, 2*(1), 1–25.

Goldner, V. (1988). Generation and gender: Normative and covert hierarchies. *Family Process, 27,* 17–31.

Goleman, D. (1990, March 6). As a therapist, Freud fell short, scholars find. *The New York Times,* pp. C1, C12.

Goodrich, T. J., Rampage, C., Ellman, B., & Halstead, K. (1988). *Feminist family therapy: A casebook.* New York: Norton.

Gornick, V. (1990, April 15). Who says we haven't made a revolution? A feminist takes stock. *The New York Times Magazine,* pp. 14, 27, 52, 53.

Gottman, J. M., & Levenson, R. W. (1986). Assessing the role of emotion in marriage. *Behavioral Assessment, 8*, 31–48.

Griffith, J. L., Griffith, M. E., & Slovik, L. S. (1990). Mind-body problems in family therapy: Contrasting first- and second-order cybernetics approaches. *Family Process, 29*, 13–28.

Haavind, H. (1984). Love and power in marriage. In H. Holter (Ed.), *Patriarchy in a welfare society* (pp. 136–167). New York: Columbia University Press.

Hare-Mustin, R. T. (1983). An appraisal of the relationship of women and psychotherapy: 80 years after the case of Dora. *American Psychologist, 38*, 593–601.

Hare-Mustin, R. T. (1987). The problem of gender in family therapy theory. *Family Process, 26*, 15–27.

Hare-Mustin, R. T. (1988). Family change and gender differences: Implications for theory and practice. *Family Relations, 37*, 36–41.

Hare-Mustin, R. T., & Marecek, J. (1986). Autonomy and gender: Some questions for therapists. *Psychotherapy, 23*, 205–212.

Hare-Mustin, R. T., & Marecek, J. (1988). The meaning of difference: Gender theory, postmodernism, and psychology. *American Psychologist, 43*, 455–464.

Hare-Mustin, R. T., & Marecek, J. (1990). *Making a difference: Psychology and the construction of gender.* New Haven, CT: Yale University Press.

Hayles, N. K. (1986). Anger in different voices: Carol Gilligan and *The mill on the floss. Signs, 12*, 23–39.

Hochschild, A., with Machung, A. (1989). *The second shift: Working parents and the revolution at home.* New York: Viking.

Hollway, W. (1984). Gender difference and the production of subjectivity. In J. Henriques, W. Hollway, C. Urwin, C. Venn, & V. Walkerdine (Eds.), *Changing the subject: Psychology, social regulation, and subjectivity* (pp. 227–263). New York: Methuen.

Jacobson, N. S. (1983). Beyond empiricism: The politics of marital therapy. *American Journal of Family Therapy, 11*(2), 11–24.

James, K., & MacKinnon, L. (1990). The "incestuous family" revisited: A critical analysis of family therapy myths. *Journal of Marital and Family Therapy, 16*, 71–88.

Jones, E. (1955). *The life and work of Sigmund Freud* (Vol. 2). New York: Basic.

Kahn, A. S., & Yoder, J. D. (1989). The psychology of women and conservatism: Rediscovering social change. *Psychology of Women Quarterly, 13*, 417–432.

Lerner, H. G. (1990, April). Problems for profit? *The Women's Review of Books, 7*(7), 15.

Maccoby, E. E. (1990). Gender and relationships: A developmental account. *American Psychologist, 45*, 513–520.

MacKinnon, L. K., & Miller, D. (1987). The new epistemology and the Milan approach: Feminist and sociopolitical considerations. *Journal of Marital and Family Therapy, 13*, 139–155.

Margolin, G., Talovic, S., Fernandez, V., & Onorato, R. (1983). Sex role considerations and behavioral marital therapy: Equal does not mean identical. *Journal of Marital and Family Therapy, 9*, 131–146.

McGoldrick, M., Anderson, C. M., & Walsh, F. (Eds.). (1989). *Women in families: A framework for family therapy.* New York: Norton.

Miller, J. B. (1976). *Toward a new psychology of women.* Boston: Beacon.

Parlee, M. (1989, March). *The science and politics of PMS research.* Paper presented at the meeting of the Association for Women in Psychology, Newport, Rhode Island.

Smith, T. E. (1990). *Lie to me no more: Believable stories and marital affairs.* Unpublished manuscript, Florida State University, School of Social Work, Tallahassee.

Stacey, J. (1983). The new conservative feminism. *Feminist Studies, 9*, 559–583.

Stern, J., & Stern, M. (1990, March 19). Decent exposure. *The New Yorker*, pp. 73–98.

Taffel, R., & Masters, R. (1989). An evolutionary approach to revolutionary change: The impact of gender arrangements on family therapy. In M. McGoldrick, C. M. Anderson, & F. Walsh (Eds.), *Women in families: A framework for family therapy* (pp. 117–134). New York: Norton.

Taggart, M. (1985). The feminist critique in epistemological perspective: Questions of context in family therapy. *Journal of Marital and Family Therapy, 11,* 113–126.

Tavris, C. (1989, December). Do codependency theories explain women's unhappiness — or exploit their insecurities? *Vogue,* pp. 220, 224, 226.

Toufexis, A. (Fall, 1990). Coming from a different place. *Time,* 64–66.

Walters, M., Carter, B., Papp, P., & Silverstein, O. (1988). *The invisible web: Gender patterns in family relationships.* New York: Guilford.

Wattenberg, E. (1985). In a different light: A feminist perspective on the role of mothers in father-daughter incest. *Child Welfare, 64,* 203–211.

Watzlawick, P., Beavin, J. H., & Jackson, D. D. (1967). *Pragmatics of human communication.* New York: Norton.

Weedon, C. (1987). *Feminist practice and poststructuralist theory.* New York: Basil Blackwell.

Worell, J. (1988). Women's satisfaction in close relationships. *Clinical Psychology Review, 8,* 477–498.

Young, I. M. (1983). Is male gender identity the cause of male domination? In J. Trebilcot (Ed.), *Mothering: Essays in feminist theory* (pp. 129–146). Totowa, NJ: Rowman & Allanheld.

5

VIRGINIA GOLDNER

Sex, Power, and Gender: A Feminist Systemic Analysis of the Politics of Passion

FEMINISM HAS BEEN PREOCCUPIED with the subject of power throughout its history. The questions about having, confronting, and combating power have been central to the development of feminist theory, to its social ideals, and to its complex practices. As our movement and thinking have grown, both in numbers and in intellectual complexity, the issue of power has been interrogated from so many perspectives that it has been virtually turned inside out by its "accusers." What began as a simple repudiation of power as being a hierarchical, Western, "male" strategy and ideal, has been reformulated, many times over. As a result, no longer does it simply represent "masculine badness," but it has come to be viewed as a *Problematic*: as an impulse and ambition that, though potentially hazardous, can also be creative, empowering, and useful. Moreover, the ambivalent, paradoxical expressions and meanings of power in intimate relationships have led most feminists away from simplistic characterizations of victims and victimizers, toward more complex views of power as a relational arrangement, buttressed by the larger sociopolitical context of gender inequality, but not reducible to it.

This is a revised and expanded version of Goldner, V. (1989). Sex, Power and Gender: The Politics of Passion. In D. Kantor & B. Okun (Eds.), *Intimate environments: Sex, intimacy and gender in families*. New York: Guilford Press.

My contribution to this evolving formulation will take the form of a detailed discussion of an initial interview with a couple along with some material from the second session. For these two people, their inevitable contest for power became displaced to and enacted in their sexual relationship. My close textual reading of this session is part of an emerging tradition of feminist postmodern theory. (See Chapter 4, Hare-Mustin.) As Hare-Mustin suggests, feminist ideas converge with those of postmodernists like Foucault by pointing to the intimate and immediate operations of power (rather than to the more obvious forms of state power) such as police, army, legislators and judicial bodies. Power is examined as it affects daily life within the kinship system (p. 64). From my perspective, the feminist appropriation of Foucault provides a formal theoretical basis for the foundational premise of "second wave" feminism, "the personal is political," because it analyzes and critiques "any axis along which power differentials are organized and distributed, such as . . . gender" (De Lauretis, 1990, p. 128).

By taking a close look at the power operations in this intimate relationship, my argument will develop the idea that what had begun as a playful, deeply passionate "sex game" turned grim and pathological because control of sex became equivalent to control of the relationship as a whole. Once the sex game came to be used to solve the problem of power in the relationship, it could no longer be playful. Instead of sex serving as a counterpoint to the couple's "out of bed" relationship, a "recreational" alternative sphere of mutual self-expression, the politics of the sex game eventually "took over" the relationship in all its aspects.

There is a significant distinction to be made here, not only about the nature and "uses" of sex, but more generally about the nature of power in intimate relationships. Think about the difference between the symbolic meanings of the terms "play" and "game." We owe our psychological understanding and respect for "play" to the English psychoanalyst, Winnicott (1971), who considered play to be a crucial intermediate zone between fantasy and reality. Both children *and adults* need play in order to explore and expand their psychic range. Winnicott liked spatial metaphors, and he thought of play (which he defined in the broadest sense) as "transitional space" facilitating a benign, regressive, "regrouping" experience. This kind of playful reverie could be solitary or relational.

For our purposes, thinking of sex as "play" means thinking of sex as open-ended, ambiguous, where no one is in charge, where process unfolds "as it will." By contrast, "game," an important metaphor in family therapy discourse, evokes "moves" and "countermoves," where the terms concern "winning" and "losing," and the process is characterized by competitive escalations, befitting the sardonic imagery of (dirty) "games without end."

The breakdown of the mutuality of "sex-as-play" into sex as a "power game" organized around the eroticization of dominance and submission is, according to many feminist scholars, inherent in the psychosocial construction of gender. The most radical formulation of this standpoint has been expressed by the feminist legal scholar, MacKinnon, who defines gender not as a marker of sexual *difference*, but as an instance of sexual *dominance*. Indeed, she argues for a painful, critical parsimony: "the eroticization of dominance and submission *creates* gender. . . . Sexualized objectification is what defines women as sexual *and as women* under male supremacy" (1987, p. 50).

This uncompromising, unsettling characterization of heterosexual relations "fits" the case story I am about to tell. The powerful, futile erotic struggle of the couple in question serves as a cautionary tale about the social relations of gender. Without this frame, the story becomes a case study of reciprocal psychopathologies, a reading which narrows its meaning, blames the victim(s), and keeps us as "untrained" observers. Their love story is, to some degree, a love story we have all known: a story of bonding turned to bondage, of pleasure to power, of reparation of trauma to its repetition.

In what follows, I shall discuss the politics of this story as it emerged in the initial interview. The couple, whom I shall call Dan and Sarah, were both attractive performing artists. Dan was 31 years old, a working actor currently between jobs. When he was working, he was already doing T.V. commercials and movies, and he had come close to being cast in a number of Broadway plays. Sarah, at 21, was a talented singer and songwriter, but she was both unfocused and unemployed. Dan and Sarah came to therapy because Sarah wanted to end their relationship of three years. She had agreed to delay her decision to see if couples therapy would be helpful.

At first, the couple's problems seemed fairly unremarkable. Sarah felt that her involvement in the relationship was draining her energies from attending to her own life and career and that Dan's moody depressions were a burden for her to cope with. Dan felt that he understood from his own experience "someone's need to consume themselves with their ambition," but he believed that a "relationship could also be a security blanket in the turbulent entertainment business." With reference to therapy, he said, "I don't want our relationship to end, but if it *has* to end, I want a *creative* separation, working it out in a place like this." (I filed away Dan's phrase about therapy offering the possibility of a "creative separation," thinking later that it was both an apt metaphor for an actor and a potential directive for how to conceptualize the treatment.)

As we explored the different attitudes held by Dan and Sarah about being together, I learned that they had been fighting a lot, that Sarah had moved out, and that they now had a weekend relationship. After tracking the early history of their romance, I began to inquire more specifically about their current difficulties. At this point, Dan inhaled deeply on his cigarette, changed postures, and launched into a description of their escalating power struggle over sex: "I've been working through some bizarre sickness where I get sexually turned on by things Sarah did with other men," he began.

As the story unfolded, it emerged that this had become an erotic compulsion ever since Sarah had told Dan, during lovemaking, that she had once slept with two men. Whenever they had sex, he would beg her to and then demand that she tell him about other sexual encounters she had had, but once he had an orgasm, he would be overcome by bad feelings and withdraw from her.

Although this sexual drama was disturbing and painful to talk about (and live with), it seemed clear that both Dan and Sarah found what I called "the talking sex game" deeply erotic. The trouble began when Dan left New York for California to shoot a movie. He was gone for six months, and, when Sarah joined him, he learned, "while interrogating her" during their first time in bed, that Sarah had slept with someone at a party while he was away. To add to his sense of betrayal was the fact that on the night in question, he had phoned her as planned. (He had been calling her once or twice a day during the entire shoot to "reassure" her that he was still committed to the relationship.) When he found she was not at home, he kept calling all night and was frantic with worry for her safety. ("She lives in a bad neighborhood.") "That night put me through so much agony," he said, "and she was out getting fucked!"

He continued talking in a tone of both anger and shame: "When she told me about it while we were making love, I got off on it sexually, but afterwards the reality would set in and I would become like a crazy man. I don't remember feeling so betrayed in all my life. I felt very much in love with her, but I felt every time I go away she's going to fuck someone else. All these things came up in me. The feeling of the 'mother figure' in my life not being there when I needed her. That, on top of the guilt I felt for getting off on the experience, was the beginning of a number of problems sexually which we've had."

What followed was an oddly gripping and sad account of Dan's attempts to regain control of Sarah's sexuality in trying to get her to, in essence, reenact the betrayal in reality, by having sex with another man while he was present. In counterpoint were Sarah's attempts to resist Dan's control, by somehow out-maneuvering him through a series of sexual escalations of her own. The details of this dangerous "game without end" will emerge in my discussion of the case.

Let us begin our analysis of this extravagant and painful relationship by locating the protagonists in hierarchical space. This will require stretching Bateson's (1958) circular view of complementarity to include the idea that the position of "up" and "down" are not a matter of perspective, and therefore they are not inherently reversible. Many social hierarchies are inscribed in the social order and cannot be changed until the world changes. These include age, sex, and class hierarchies.

For this couple, a comparison of their relative social positions in the world at large locates Dan as "up" and Sarah as "down." He is 10 years her senior, a man, well-launched in his acting career, capable of earning "good money." By contrast, Sarah is young indeed, barely out of adolescence, and is a woman with no training, no money, and no professional contacts or role models other than her boyfriend.

If we move the lens in closer and look at the organization of their relationship, another unequal complementary organization comes into focus. This involves their division of emotional labor. In terms of their system, Dan is "figure," Sarah is "ground," Dan is "subject," Sarah is "facilitating environment."

SARAH   I lose myself in romantic relationships. If I didn't have someone to be always concerned about, I'd be so miserable that I'd be forced to go out into the world.

DAN   There is a tremendous value in having a security blanket in this turbulent entertainment business.

Sarah is tending the relationship, Dan is being tended. For him, the relationship *is* a security blanket, where love facilitates work; for Sarah, love compromises it—she must choose one or the other.

DAN   I have a lot invested in Sarah—dependency, selfish need; seeing her on weekends kept me in contact with this NEED. It's very hard to be with me. I'm very high when I'm working, very low when I'm not . . . I take it out on who I'm with.

SARAH   If Dan is in a bad mood, I don't exist. The whole weekend there's a weight on me.

Dan's primary relationship is with his career. When he is working, he is happily obsessed; when he is not working, he is morbidly preoccupied. Sarah's subjectivity is not a part of their relationship, Dan's *defines* it. To find herself, she must leave him. If she leaves, it is not "her" he has lost, but the "need satisfier" that he can keep contact with on weekends.

What is sad and interesting about this arrangement is that, looking back, we can see that things were not always so skewed. This standard gendered arrangement of male subject and female facilitator evolved out of a more genuinely reciprocal exchange. Indeed, in the early phases of their relationship, we can find evidence of a fragile mutuality—the provision of reparative empathy and mutual idealization.

DAN   Sarah helped me find qualities in myself I had no access to. I'm more intellectually capable now than when I first met her.
SARAH   He was so different from anyone I'd ever met. He really listened. I could tell him anything, there was no pressure to be normal.

But the language, even early on, anticipates the subversion of reparative empathy into exhibitionism, voyeurism, and domination. Let's look first at the way in which both partners "misuse" Sarah's empathy.

DAN   What drew me to Sarah is that she has a tremendous intellect. I was attracted but that wasn't the most important thing. It was that she understood *pain* in a very intelligent way. She has tremendous insight into *life itself*.

As Sarah articulated his pain, Dan felt freer to then idealize it, and to idealize her as the vehicle through which his morbidity was to be elevated. It eventually became an ideal unto itself. "I don't want to have fun. I just want to sit and brood."

For her side, we can see, even in the session, how Sarah protects Dan's self-esteem at the cost of the truth and of her own narcissism.

SARAH   He fell in love with me first—no not really. . . . It's a drag to be with him when he would mope. . . . That's a mean thing to say.

To look now at the subversion of Dan's empathy, we can begin with Sarah's memory of that early period:

SARAH   I could tell him anything and he wouldn't be shocked. Any fantasy, any weird thing I would want to do or had done—like getting up and dancing around.

Dan's acceptance of her playful, body-exuberant narcissism became transformed by both of them into material for sexploitation so that his provision of a "maternal environment" became voyeuristic, and her self-expression became exhibitionistic. A motive for her can be found in the line, "Sometimes he doesn't seem there, and I feel like shaking him."

What had been, for a short while, a reciprocal arrangement of positions, each being a subject to the other's empathic recognition and appreciation, eventually became a rigid, mutually objectifying process. Sarah is now cooperating in having become a sexual object, and Dan has transformed himself into the split-off, dissociated voyeur that Khan (1979) and, more recently, Benjamin (1985) write about so evocatively. As Benjamin puts it, "the male posture, whether assumed by all men or not, prepares for the role of master. He is disposed to objectify and control the other . . . in order to deny his dependency. The female posture disposes the woman to accept objectification and control in order [to remain emotionally connected]" (p. 63).

Situated in this emotional and social context, the couple's fragile equilibrium is, not surprisingly, easily destabilized by the threat of separation. Moreover, although the two do not think about it in these terms, once Dan has left for California, the power differential between the two lovers becomes even more exaggerated, thereby adding to the strain. Dan was in California shooting a movie. Sarah was left in New York with nothing specific to do and without any money, not even enough to call him when she wanted.

Dan's calls, characterized as "reassurance," were actually a means of controlling her. Since his calls were framed in terms of emphasizing that Sarah was still his sexual ideal, Dan could deny the humiliation of his dependency and *his* need for reassurance—reassurance that he would not be abandoned. Since he did not want to suffer what he called "the mother figure in my life not being there when I needed her," he arranged that Sarah would always be at the other end of the phone line. (By calling her twice a day, he prevented her from being and feeling alone.)

By denying and eroticizing his dependency, Dan, in de Beauvoir's (1949) terms, is "objectifying" Sarah. In a recent issue of *Feminist Studies*, de Lauretis (1990) captures the essence of de Beauvoir's thinking on this point:

The male subject casts women as object . . . but because he continues to need her as "the sex," the source of sexual desire, he remains related to her, and her to him, by a reciprocal need. Hence, the paradoxical definition of woman as a human being fundamentally essential to man and at the same time an inessential object, radically "other." (p. 117)

Sarah's reciprocal form of existential bondage also follows de Beauvoir's paradigm in that she enacts it in sexual terms. First, we can see that Dan's telephone control strategy "works." Sarah remembers feeling relieved when Dan first leaves, thinking "OK maybe it'll be better for me, good for me to be alone, to know myself better." But instead, Dan insinuates himself into her solitude so that now everything in her mind and life is geared to *her* one big scene: Getting Off The Plane.

SARAH   The time he was gone, I lost 20 pounds for *him*, all I could think of was exercising so I could look really good when I got off the plane for *him*.

Sarah is no longer a subject in search of herself but has transformed herself into a subject-as-object. This construction by Muriel Dimen (1986) captures the truth of Sarah's situation. She writes: "Women are not men's slaves, but they know, as subjects, that they are treated as objects, into which they must sometimes also transform themselves" (p. 5). De Lauretis (1990) elaborates this concept in terms that (sadly) seem written for Sarah:

A woman must always continually watch herself. She comes to consider the surveyor and the surveyed within her as the two constituent elements of her identity as a woman. . . . Men look at women, women watch themselves being looked at. . . . The constant turn of subject into object into subject is what grounds women [in a different relation to heterosexual relationships than that of men]. (p. 119)

For Sarah, this constant oscillation between subjectivity and subjugation organized her will and determined her means of self-expression.

Sarah's one form of rebellion (not independence) was to sleep with someone else. She strikes a defiant tone in the interview, saying, "I don't feel I did anything wrong," but, in truth, Sarah is compliant even in her rebellion. Her behavior is no more than a pseudo-independent act already cast in terms of the game.

Note that she does not try to free herself from Dan by devoting herself to theater classes, auditions, or even some form of structured self-observation like therapy. Even more to the point, she says, by way of proving her "good faith," that she was thinking of Dan all the way through her one-night stand, not her lover or herself!

Finally, we can see this act as Sarah's move from complementarity to symmetry since it contains a competitive impulse. She surely knew that Dan would "catch" her, since he said that he would call at 10 p.m. that night. Further, we can surmise from the way she discusses issues of control in the session that, even if she were unaware of the feeling at the time, she must have been chafing against his subtle forms of control and her obsession with his affirmation.

Thus, part of her motive must have been to derail him, just as she has been derailed. For this one night, and for some of the next day, Sarah has arranged it so that Dan will be thinking of her—not only when he wants to, for example, at night at a club when he is feeling seductive, but when he is trying to sleep, or rehearse, or "hang out" with his friends.

In objectifying her subjectivity by acting out her resistance to Dan within his categories, Sarah loses her personal voice and "speaks" only in Dan's language. This silenced form of speaking has been written about often in feminist commentaries of "women's place." De Lauretis (1990) calls it

the paradox of a being that is at once captive and absent in discourse, constantly spoken of, but itself inaudible or inexpressible, displayed as spectacle and still unrepresented or unrepresentable, invisible, yet constituted as the object of vision: a being whose existence and specificity are simultaneously denied, negated and controlled. (p. 115)

We can see this form of objectification in an earlier stage of the game. When Dan insults and challenges her during sex by saying, "Let's get your roommate," Sarah counters with, "Let's get a man." In talking to the therapist, she explains, "I just wanted to show him how it felt for him to ask to have another girl there. I didn't really mean it." Instead of "giving voice" to her own particular experience of Dan's request, Sarah mimics him to make her point. And this is how their game goes; ultimately this escalating mimicry becomes a dangerous "game without end."

It is also important to see in this incident that, for this couple, there is already a presumption of differential entitlement to narcissistic protection from sexual or gender injury. When Sarah mimics Dan by suggesting that they get another man, he becomes furious. Dan's freedom to hide his masculine vulnerability in rage and to rage about being reminded of his vulnerability, once again constitutes him as the subject and star of this melodrama. Sarah's form of self-expression is restricted to analogy.

Sarah's use of her sexuality as a substitute for speech and independent action is to be found again in the incident that Dan remembers as starting the game.

DAN   It was when we knew I was going away, we did coke and she told me she'd once slept with two men.

Here, one can speculate that the impending separation, which threatened each of them in different ways, created the need for a ritual, and the sex play provided the material.

For Sarah, we can imagine that Dan's leaving her to do a Hollywood movie, trampled on her narcissism. It shattered the illusion of the romantic twinship—of the two songwriting performers on their way to the top—and dumped her back into the reality of being a 21-year-old, untrained, unemployed "unknown." Her only forum for stardom now was sexual, with Dan cast as her enraptured audience. So she used her exhibitionism, which until now had been a shared activity with Dan, *against* him, to put him in his place. She had been a star *before* she knew him, a sex star, with two *other* men adoring her.

For Dan, we can say that Sarah's revelation, to borrow Stoller's (1979) telling metaphor about the sudden, unexpected ways that Eros strikes, "stabbed him with excitement" (p. 15).

DAN   That fantasy had never occurred to me in my sexual existence as a man. I proceeded to always want that to happen. I began to feel, "maybe she *deserves* two men, she's a beautiful woman."

A process unfolded by which Dan turned humiliation to triumph.

What he describes as a "fantasy [that] had never occurred to [him] in [his] sexual existence as a male" was *not* fantasy. It was fact, and it was two *other* men who had slept with *his* lover. By proceeding to "always want that to happen" in bed, Dan gets Sarah to undo his exclusion and emasculation. By casting himself as a slave of love, he orchestrates his humiliation and sexual subjugation ("maybe she *deserves* two men"), and, via his erotic domination, he neutralizes his enemies because he is now directing a pornographic scene starring his girlfriend and a couple of extras.

At this point, the mutual, symmetrically competitive uses of the sex game are in place, and each move will now inspire a counter-move in a dangerous, escalating spiral. The next move took place when Sarah arrived in California. Dan wanted to play the game again to reassure himself and reestablish to Sarah that she belonged to him. Sarah has a sexual secret, but cannot resist telling him, since her sexual potency is her only source of self-assertion, power, and revenge in the relationship.

SARAH   I tried not to tell him, but he'd make it that I'd *want* to tell him because he'd get really turned on.

But the problem the sex game was supposed to solve was not solved, because once the erotic spell was broken, Dan had to face the reality of Sarah's betrayal and, with it, the realization that he truly could not control her, no matter how hard he tried.

DAN   So after I had an orgasm, even though I got off on it in fantasy, the reality set in and I became like a crazy man. I thought, "This is what's going to happen with this girl." I was very much in love with her, but every time I go away, she's going to fuck someone else.

Since Sarah's escalation was "real," it could not be symbolically nullified by being taken into their bed. But we also know that Dan's narcissism was sufficiently damaged so that he could not even tolerate the knowledge of Sarah's having any sexual past that did not include him.

SARAH   Even when I'd tell him things I did before I met him, he'd have that reaction after he'd have an orgasm. I'd be lying there and he'd push me away.

If Dan was compelled to rewrite Sarah's sexual history every time they made love, then how would he undo the actual exclusion created by her sleeping with another man now that he *was* in the picture? This could only be accomplished by a symmetrical escalation.

DAN   It was always gnawing at me, the PAIN of it.

SARAH   But every time in bed he'd ask me to talk about the same thing.

Clearly, it was no longer sufficient for Dan to reestablish his authority by controlling Sarah via an "acted in" sexual fantasy—the "talking game"—in bed. Since Sarah had acted out the scene without him in the real world, Dan's next move was inevitable. He would have to now cast and direct the scene himself, in the real world. He selected a man, "convinced" Sarah to dress in "slutty" black clothes, and brought her to the nightclub where he wanted her to seduce the man in question for the *menage à trois*. Sarah, however, was ready with a "counter-move."

SARAH   I didn't want to do it, but he got so determined. I knew I had to get away from him that night. I thought, "What could I do to get him not to want to be with me that night, or maybe ever?" So I told a lie. I said, "I'm sleeping with someone else."

Note what is significant about her attempt to free herself from Dan's domination: Once again, she can only assert her subjectivity and her will not to play Dan's game in Dan's terms. She cannot simply say "No" in her own voice and leave on her own terms. She can only free herself within *his* categories of domination and humiliation. In this case, her "solution" is particularly bizarre. Now, not only have the categories of play and reality been corrupted by the struggle for control, but even the distinctions between lies and truth have lost their meaning. Sarah's escalation is constructed out of the ostensible revelation that she has slept with another man, even though Dan has not gone away (one step worse than his worst fear), only it is *not true*.

We can see the reasons for this "fraudulent" maneuver in Sarah's view of her options. Both she and Dan agreed that, in a direct battle of wills, Dan would prevail. Sarah's only alternative to submission was to leave the field, but because of her gendered commitment to romantic attachment, she cannot leave without the help of therapy. (Note that in her scanning for a way out she can only think of how she can get Dan to reject her. The idea that *she* can walk out is not even in her calculations.)

This sad and complex incident "embodies" many of the themes feminists have decoded in male-female relations. Hare-Mustin (Chapter 4) refers to the "male sexual drive discourse" which constructs male desire as "driven," impulse-ridden, and "caused" by arousing women. Because, as she puts it, "men's sexual urges are assumed to be natural and compelling . . . the male is expected to be pushy and aggressive in seeking to satisfy them" (p. 71). Thus, she suggests, the "male sexual drive discourse," coupled with what she calls "the permissive discourse" (a view of sex that focuses on male sexuality and sets a standard of sexual compliance for women) authorizes men to do whatever they want ("need") to satisfy their desires.

In her summary of Hollway's research, Hare-Mustin reports Hollway's finding that women often give in to a kind of interpersonal coercion, to men's pleading for "free" sexual activity, because it seems so important to men. Thus, what is expected of women is to *appear to consent freely even when they do not*.

SARAH   I didn't want to at the beginning of the night. I said, "No coke, no sex." I took a stand. But he got so determined. . . . He's so persistent. . . . And I knew he was in that mood. . . . After I lied to him about sleeping with someone else, he hit me. I was upset, but then we laughed about it. I wanted to be with him, and I wanted him to be normal. Somehow, I started losing my will. . . . He wanted it so *badly*, nothing was going to stop him.

Given his resolve, her oscillation between subjectivity and subjugation, and their proclivity for erotic solutions, it is not surprising that they eventually acted out an Oedipal drama in which no one was excluded. And also it was no surprise when the night was over, Dan once again constituted himself the victim of Sarah's sexual potency and emotionally abandoned her.

SARAH   After that happened, Dan was totally distant and cold. I felt totally abandoned. He wanted it *so* badly, and then he *hated* me for it.

With the sex drama now taking over their lives and their relationship, Sarah's next move was the ultimate bid for control, and the only moment in which, although still situated within Dan's narrative, one could speculate that Sarah was aiming to reclaim some independent stance. I framed this for them in the interview as her attempt to "compete for authorship of the script."

SARAH   The idea of sleeping with two men is nice, it bothers me that *he* wants me to. I don't want him to have such control.

THERAPIST   You want to feel if there is a game you both play, there
   should be *two* script-writers. (to Dan) When she wants to write the
   scene, you feel there is something unfair about that?

DAN   She didn't flirt with that guy that night when I asked her to. . . .
   but she has since flirted with him when I didn't want that to happen
   . . . which she knows makes me upset . . . but she does it anyway. I
   don't think that's *fair play*. (Note this metaphor in terms of the play vs.
   game analogy discussed earlier.)

At this point, we can say that there is no longer even an analogical
separation between sex and power. The struggle for control over the
definition of the sex game *was* the struggle for control of the relationship.
Fantasy has now lost all its interiority. What was once repressed or suppressed has now become spoken, acted-in, acted-out, and has eventually
absorbed the protagonists and some innocent bystanders. Even an unexpected pregnancy gets absorbed into the control drama. Dan wants the
fetus aborted because he cannot make love to her in his "dirty" way if she
is pregnant (a "mother" figure), and Sarah, who says she does not want the
baby for itself, still wants it because it represents external proof of her
value to Dan as an "object of desire."

SARAH   I didn't want the baby, but I wanted him to want it, to want
   me and it. I'm happy I don't have a baby.

In the final sequence, we can see all the elements in the competition
playing out at fast forward. Dan must restore his authority after Sarah
starts up a friendship with the other man in their one-night stand, so he
plays the talking sex game with her while preparing for a Broadway
audition.

DAN   I pulled the same shit. I fucked her, got off on my fantasy, and
   rolled over to work on my script.

Now it is Sarah who is jolted out of the erotic spell by this insult—she is
nothing more than a five-minute study break. She retaliates with the next
possible escalation: acting-out the drama of betraying and excluding him
in reality, in the present, while he is in town, and on the night before his
big audition. (She also makes sure that he gets no sleep by calling twice in
the middle of the night.) When Dan is finally provoked into ending the

game, a step Sarah cannot take, ("I had to think of something SO bad, that he'd break up with me.") Sarah, using Dan's strategy, stops him from kicking her out the next morning by eroticizing her betrayal. She seduces him into getting off on it. Dan loses his resolve, fucks her, and then, in the aftershock, flies into a rage and kicks her out.

Somehow, as is always the case between them, Dan gets the last word and manages to claim for himself the victim position.

DAN   How could she do this to me the night before my big audition? I feel like such a victim!

The following short excerpt from the end of the second session illustrates how we (after the first session, the therapy was conducted jointly with Jorge Colapinto) positioned ourselves in relation to this couple, in order to shift their center of gravity. This coda from the second session helps place the sordid politics of the sex game into a psychologically humane and poignant context. As we learn about the larger context in which the sexual control struggle was enacted, we come to view the couple's erotic struggles as a melodramatic diversion and displacement from the formative issues in each of their lives. Most importantly, we learn early in the interview that Sarah, for the first time since she ran away from home at age 14, is moving back in with her mother.

End of Session Two

COLAPINTO   You, Dan, would like this therapy to work so that you and Sarah can remain a couple, so that Sarah will stay. You, Sarah, want this therapy to work so that you can leave without his being angry at you, so that you can have a friendly goodbye. (They both nod.)

GOLDNER   (to Colapinto) It just occurs to me now, Jorge, that if Sarah were to choose to stay with Dan, she would be leaving her mother alone again after all these years.

SARAH   (nodding) She feels obligated to take me back because she feels so guilty.

GOLDNER   What does she feel guilty about?

SARAH   Because our family, for the second time, broke up when I was 14, and I ran away from home. I had to take care of myself, but I really wasn't grown up at all, I was a kid.

GOLDNER   (to Colapinto) So you see, by coming back she gives her mother a chance to repair this, and if she chooses to move back in with Dan, she deprives her mother of the chance to make up for all that lost time between ages 14 and 21.

DAN   And I could be in the way of that. I could just be in the way. I'm *glad you said that*, because I feel less, uh, *angst* about the situation now that you said that I could be in the way of something that she's trying to complete with her mother. And that has nothing to do with me. I am *not*, I did wrong by her, I have hurt her badly and I've done a lot of things that are possibly irreparable. I don't know, that's what I'm trying to find out. But that aside, if I didn't do *anything*, if I was the greatest guy in the world, if I never hurt her once in the three years I've known her, I could still, possibly, just simply be in the way of her completing something with her mother, which I would have never thought of if you didn't make that point. And I appreciate that. I don't know if it's of any use to Sarah, but it's useful to me. . . . I think you're *onto* something, that is bigger than both of us and our problems.

COLAPINTO   (to Sarah) For the first time since you were 15, you are living in a home —

SARAH   — with my mother, it's weird . . . which is a drastic change from what it was in the last three years.

GOLDNER   You said that your mother's new boyfriend, a musician, that that relationship is also a little rocky —

SARAH   He's not really new, they've been together three years.

COLAPINTO   So you and your Mom started together. Wasn't it three years that you and Dan have been together? (Dan laughs loudly.)

SARAH   Yeah. . . . It's rocky because he's an alcoholic and kind of crazy. She's moved out because she wants to break up with him.

GOLDNER   Oh, is that so? (Everyone laughs loudly at the growing analogy.) They're both helping each other — breaking up with these —

DAN   It's team work!

GOLDNER   Yeah. . . . How do you think your relationship with your mother would go if there were no boyfriends, if she didn't have a boyfriend and you didn't have a boyfriend?

SARAH   It would be different. We both wouldn't be concerned with other people as much. She calls Jim, I call Dan. . . . We're still involved with other people.

GOLDNER   Would there be more conflict or less conflict between the two of you if there were no boyfriends?

SARAH   I'm happy she has a boyfriend, she puts less demands on me time-wise. It won't be like she'd need me, need my affection—

GOLDNER   If your mother breaks up with her boyfriend, she'll put more pressure on you?

SARAH   I don't think she'll break up with him.

GOLDNER   You don't think that she will. What would she say about you and Dan? Does she think you'll break up with him or not?

SARAH   She thinks I *might*.

GOLDNER   If she were here, and I asked her that question, as I just did to you, . . . if I were to ask her to "call it" about you and Dan?

SARAH   She would say I *might*. She thinks I'm stronger than she is.

DAN   (Laughing) So she's trying to get you to do it first!

SARAH   Before my mother and I got our apartment together, we were in a cab and I said, "Are you going to break up with Jim?" She said, "I don't know, I have to see how I feel when I'm alone, in my own apartment. What about you, are you going to break up with Dan?" And I said, "I don't know."

GOLDNER   So she and her mother are taking each other's pulse here!

COLAPINTO   Yeah, you're right! Is your father remarried?

SARAH   He lived with a woman for eight years, now he's with a girl named—

GOLDNER   You call her a girl because she's much younger?

SARAH   *Quite* a bit. (Everyone laughs at the analogy.)

COLAPINTO   So, he knows about these kind of women!

DAN   Yeah, he knows about these kind of women!

SARAH   He feels he's been fucked over by all the women he's been with, that they've all lied to him. He feels totally like a victim. I thought he just left my mother, but he told me that he found her in bed with another man and said, "Forget this!", and he left and went back to New York when I was three years old.

GOLDNER   Rings kind of a bell?

DAN AND SARAH   Yeah. Right!

SARAH   Dad said he could never be with someone if he found out she did that!

GOLDNER   Would you like to help your mother get stronger with men?

SARAH   I like it when she does. I don't encourage her *too* much, but I think it would be really good if she broke up with Jim. I think he's stopping her in her career.

GOLDNER   And does she think that Dan is stopping you?

SARAH   She doesn't really know.

COLAPINTO   You said she thought Dan was a little possessive? Is that what her boyfriend is to her?

SARAH   Yeah, she says he's clingy, needy, like a little baby.

GOLDNER   I'm thinking that, as we said before, there are risks in coming here, and I'm an agnostic, I don't know how things are going to turn out between you. (To Colapinto) But what intrigues me is Sarah's return home to her mother . . . and I would like to invite her mother to come in here so that the two of them could talk about their dilemmas together. (To Sarah) If you were to ask your mother to come in, to sort out some important choices, do you think she would?

SARAH   She would want to. She feels she wants to talk to me and tell me things she wouldn't otherwise. There are things she wants to talk to me about, I know.

GOLDNER   Would that be a risk for Dan?

DAN   I'd feel a little abandoned, a little left out (laughs) but I feel it would be good for them and helpful. I need attention, too, but I think it would be *great*, because I think you're *onto* something that's bigger than both of us and our problems.

COLAPINTO   Let's have that session, and then let's think of a significant man for Dan to have a session with.

GOLDNER   What about your father?

SARAH   Would he come?

DAN   My father . . . he's a very intense man. I would love for him to do it. One time I said to him, at my brother's ordination (to become a priest) I said, "If I had one gift in the world, it would be (his eyes tear up) to make you smile all the time." I also said, "I want you to go into therapy." He said, "You mean a headshrinker?" I said, "Yeah," because he's been through *so much*, and I do the same thing. . . . I'd love to do it with my father, but he'd never do it, because he'd never take a day off from work to come here and do that for himself.

COLAPINTO   How about for you?

DAN   (cries silently, with his head down) I don't know.

Long silence

GOLDNER   (to Sarah) Do you know what it is about what we are talking about that is so painful to Dan?

SARAH   His relationship with his father.

GOLDNER   What about that is affecting him so strongly?

SARAH   He doesn't feel his father would care enough about him to come here.

GOLDNER   Maybe we can help Dan with his father, and with that question mark.

DAN   (looking up slowly) I don't know why all of a sudden I did that. . . . You're doing a good job and you've helped us both already. Thank you for that, you're good at what you do.

As the interview unfolded, the most startling information was the revelation that Sarah's mother's marriage to Sarah's father was abruptly severed when he caught her in bed with another man. Here one can see (although we chose not to comment on it *directly* at this early stage) a possible meaning to Sarah's pursuit of triangles and to her odd remark early in the first session that, although she was sleeping with Dan, she did not want him to leave his girlfriend because she "hates to see people break up." In a subsequent session with Sarah and her mother, we learned that mother's sexual "betrayals" and preoccupations were, even in her own view, feeble attempts to gain attention and recognition from her husbands. In the context of this history and its meanings and consequences, Sarah's sexual triad could be framed as her attempt to use sex, as her mother did, to accomplish in her generation what her mother could not achieve: admiration, recognition, and attention. She repeated the trauma of the exploded triangle by going to bed with two men, in the hopes of waking up with both of them still there and still committed.

But, in the wake of the predictable debacle of the sexual enactment, Sarah is moving back in with her mother, for the first time since she ran away from home at 14. By framing this event in terms that elevated the importance of the newly evolving mother-daughter relationship, we "seeded" the idea that *this* couple is, has, and can be central for both women and that they have an opportunity, if they "put each other first," to construct a reparative experience that is not detoured through men.

The two women (and a sister, one year older than Sarah, who eventually joined the therapy) have clearly been operating along parallel tracks, indeed, in a kind of parallel play. Remarkably, the mother and both daughters had all moved to New York from rural areas and were all struggling to get musical careers launched. (The mother had been a bit of a singer and pianist before getting buried in children, romance, and domestic debacles.) All three felt compromised in their goals by their need for men and their need to give to men. Beneath it all, each of them, in a variety of coded actions and remarks, blamed the other two for the breakup of the family and yearned for an overt position of importance in the others' lives.

By listening to the "gaps" in the conversations between mother and daughter, one can speculate how men and careers had become the displacement language through which the two women "talked" and avoided talking about their own relationship. It comes through in the sad and funny way Sarah reported how she and her mother discussed their lives and choices in the taxi. Neither speaks of her fears and wishes about living together, but instead they discuss the two "needy" men whom they cannot abandon or be abandoned by. Indeed, they talk about living together as if it were merely a way station between boyfriends or a means to get enough money together to live alone, so they can gain the solitude necessary to forge ahead with their respective love and work agendas.

By elevating the mother-daughter couple as its own reward, and not a means to an end, we not only grant this relationship the centrality and dignity it deserves, but we set the stage for the women to face their love and need for one another directly, rather than expressing their filial desires and disappointments metaphorically by displacing the issues onto men. This repositioning of the mother-daugher dyad is not only potentially useful to Sarah but to her mother as well. This is because mother had chosen "sexual liberation" over personal and career development, and had ended up still preoccupied with men and sex at age 40, no better positioned financially or professionally than her 21-year-old daughter.

But, beyond the feminist reformulation of the problem and its reparative potential for mother and daughter, the frame was unexpectedly liberating for Dan. In our making mother and daughter the central relationship and his romance with Sarah peripheral, he quickly sensed the possibility for a face-saving "way out" of the addictive cycle. Where Dan could not remove himself from any real or imagined heterosexual couple Sarah formed, he *leapt* at the chance to define himself as peripheral to Sarah and her mother. ("I'm *glad* you said that I could be in the way of something that she's trying to complete with her mother. . . . And *that* has nothing to do with me.") *Theirs* is a triangle Dan can walk away from, with his self-esteem intact. Thus, with our frame, Dan creates what he had asked for in the first session: a "creative separation."

Our definition of Dan and Sarah's relationship (one that is situated in a context which, as Dan says, "is bigger than both of us and our problems") set the terms for the therapy. We conveyed, and they accepted and worked with the idea, that they were a kind of "pseudo-couple" who had gotten caught up in a form of sexual competition that was an enactment of dilemmas best addressed out of bed and with the original cast of characters: parents and siblings.

By virtually ignoring the seductive, compelling presenting problem, the therapy underlines the illusory power of sex. Freedom to enjoy and elaborate the possibilities of a regressive experience like sex creates the fantasy of power, but only for as long as the erotic moment lasts. These two young people are casualties of the sexual revolution my generation fought to accomplish. Their freedom to pursue pleasure, fantasy, and variety is constrained by the structures of domination that organize their relationship and define the contours of their imagination. Their pleasure cannot be playful because it has become the medium through which their gendered struggle for power was enacted.

There is a cautionary tale here for all of us. Unless we can face the painful realities of gender inequality in intimate life, the use of sex to gain and maintain power will remain a central motif in all of our lives.

REFERENCES

Bateson, G. (1958). *Naven* (rev. ed.). Stanford, CA: Stanford University Press.

Benjamin, J. (1985). The bonds of love: Rational violence and erotic domination. In H. Eisenstein & A. Jardine (Eds.), *The future of difference* (pp. 41–70). New Brunswick, NJ: Rutgers University Press.

de Beauvoir, S. (1949). *The second sex*. New York: Vintage.

de Lauretis, T. (1990). Eccentric subjects: Feminist theory and historical consciousness. *Feminist Studies, 16*(1), 115–150.

Dimen, M. (1986). *Surviving sexual contradictions*. New York: MacMillan.

Khan, M. (1979). *Alienation in perversions*. New York: International Universities Press.

MacKinnon, C. (1987). *Feminism unmodified: Discourses in life and law*. Cambridge, MA: Harvard University Press.

Stoller, R. (1979). *Sexual excitement: The dynamics of erotic love*. New York: Pantheon.

Winnicott, D. W. (1971). *Playing and reality*. New York: Basic Books.

III
STORY AND RITUAL

6

CHERYL RAMPAGE

Personal Authority and Women's Self-Stories

AFTER WORKING IN marital therapy for several months, a woman begins a therapy session with the startling announcement that her husband has taken on the task of hiring a new gynecologist for her. She had been scheduled to undergo a minor surgical procedure in her former gynecologist's office the previous week. Her husband had accompanied her to the doctor's office, and, upon arrival, he had become acutely uncomfortable with the fact that it was not located adjacent to a hospital. He had insisted that the surgery be cancelled and rescheduled as an inpatient procedure. She agreed not to have the surgery as scheduled, even though she had had the same surgery on two previous occasions, and even though she believed that her husband's fears were unrealistic. Later, she said that she would be too embarrassed ever to see her gynecologist again and extracted a promise from her husband that *he* would find her a gynecologist of whom they could both approve.

As I listened to this story, my first reaction was that it sounded as if the woman was manipulating her husband into taking responsibility for managing her health care as a means of avenging herself for the insult she experienced at his hands in front of her physician. However, as I explored the issue, I detected in her a real doubt that she could manage this issue better than her husband could manage it for her. Although she had a long-standing relationship with her physician and had never questioned his competence or felt poorly treated, she found it difficult to hold onto her sense of certainty about her choice or her entitlement to choose at all.

PERSONAL AUTHORITY AND GENDER

What can explain this woman's pathetic lack of ability to see herself as an effective, competent agent regarding her own self-interest? The most parsimonious explanation is that this woman lacks a well-developed sense of *personal authority*, the ability to know one's own needs and desires and the ability to act so as to satisfy those needs and desires, even in the face of pressure from others to conform to their wishes or expectations.

Personal authority is the most fundamental form of power, the power to be *self*-determining, to act rather than react, to choose the terms on which to live one's own life. It is thus distinguished from the more common understanding of power as the ability to exercise control over others. Personal authority must also be distinguished from authority which comes by virtue of an association with another in authority (e.g., a powerful person), or with an institution which is vested with authority by some common or formal agreement among members of a society (e.g., the Supreme Court).

Nature vs. Nurture

Not surprisingly, personal authority is more frequently displayed by men than by women, for it requires a way of being in the world that is consistent with the prevailing gender expectations for men, while it is antithetical to the culturally defined norms for female behavior. A man of independent mind who lives life on his own terms may be a hero, a leader, or a visionary, but such a woman is typically seen as odd, dangerous, or evil. Shakespeare might be regarded as an example of a man with personal authority. A woman possessing Shakespeare's talents and ambitions would likely have met with a tragic fate, as Virginia Woolf described in her classic essay *A Room of One's Own* (1957).

Social norms. In the past few years, a number of feminist theorists have advanced hypotheses which help to explain the general lack of personal authority among women. These theorists place heavy emphasis on socialization rather than biology as determinative of women's character and behavior. Gilligan (1982) was among the first to demonstrate that women tend to see themselves as embedded in their social context and make moral decisions based on their assessment of how everyone involved will be affected. This social embeddedness sometimes makes it difficult for women to recognize their own self-interest. It is impossible to enact personal authority without the recognition that one's self-interest exists independent of and potentially in contradiction to the self-interest of others.

Belenky et al. (1986) noted that a woman develops a sense of herself as an independent thinker/knower (a prerequisite of personal authority) on the basis of accumulated personal experiences in which she is told that her opinion matters. To be authoritative requires both knowing one's knowledge and feeling entitled to act on it.

Others have pointed out the ways in which predominant patterns of child raising discourage independence in girls, teaching them to believe that happiness is only to be found in selfless service to others (Miller, 1976; Dinnerstein, 1976; Chodorow, 1978). The thrust of all these authors' arguments is that *social* norms and expectations regarding appropriate female behavior, rather than biology, discourage women from seeing themselves as capable, independent knowers, able to make choices about their lives regardless of the approval or disapproval of others.

Codependency. One disturbing consequence of the recognition that women have difficulty living at the center of their own lives has been the recent phenomenon of giving women a diagnosis of codependency because they put others' needs ahead of their own and do not feel entitled to pursue their own goals (Beattie, 1987; Schaef, 1986). This purported illness, codependency, labels women as sick for demonstrating the very traits that are culturally presented as proper female behavior. Since it is true that women in this culture are trained to believe that it is appropriate to live in the service of others (especially husbands and children) and inappropriate to live at the center of their own lives, it is hardly fair to tell them that they are sick for doing precisely what they have been trained to do. A more useful approach for women regarding their difficulty in making the best personal decisions for themselves is found in the work of Lerner (1985) and Bepko and Krestan (1990). These authors acknowledge that women are trained to be self-effacing and conflict-avoidant, and then move on to discuss how women can change their lives in the direction of being more independent and authoritative without renouncing their skills and interest in relatedness as a key element of their lives.

Women's Learning

There are three primary ways that women learn about personal authority. The first involves direct experience. From the time the infant is mobile, she is an active explorer of her environment. She reaches for objects to put in her mouth, crawls toward stairs and electrical outlets, wails when she is tired or hungry. These behaviors do not need to be taught, and the infant has no sense of impropriety about pursuing her goals or getting what she wants.

However, as time goes on, the infant hears more messages from powerful adults that some behaviors are inappropriate. To a greater extent than boys, girls hear that being good (i.e., docile, sweet, cooperative) is desirable and that wanting her own way too much is not (i.e., it is seen as headstrong, selfish, spoiled). Parents and teachers respond differently to girls and boys, reinforcing girls for their generosity, caretaking, and helpfulness, while praising boys for being inventive, clever, independent, and self-sufficient.

Modeling. A second method by which girls learn about personal authority is through the modeling of significant adults. The daughter observes her father expressing his opinion, making decisions, being in charge, while she is likely to observe a mother who placates, defers to her husband, and serves rather than leads. How often does the little girl observe Mommy driving the car while Daddy sits on the passenger side? How often does she hear Daddy say to a salesperson, "I'll have to ask my wife about it" before making a purchase? What conclusions does the child draw from such interactions about who feels entitled, powerful, authoritative?

Stories. A third way in which lessons regarding personal authority are taught is through stories. There are two categories of instructive stories. The first is cultural stories, conveyed through legends, fables, novels, plays, operas, films, and television. The second is family stories, told by parents, grandparents, and other relatives. Both kinds of stories carry implicit and explicit messages about personal authority for women. The purpose of this paper is to explore how women learn about personal authority from stories, and how therapists might work with their clients' stories to increase the clients' sense of personal authority.

WOMEN'S STORIES

Cultural Stories

Most of the public stories throughout history have been authored by men, and so represent the male viewpoint, even if the subject matter is female. Usually, however, the stories themselves have been primarily concerned with men's lives rather than women's. The vast majority of recorded history is the history of *men's* lives. Men can look to the countless stories of other men, from Tutankhamen to Gorbachev, to inform their lives. Among those stories are the stories of heroes, villains, saints, rogues, workers, inventors, athletes, artists, philosophers, adventurers. These are but a few of the background narratives against which men can create, measure, and interpret their own unique stories.

Until the 19th century, the number of public stories about women was extremely limited, and the majority of those were written by men. In keeping with their historical context, most of the stories about women extolled the virtues of piety, obedience, and selflessness (e.g., stories about the Virgin Mary), and warned of the harsh consequences of choosing a different path (e.g., *The Scarlet Letter*). Few stories were authored by women, and even fewer held out a vision of women's lives that departed from the standard portrait of devoted subservience to men.

Children begin hearing about life's possibilities while sitting on Mother's lap, listening to her read stories. Thus, at a tender age, the little girl learns that her life will be made happy by a man who will rescue her from dire circumstances (Cinderella, Sleeping Beauty, Snow White); that to be adventurous will bring her certain peril (Little Red Riding Hood, Goldilocks and the Three Bears); and that duty to family constitutes the highest good (*Little Women*). Even in 1990, a mother looking for less blatantly sexist literature for children sets a difficult task for herself. Such literature does exist (cf., *The Paper Bag Princess*) but not in the same abundance.

Television does little to challenge the theme that females should be deferential, other-directed, and powerless. From *Leave It to Beaver* to *Dallas*, the message is that women's place is in the home, and that if a woman should exercise authority, it must be indirect (i.e., manipulative) or in the service of others. Popular films carry much the same message. As they view these programs and films, females are receiving instructions as to gender-appropriate behavior, feelings, and attitudes. When Ingrid Bergman leaves Humphrey Bogart to follow her husband at the end of *Casablanca*, women viewers everywhere are receiving a powerful message about the priority of wifely duty over personal desire. Likewise, watching Glenn Close be killed by her lover at the end of *Fatal Attraction* sends out an equally powerful message about the danger for women of following their selfish interests.

In writing of literature by and about women, Heilbrun notes:

Because [having power and control] has been declared unwomanly, and because many women would prefer (or think they would prefer) a world without evident power and control, women have been deprived of the narratives, or the texts, plots or examples, by which they might assume power over—take control of—their own lives. (1988, p. 17)

Heilbrun makes the case that while there are many narratives available for men to live their lives by, women have been essentially limited to one. The story of women's lives is the story of marriage. Almost all of the literature about women supports the idea that wife and mother are their only appropriate roles. Furthermore, not just any marriage will do: The correct marriage is one in which the woman is the helpmate, the emotional caretaker, dependent and essentially passive. Most literature instructs women that their choices are limited, that marriage is most desirable, that a life of selflessness, sacrifice, and devotion to the needs of others is the paramount duty and joy of all women. Few literary heroines have escaped this fate, and those who have (by rejecting marriage or failing to carry out the role of proper wife) are usually punished.

Biography. There are two sets of texts outside the traditional marriage narrative. The first consists of biographies of women who have chosen to live a different sort of life. Thus, women can read about the lives of Joan of Arc, Elizabeth Blackwell, Susan B. Anthony, and others. Many of these women lived outside of social convention. They did important work, often accomplishing great good. They exercised enormous personal authority. Yet their stories seem to have little impact on the prevailing mores or on the sense women carry about the possibilities for their own lives. The reason is simple: For a story to be instructive it must be possible for readers to identify with the protagonist, to recognize some common bond through which her entitlement to live a different sort of life becomes our entitlement to do so.

Unfortunately, most of the biographies of women emphasize exceptionality or coincidence rather than choice or entitlement. These women either see themselves as different, unlike other women and, therefore, are of little use as models, or else they see their accomplishments as having been forced on them by necessity, not as chosen goals, consciously selected, consciously pursued. In neither case can the reader use the story to inform her *own* strivings toward accomplishment, her *own* desire to be in charge of her life. Thus, to a large extent, the genre of women's biography has had little impact on women's lives.

Women's literature. The second set of texts that stands apart from the marriage narrative is loosely grouped in bookstores under headings marked "Women's Literature." These texts, including both fiction and biography, are distinguished from the many other works by or about women precisely by their rejection of the marriage narrative as the only plot for women's lives. While the heroine in these texts may be married (e.g., Lessing's *Summer Before the Dark*, Gilman's *The Yellow Wallpaper*, or Chopin's *The Awakening*), the plot of the text is a critique of the ways in which traditional marriage confines, trivializes, and makes intolerable women's lives. Also represented in this literature are alternative narratives in which women envision and create meaningful lives quite apart from marriage (e.g., Walker's *The Color Purple*, Gilman's *Herland*, and Atwood's *Cat's Eye*).

This body of work is not only instructive but liberating in that the stories it tells about women invite the reader to identify with the heroine and to evaluate critically the prevailing gender arrangements that constrain her life and limit her opportunities. Perhaps precisely for that reason, these texts are often marginalized, categorized not as literature but as "women's literature," and likewise taught not in required university courses but only in elective "women's studies" courses. Becoming a part of the literary canon is a highly political process. Because this body of texts is not part of the canon, these works are unknown to the majority of women who still live under the spell of the marriage narrative.

Family Stories

The second major type of narrative from which we learn about life's possibilities is the personal or family story. These stories are oral accounts, handed down through generations of a family, which create a communal understanding of who the family is, as well as provide instruction regarding what constitutes appropriate personal conduct.

> One of the family's first jobs is to persuade its members that they are special, more wonderful than the neighboring barbarians. The persuasion consists of stories showing the family members demonstrating admirable traits, which it claims are family traits. Attention to the stories' actual truth is never the family's most compelling consideration. Encouraging belief is. The family's survival depends on the shared sensibility of its members. (Stone, 1988, p. 7)

Congruency. As I have read and heard the hundreds of family stories recounted to me by students and clients over the past fifteen years, two characteristics of the stories stand out. First, the stories are always consistent with the fundamental sense of life held by the storyteller. Depressed clients never spontaneously tell uplifting or triumphant family stories; conversely, optimistic, hopeful people tell no defeatist or tragic stories. Clearly, even the simplest, smallest, most ordinary of families accumulates enough experience across three or four generations to inspire thousands of possible stories. What accounts for the particular stories that are remembered and retold? One possibility is that the stories recounted now are *the* formative stories, the stories about the events that created or caused the current life experience of the storyteller. Obviously, this interpretation poses a linear connection between the history that the story represents and the current life experience of the storyteller.

Another possibility, in keeping with a more constructivist viewpoint, is that the client actively (albeit, perhaps unconsciously) *creates* a background or field against which to place her current experience. The client who is feeling depressed and hopeless will thus recall stories which are consistent with that experience: stories about devastating loss, impossible choices, shattered dreams. At a different point in her life, the client might report an entirely different set of stories. The idea that people actively construct stories for their lives has recently gained currency in family therapy partly through the work of White and Epston (1990). These authors have postulated the extremely useful concept of the "problem saturated story" that mires clients in their difficulties and makes it hard to imagine any solutions.

Elaboration. The second notable characteristic of family stories told by clients and students is that women have more numerous and more elaborate stories to tell. Perhaps this circumstance is best understood as a consequence of the politics of story making. Men have made and told their stories in the public arena where the stories have (sometimes) been endowed with meaning and could therefore be instructive to a wide audience. Women's lives have also needed the kind of moral and cognitive instruction that comes from storytelling, but the arena of women's storytelling has been restricted (until recently) to home and hearth.

In contrast to public story making, the telling of family stories is largely a female enterprise. It is women who sit around the table at family gatherings, after the men have gone off to play cards or watch the football game, and weave together the stories that become the fabric that defines the family. It is mothers who are most likely to hear and respond to a child who requests a story about when she was a little girl, or asks what it was like when she was born. Women are both the makers and the guardians of family stories. By hearing about her mother's and grandmothers' lives, a daughter first learns to define the possibilities of her own life. Laird (1989) points out that this very fact has been used to disparage women's stories, denigrating them as gossip, old wives' tales, or coffee klatching. Perhaps family stories have been more important to women than to men because they are the only stories women have had to shape their lives by.

THERAPISTS' USE OF STORIES

A client tells the following story about her mother:

When my mother was 16, she was raped by her father while her eldest brother held her down. After they released her, she went and got her father's shotgun and held both men at gunpoint for eight hours. Eventually the police came and drove the two men off. They never returned to the family.

It is possible, perhaps even compelling, to read this story in heroic terms. A young woman, having been brutalized by two of her own kinsmen, turns the tables and seizes control of the situation. As it stands, the story could be a powerful exemplar of personal authority, a foundation on which to build a life of competence, independence, mastery. The actual outcome, however, is quite different. The client continues:

Later my mother was engaged to six different men. Every time the wedding approached, she would break off the relationship. Finally, her mother locked her in her room for a week before her wedding so she couldn't run away or get out of it. After she and my father married, she became an alcoholic. She never really functioned very well as an adult.

So the achievement of the young woman, her ability to act powerfully on her own behalf, does not sustain her. Eventually she is defeated and sinks into a life consistent with that self-appraisal. She becomes depressed, silent, and addicted.

The client who tells this story is a successful professional woman who struggles endlessly with her own feelings of inadequacy and despair. She relates most obviously to the theme of insurmountable hardship in her mother's story and has difficulty trusting her own ability to make good decisions for herself. This doubt is fed by the response she often gets from others who tell her that she is too tough, too independent, too willful.

Opening Up Meaning

In working with the family stories of women clients, the therapist must be ever mindful of the cultural biases that might hinder her ability to understand the story apart from the predominant cultural narratives for women, just as those biases hinder the client's ability to tell the story. Since women's stories have been so limited to stories of marriage and service to others, it could be compelling to understand this client's story as the story of a woman so damaged by the violent incest she experienced that she was unable to recover, even through the safety and protection offered her by marriage.

A quite different interpretation, made possible only by standing outside the marriage narrative, is that for this client's mother, the thought of marriage did not bring to mind a safe harbor, but rather recreated for her the coercion and powerlessness she experienced with her father and brother. Her breaking off the engagements to six different men could be her repeated attempt to assert her right to say "No," to control her body and her destiny. Likewise, her alcoholism might have represented her final declaration that she would not be controlled by others, would not live out someone else's fantasy of how or what her life should be.

This interpretation does not alter the loss suffered by both my client and her mother, but it points to a different source of the trouble: not that sexual violence destroys a woman's life, but that a life without choices, without power to determine one's own destiny, is a life from which escape seems the only possible solution. This interpretation validates the client's strong desire to make her own choices and to be in charge of her own life, and allows her to see her mother as someone she can admire rather than merely pity.

Sources. When clients bring their personal stories into the therapist's office, those stories are already endowed with meaning. That meaning is drawn from two sources: First, the story is coherent with and often a metaphor for the client's current life experience. Therefore, it has diagnostic significance because it provides information regarding the extent to which the client feels hopeful or despairing about her life. Second, the story takes place within the dominant cultural narratives available and therefore will most likely be interpreted by the client in a way that is consistent with that narrative. Women will have difficulty seeing positive value in stories that do not support marriage as the ideal state, and will tend to pathologize stories, even their own stories, which take place outside of that narrative.

A woman in her mid-thirties with a highly successful career as an investment banker came to therapy seeking assistance in her efforts to change the nature of her relationships with men. She was eager to marry and have children, but had a history of becoming involved with men who were dependent and manipulative.

She complained that she was always trying to help the current man in her life to reach his potential. In her own family, she had always looked up to her father, a charming but authoritarian man. When the client was in her early twenties, her parents separated unexpectedly. Soon after, her mother moved to Florida, where she had resided ever since. The daughter took her mother's side in the separation and had not spoken to her father again. A few years later, he died suddenly of a heart attack. The daughter was devastated and guilt-ridden. She vaguely believed herself to be responsible for her father's death and was angry at her mother for having thrown him out.

Clearly, the daughter in this case was trying to solve the problem (as she understood it) of having abandoned her father by being absurdly patient and loyal to men who exploited her financially as well as emotionally. In addition, she now saw her mother as somewhat pathetic. Sometimes working with clients' stories to increase their sense of personal authority involves discovering missing elements to the story as much as creating new meanings. Because I sensed that there were important pieces missing from this story, I asked the client to write her mother's biography, a task that necessitated some renewed inquiry into the family history.

The client went to visit her mother, equipped with a set of questions to be explored. She returned from this trip in a state of confusion and surprise. Her mother had been quite eager to talk about the family. She recounted for her daughter numerous incidents of the father's gambling addiction, which had culminated in a telephoned threat on his life over a gambling debt. Upon putting down the phone, and without a word to his wife of 25 years, he walked out the door of their home forever. Far from being permanently damaged by her husband's departure, his wife felt liberated from the consequences of his addiction and had been living a very satisfactory life in Florida. She assured her daughter that her life had never been happier.

The effect of this new information on my client's sense of her own possibilities was immediate. A week after returning from the visit, she presented her current lover with a bill for the several thousand dollars she had lent him and a promissory note for him to sign. His expression of outrage at her lack of trust did not dissuade her. She declared herself no longer willing to be responsible for his life or his debts. Eventually, he signed the note and shortly thereafter the relationship ended. Although it was difficult, this loss did not create panic for the client, who was also starting to believe that a satisfactory and meaningful life outside of marriage might be possible. This belief was a direct consequence of the discovery she had made about her own mother's life.

Search. It is important for the therapist to listen carefully to the client's stories, not only to understand the meaning the client derives from the story, but also to discern alternative, potentially more liberating meanings. In the area of personal authority, it is essential to discern the limitations that the client's current understanding of the story places on her sense of power and control over her life. Sometimes creating a shift regarding the client's personal authority depends on emphasizing a different aspect or character of her story than the client has emphasized. As the following case illustrates, even the bleakest of stories usually contains some redemptive feature.

A woman came to therapy after failing law school. Depressed, she saw her failure as consistent with her family story. Both of her parents had been unsuccessful in their lives. Her father, a businessman, was always working on a deal sure to make him rich; her mother was a homemaker with no interest in housework and very little energy for her children. The client experienced herself as being pulled into what she believed would be the next chapter of the family story, in which she would also be marginal and unhappy. Only after some exploration was a different theme in the story detected. There was a favorite great aunt who, although totally lacking in formal education, had successfully run the one-room school in her hometown for many years. "How had she found the courage to defy convention and engage in such blatant self-determination?" I wondered aloud to my client. What lessons did her story suggest for my client? With some encouragement, the client embraced her great aunt's story for herself, taking it both as a model and validation of her own ambition. Within a few months, she established a nonprofit child advocacy agency and secured state funding to work with children placed in foster care because of abuse in their family homes.

Rashomon. The creation of belief is a more complicated task than the sharing of facts, and it is in the realm of belief that family stories have their greatest effect. As the play *Rashomon* demonstrates, a particular set of events may lead to the creation of multiple stories, and those stories may contradict each other. The same set of events in a family can inspire a story in which great personal authority is demonstrated, as well as stories emphasizing passivity, weakness, or deprivation.

As a child I heard the same apocryphal story told in two different versions by my mother and her mother. The story concerned the end of my grandparents' marriage during the Great Depression, when my mother was a small child. My grandmother's version of the story was heroic.

Faced with the responsibilities attendant to raising two small children and having a husband whom she suspected of being unfaithful and knew to be a poor provider, she took action. First, she borrowed a new pair of cotton gloves from a friend, the lack of her own gloves being a sign of the distressed circumstances in which she found herself. Then, she left her children with a neighbor for the day and went out to find work. Within six hours, she had persuaded the director of personnel at a manufacturing plant to hire her (an extraordinary feat for a young mother in 1931), explained her situation to her parents, secured temporary living quarters with them for herself and the girls, and gone home to confront her husband about his failures as both husband and father. He left shortly thereafter.

My grandmother never looked back with the smallest degree of regret and told the story proudly (and often) to me as a child. To her, the experience demonstrated the possibility and the importance of exercising personal authority in her life. Certainly I received the story as evidence that it is sometimes necessary to take control of one's life, even if it means going beyond the normal rules of comportment and loyalties in order to create one's own future.

There was another version of this family story, told by my mother. Her version was briefer, given her young age at the time of its occurrence, and more poignant than heroic. My mother's story was about losing her adored father for reasons she could not fathom and feeling devastated and vulnerable as a consequence. She believed herself to have been permanently damaged by the loss of her father and spent much of her life trying to replace him. To her, my grandmother's actions were selfish, rash, and incomprehensible.

Although I was troubled by my mother's pain, it was my grandmother's story that held sway over me and allowed me to consider possibilities for my life that my mother's story would not have permitted. My grandmother's establishing her right to self-determination was my model and my support for choosing to be the first in my family to go to college, for enduring the political rigors of attaining tenure, and for speaking out and writing on topics that stir controversy and create disapprobation towards me.

Receiving and Questioning

The therapist's role in the work of reinterpreting and creating new stories for clients' lives is, first of all, the role of the empathic audience. Clients must feel that their stories will be received with respect and care. Second, the therapist takes on a critical role, not of the story itself, but of the meaning attributed to it by the client. Is the currently understood meaning the only one possible? Are there themes inaudible to the client's ears which might suggest different meanings? Are there chapters of the story missing and, if so, how could they be retrieved?

If a particular goal of the work with the stories from a woman client is to assist her in increasing her sense of personal authority, then the therapist must also stay cognizant of the background narrative for women's lives which makes personal authority so difficult for women to achieve. To pursue this goal with a client requires that the therapist have a perspective that enables her to stand apart from the marriage narrative with its empha- sis on passivity, selflessness, sacrifice, and dependency. This is not to sug- gest that the therapist must be anti-marriage or that marriage per se pre- vents women from acting with personal authority. Rather, it is to suggest that therapists must be conscious of the extent to which we too have internalized the marriage narrative as the "best" or most appropriate story for women, as well as the extent to which we might inadvertently discour- age women clients from acting with personal authority by not challenging the goodness of fit between that narrative and the clients' needs, feelings, and ambitions.

REFERENCES

Beattie, M. (1987). *Codependent no more*. Center City, MN: Hazelden.
Belenky, M., Clinchy, B., Goldberger, N., & Tarule, J. (1986). *Women's ways of knowing: The development of self, voice and mind*. New York: Basic.
Bepko, C., & Krestan, J. (1990). *Too good for her own good*. New York: Harper & Row.
Chodorow, N. (1978). *The reproduction of mothering: Psychoanalysis and the sociology of gender*. Berkeley: University of California.
Dinnerstein, D. (1976). *The mermaid and the minotaur: Sexual arrangements and the human malaise*. New York: Harper Colophon.
Gilligan, C. (1982). *In a different voice: Psychological theory and women's development*. Cam- bridge, MA: Harvard University Press.
Heilbrun, C. G. (1988). *Writing a woman's life*. New York: Random House.
Laird, J. (1989). Women and stories: Restorying women's self-constructions. In M. McGold- rick, C. Anderson, & F. Walsh (Eds.), *Women in families: A framework for family therapy* (pp. 427–450). New York: Norton.
Lerner, H. (1985). *The dance of anger*. New York: Harper.
Miller, J. B. (1976). *Toward a new psychology of women*. New York: Beacon.
Schaef, A. (1986). *Codependence: Misunderstood, mistreated*. New York: Harper & Row.
Stone, E. (1988). *Black sheep and kissing cousins: How our family stories shape us*. New York: Times Books.
White, M., & Epston, D. (1990). *Narrative means to therapeutic ends*. New York: Norton.
Woolf, V. (1957). *A room of one's own*. New York: Harcourt, Brace, Jovanovich.

7

JOAN LAIRD

Enactments of Power Through Ritual

THE RELATIONSHIP BETWEEN ritual and power is a complex and intimate one. Human beings draw upon the power of ritual to enrich their lives with meaning, to heal from overwhelming losses, to move from one status in life to another. The power of ritual is used by some to dominate and oppress others and by those who are oppressed to struggle to maintain definition and coherence in the face of oppression. Because power plays such an important role in the relationships between men and women, ritual is a mode of social action fundamental both to gender identity and to the maintenance of the sexual social order.

In this chapter, I examine the relationship between ritual and power in terms of ritual's relevance in the lives of women and in the relationships between the sexes. As part of this exploration, I look at the role of ritual in the cultural construction of gender and at the uses and misuses of ritual in maintaining sexual dominance. While the power of ritual is used by both men and women to maintain particular social positions of dominance, status, and prestige, here I pay particular attention to the ways ritual is used in this society to oppress women. Examples are drawn from the larger sociocultural context and from the field of family therapy.

Portions of this article have been excerpted from Laird, J. (1988). Women and ritual in family therapy. In E. Imber-Black, J. Roberts, & R. Whiting (Eds.), *Rituals in families and family therapy* (pp. 331–362). New York: Norton.

POWER AND OPPRESSION

Anthropologist Eric Wolf, who calls power "one of the most loaded and polymorphous words in our repertoire" (1990, p. 586), posits four different modes of power. The first is power as the attribute of the person, a *personal power* or capability. This kind of power "draws attention to the endowment of persons in the play of power, but tells us little about the form and direction of that play" (p. 586). Wolf sees the second kind of power as *interpersonal power*, the ability of an ego to impose its will on another in interpersonal and other social interactions. This definition, in his view, says little about the arena in which these interactions occur. In the third mode, which he calls *tactical or organizational power*, power is seen as controlling the settings in which people exert power and interact in powerful ways with others. The fourth mode of power he calls *structural power*, which is power that organizes and orchestrates the settings themselves. Wolf likens this kind of power to Marx's idea of the power of capital to harness and allocate labor, and to Foucault's notion of power as the ability to structure the possible field of action of others, to govern the consciousness, or to shape and control social discourse.

All of these modes of power are, of course, relevant to the concerns of family therapists who must be attuned to differential power within families, the various aspects of power in the therapeutic relationship, and the larger contexts of power which shape thought and action for family and therapist. Whether power exists as some kind of objective entity and, if so, where it should be located, has long been debated in the family therapy literature, dating, perhaps, from the famous encounter between Haley and Bateson. White and Epston (1990) draw upon the work of Foucault to point out that power, which is intimately linked to knowledge, may be both repressive and constitutive—i.e., shaping—of people's lives. As they interpret him, Foucault "is subscribing not to the belief that there exist objective or intrinsic facts about the nature of power but instead to constructed ideas that are accorded a truth status" (p. 19). For Foucault, power concerns the ability to construct "truths" that shape and control social discourse. Power and knowledge are thus inseparable. As Foucault (1980) phrases it, "We are subjected to the production of truth through power and we cannot exercise power except through the production of truth" (p. 93). We are all enmeshed in a web of power/knowledge and cannot act apart from this domain. Furthermore, argue White and Epston (1990), "we are simultaneously undergoing the effects of power and exercising this power in relation to others" (p. 22).

It is important to emphasize, however, that all discourses are not equal; some knowledges are consistently suppressed, never moving from private to public consciousness, while others are consistently sanctified and receive widespread public acknowledgment. In other words, some knowledges are used to suppress alternative ways of knowing. Here we need think only of the dominance of the "power/knowledge" of particular branches of science, religion, or psychology, knowledges whose hegemonies are maintained through elaborate self-aggrandizing processes that successfully ward off, challenge, and define as deviant alternative narratives. Through the sanctification of particular "languages" or discourses, human experiences are either storied or not storied, validated or invalidated, as certain systems of thought become privileged standards by which all behavior is defined and evaluated.

Weick (1990) describes the hidden dynamics of oppression. First, certain ideologies support particular worldviews as the only acceptable ones. Through socialization to prevailing ideologies, we are taught to adopt the dominant worldview, which is enforced in various social structures through an elaborate system of sanctions, prescriptions, proscriptions, myths, and so on. Second, we learn to look outward to external authority as arbiter and interpreter of our own experiences. Third, we learn to "live the lie," to ignore or deny our own lived experiences that fall outside of the dominant story and that contradict it. This process of exclusion closes off the development of alternative stories or solutions. As White and Epston point out, many of us recognize that our "lived" experiences contradict the "truths" that make up the dominant, culturally available discourse and that can limit our opportunities for personhood and relationship. Finally, Weick details some of the social costs, the systems of hypervigilance that must be kept in place to identify and punish recalcitrants, the pervasive fears of difference (and thus the stifling of change and creativity), the shoring up of illusions, and the shriveled notions of human experience that remain.

RITUAL AS A SOURCE OF POWER

What is it that makes ritual such a source of knowledge and power? One of the central ways that particular languages or discourses are accorded special status, whether for good or evil, is through the medium of ritual, for ritual is fundamental both to the elevation and subjugation of particular discourses and, thus, to the interests of particular segments of society.

Along with story, folklore, and myth, ritual is a powerful force in the formation and shaping of meaning and belief, as well as in the maintenance and transmission of what we come to call "culture." Thus, ritual is not only revelatory of our personal and social meanings—a form for expression—but also creative and recreative. Ritual, like myth, is what anthropologists term a "packed" social category or mode of action, because it operates on and must be understood on so many levels at once. Rituals have both content and form, overt and covert meanings that communicate analogically and metaphorically. They operate on both conscious and unconscious levels with their multiple layers of symbolic richness and often mesmerizing actions, catching us up in them and pulling us along, structuring the very ways we think about and walk through our lives. Moore and Myerhoff (1977) list the following features, which together define ritual and lend it uniqueness:

1. repetition
2. acting (saying, thinking, doing)
3. special behavior or stylization (using action or symbols that are extraordinary or using ordinary ones in an unusual way)
4. order (a ritual may be ordered according to beginnings, ends, and prescriptions for behavior and still be capable of containing elements of chaos and spontaneity that may be expressed at particular times and places)
5. evocative presentational style
6. a collective dimension (that is, a dimension charged with a social message, even if it is the self sending a message to the self)

Ritual may also be defined in terms of its multiple functions. These symbolic enactments not only communicate the group's shared construction of meanings or its worldview, but, at the same time, they legitimize them as "truths." Thus, they are uniquely useful in helping to perpetuate particular "knowledges" and particular vested interests.

We cannot live without ritual, for ritual brings order and coherence to our lives. Collective rituals not only organize and bring under control our life experiences, but they can also serve to rigidify certain patterns of interaction, to minimize difference, to gloss over paradoxes, to deny conflicts, and to subjugate some to the will of others. At the same time, they can bind us to particular goals and strategies for living, while they blind us to alternative ways of knowing and doing, for we are creatures of habit who become utterly caught up in the important rituals in our lives. Most demagogues—the Hitlers, Stalins, and Perons of our century and other inquisitors and enslavers throughout history—have manipulated the power of ritual to bind loyalties and to stifle difference. Even the most benign of political, religious, or professional leaders have understood how to marshal the drama of ritual to inspire allegiance, to sell an idea, or to promote their position or cause.

Ritual and Gender

It is clear that many social rituals, particularly initiation and other rites of passage, help us prepare for and move through the various stages of our lives, by readying us to leave behind the old and incorporate the new. Such rites are usually concerned directly with the construction of the self, with definitions of gender identity and social role, and, at the same time, with definitions of social power and status.

Ritual is probably the most potent method of socialization available to kin and other such groups for preparing individual members to understand the group's meanings, to carry on its traditions, and to perform those social roles considered essential to its continuation. Through ritual, we learn who we are to be as males and females, what words we may speak to whom and on what occasions, what we can and will do and how we shall do it, with whom we are to be, and to what we can aspire. Our identities are not only reflected in the rituals we perform, but are reinforced, changed in some ways, and created anew in each action. Ritual *implies* action and performance, catching us up in its choreography or, as Kenneth Burke once said, "Ritual is dancing an attitude" (quoted in Myerhoff, 1983).

Anthropologists Gregory Bateson and Margaret Mead were among the first to attend to the cultural worlds of women and to suggest a cultural conception of gender, a conceptualization that emerged largely from their study of ritual in traditional societies. Bateson, in his effort to interpret the *Naven* ritual, demonstrated that the analysis of such a complex ceremony required multidimensional perspectives on ritual, culture, and mind. To understand a single ritual, in even the least complex of societies, requires an exploration of the rituals in terms of the society's ecology, its economy, its psychology and sociology, its sexual politics, and its worldview and symbolic systems. Further, it requires a vision of "how such partial modes of understanding can be fitted together in a coherent process of explanation" (Keesing, 1982, p. 17). Keesing warns that "bridge building between partial explanations itself entails further dangers. We are likely to be left with nothing more than an ever more complex functionalist matrix of interconnection, ultimately static and circular: 'the system' endlessly reinforcing and perpetuating itself" (1982, p. 33). Careful attention to the social construction of gender and the relationships between the sexes is an essential part of that vision.

As is evident above, in traditional anthropological analysis, rituals have been seen as taming chaos and imposing order, as reinforcing social integration and society itself. However, in his review of studies of the Eastern Highlands of New Guinea, Keesing has observed that what the central social rituals of these societies actually celebrate is the unity and power of *men*. As he points out:

They celebrate and reinforce male dominance in the face of women's visible power to create and sustain life, and in the face of the bonds between boys and their mothers which must be broken to sustain male solidarity and dominance. Women's physical control over reproductive processes and emotional control over their sons must be overcome by politics, secrecy, ideology, and dramatized male power. (1982, p. 23)

Male initiation rites in the Highlands not only transform boys into men, but are transformations in which the senior men define themselves as special in relation to women and to uninitiated boys. Langness (1974) argues that "the social solidarity [expressed in ritual] rests upon a power structure entirely in the hands of males, a power structure supported where necessary by a variety of acts that are magical, pure and simple, and designed to keep power in the hands of males" (p. 19). Such power is obtained through maintaining a clear sexual polarization in the world of economic production and through controlling women's productive and reproductive powers, as men or male-dominated kinship groups exchange women and bridewealth. Since male power, status, and prestige are dependent in large part on women's labor, "it is ties with women that pose the greatest threat, from both within and without. The bond between mothers and sons could keep boys from becoming men: it must be broken dramatically and traumatically" (Keesing, 1982, p. 24). Men's shared secrets of ritual contribute to the maintenance of a supercommunity in which women are either excluded from the central rituals of the society or play roles complementary and subordinate to those of men, "as spectators and fringe participants in male-dominated ritual pageantry and politics" (Keesing, 1982, pp. 24–25).

While the Eastern Highlands of New Guinea may seem far removed, it is the case that male rituals throughout the world, including of this society, tend to be more public and more central to social cosmology than female ones. Women's rituals are usually less dramatic or colorful, less important in terms of power definitions, and in the great majority of societies tend to reify women's domestic roles. What rituals that do exist for women tend to celebrate woman's role as nurturer or caretaker and her assignment to a particular lineage and a particular male. Rituals that endow certain knowledges with great authority, auguring the accumulation of social and personal power, are not generally as available to women. Whatever contributions women make to public life are rarely made explicit; their social personae are usually defined by virtue of their relationships to men.

While the above interpretations and generalizations tend to emerge from the study of less complex and diverse societies than our own, societies in which ritual experiences rather than written words or abstract concepts are the primary sources of learning, they nevertheless draw attention to some of the issues of knowledge, power, and gender implicit in American ritual. A few observations about our own cultural rituals may be made and briefly illustrated.

1. Women's rituals in the United States are less central and less definitional in terms of national values than those of men.
2. National rituals tend to define and confirm the assignment of the public domain (and thus greater power and prestige) to men, the domestic domain to women.
3. Many rituals, both societal and familial, continue to define women's deference and subordination to men.
4. Women's power, in this society, continues to be feared by men; in many traditional societies, women are seen as dangerous and polluting and thus must undergo elaborate purification rituals.
5. Women who choose to march to a different drummer, that is, women who choose not to define themselves in relation to men (e.g., unmarried or lesbian women) are excluded from major social rituals, their lives are largely unstoried, and their own rituals are defined as unimportant or deviant.

Power and Authority

In this country, our most colorful national pageants, which send powerful messages concerning what is to be most celebrated and valued, are associated with the military and with male-dominated spectator sports, particularly football and baseball. These public enactments celebrate the corporate-military complex as well as characteristics associated with males, such as aggressiveness and physical prowess. Women tend to play subordinate and supportive roles in these elaborate pageants, cheering on the real actors in the drama. There are no rituals, equivalent in visibility or drama, that celebrate female symbols, roles, or characteristics. The public domains (and thus the public rituals) that are associated with power in this society—those of politics, the courts, the military, banking, the corporation, and even academe—remain largely under the domination of men. It is difficult for many, if not most, women to see themselves reflected or recreated in the rituals associated with these domains.

Questions may be raised as to whether even those rituals in our society highly identified with women and usually located in the family clearly celebrate women's lives and contributions or are under women's control. Reproduction provides one example. In preindustrial societies, argue Paige and Paige (1981), the rituals of reproduction are essentially political, a means by which men control the reproductive powers of women in order to gain political and economic power. Rich (1986) vividly describes how the control of birthing in our own society was stripped from women and how it became an experience in which women were forced to lie down, to take a passive role, and to be isolated from the support and comfort of other women. Women were also encouraged to relinquish breast-feeding, which became an isolating, embarrassing, and somehow "primitive" practice in this age of "scientific" mothering. In spite of what appears to be a contemporary reclaiming of birthing and nursing on the part of women, Paige and Paige maintain that the male-dominated medical profession still controls the processes of childbirth; the "natural childbirth" movement has offered only minor modification and, in fact, its major innovation is paternal participation in delivery, a practice they see as a new form of *couvade*. Furthermore, while some women may have assumed more control over their own rituals of birth, it is men who dominate the legislative and judicial bodies that will ultimately decide whether women can make decisions to terminate pregnancy, to whom and under what conditions birth control will be available, to whom custody will be granted, and so on.

In Levi-Strauss's theory of kinship, marriage was seen as "the most basic form of gift exchange, in which it is women who are the most precious of gifts" (Rubin, 1975, p. 173). Rubin believes that "kinship and marriage are always parts of total social systems, and are always tied into economic and political arrangements" (p. 207). The marriage contract and the obligations of kinship serve as charters for bestowing or limiting rights of person and property. In Rubin's view, if, in precapitalist society, women were kept in their place by men's cults, secret initiations, and so on, "capitalism has taken over, and rewired, notions of male and female which predate it by centuries" (1975, p. 163). The notion of the exchange of women is still enacted in the traditional marriage ceremony, in which the daughter is "given" to the groom by her father and, in the process, exchanges the name of one male for another. It can be argued that, in our society, the powerful symbolism and language in this rite lack the literal meanings of ownership and connotations of women as property found in many traditional societies. Nevertheless, such words and symbols create recursive worlds of meaning which act on the unconscious level, telling women who they are and what they may become, as Starhawk (1987), Imber-Black (1989), and others have so convincingly argued in their interpretations of contemporary women's rituals. In fact, in many marriages it is clear that what has been purchased is women's domestic labor.

The notions of exchange and control of women by men through marriage and kinship alliances have other, very concrete, applications in American marriage and family patterns. For example, men continue to earn far more money than their wives, whether or not the wives work outside of the home. As Schwartz (1987) points out, in marriage as well as in the larger society, "money talks." In marriage, money or earning power buys the right to make decisions—decisions concerning whether to stay or leave, what the family will purchase, where they will live, how the children will be educated, whether there will be therapy, whether father will attend, and so on. In many cases, money buys the right of men to bind women to unhappy marriages and, in some families, to rituals of violence and humiliation, since many women lack the resources to live independently or the skills to compete in the public world.

Public = Male : Domestic = Female

Male rituals everywhere seem to celebrate men's entry into and participation in public life. Female rituals everywhere seem to celebrate and define women's entry into and participation in domestic life. Rosaldo (1974) points out that in many societies there are radical divisions between the lives of men and the lives of the domestic group. Such arrangements leave men free to design rituals of authority that define them as superior, as special, and as separate. These rituals increase the distance between men and their families, thus creating barriers to the demands for intimacy that family life implies. She argues that "because men can be separate, they can be 'sacred'; and by avoiding certain sorts of intimacy and involvement, they can develop an image and mantle of integrity and worth" (1974, p. 27). An analogy may be made to American society, for it is clear that even in dual-career families, women continue to carry much greater responsibility for the care of the children and the maintenance of the home. It is much more difficult for women, even for those who work outside of the home, to construct or control public images of authority, since they are weighted down with the demands of caretaking and the burdens of domestic life. In public life, men are the authors, women the helpers; in domestic life, the reverse is the case. For Rosaldo, as for many feminist scholars, the distribution of work roles is key to issues of gender equality and distribution of power.

Women's Rites of Passage

In our own society, no clearly defined or universal initiation rites of passage exist for men or for women, a phenomenon that contributes to the difficulties young people face in leaving home and defining adulthood. The period of adolescence is prolonged and poorly marked. For many, high school graduation serves as a diffuse transition rite; for others, entry into the military; for still others, marriage.

Those rituals that do exist for the young female in our society carry confusing and ambiguous messages that fail to ready her for public life, that continue to define her in relation to and as contingent upon males. The imagery from the "sweet sixteen" party and the debutante's "coming out" party emphasize beauty, femininity, and grace—and the availability of young women for potential husbands. These messages are most powerfully portrayed and best exemplified in the national Miss America pageant, that male-directed annual rite of Fall in which women parade their bodies in a ritual somewhat reminiscent of the slave or cattle auction.

With the exception of her wedding, her birthday, and her own funeral, there are few rites that help a woman mark *any* of the major transitions in her life, or at least few rites for which cultural material is available to the individual family. The married woman's life is most clearly marked by family rites that celebrate the movement through life of her children. While childbirth brings special privileges and recognition for the new mother, it often lacks symbolically rich rites of passage which help women incorporate the new status of motherhood. Twenty years ago, in most medical settings, it was the ritual of hospital routine that regulated new mothers' access to their own infants; mothers were restricted from holding or seeing their babies, from feeding them when they were hungry, and thus were stripped of important parts of the mastery and gratification that come with this act of creativity. Even now, it is women's reproduction (product) that is celebrated, rarely her own transition to a new and challenging role that will likely consume much of her energy for many years to come. Similarly, the transition to post-childrearing is inadequately honored as women enter a new phase in their lives with a new set of self-definitions and interpersonal relationships to be mastered. In family therapy, it has often been the "emancipation" of the child from the enmeshing or overinvolved mother that is the central goal of treatment. In few published cases is the mother helped to reconceptualize, incorporate, redefine, and celebrate her own changed status. The fact that these transitions are so poorly marked through ritual may contribute to the common occurrence of depression during both of these life phases.

Neither are there widely sanctioned rituals that help women incorporate public roles, that move them into the company of senior women, or that venerate their achievements and wisdom as they move to old age. Since rites of passage are important facilitators in the definition of self in relation to society, there is clearly a need for women to reclaim, redesign, or create new rituals that will facilitate life transitions and allow more meaningful and clear incorporation of both familial and public roles. For women who do move into the public domain, into male-defined and male-dominated professions, the risks are often heavy and some gains are made with substantial costs in ritual degradation and humiliation, reminders that the public sphere belongs to men. The contemporary heroine is often criticized and ridiculed by both men and women in a male-controlled mythmaking process, which reminds us all continually that the public sphere belongs to men. For example, Eleanor Roosevelt was villified repeatedly for overstepping her bounds, her appearance and her mothering held up for public approbation. More recently, the attack on Margaret Mead's work by Derek Freeman (1983) excited the media for many months, while the occasion of Mary Catherine Bateson's (1984) loving and eloquent memoir of her parents gave male reviewers license to disparage not only Mead's contributions to social science but her abilities as wife and mother. Furthermore, women in the public eye, no matter how successful, are chained to their husband's choices. While neither Gerald Ford's nor Michael Dukakis' careers seem to have been adversely affected by their wives' drinking, Geraldine Ferraro's bid in part faltered on her husband's financial decisions. And Elizabeth Dole, the only woman in Reagan's cabinet, resigned to devote her energy to her husband's run for the presidential nomination. It was clear whose career came first.

Dominance and Submission

Another theme repeatedly enacted in both domestic and public ritual is one of dominance and subordination, as women perform in ritual roles that define their supportive and ancillary positions in relation to men. For example, in many societies, women's deference to men is demonstrated symbolically by walking several paces behind their husbands, covering their faces in the presence of men, keeping their eyes downcast, or sleeping at the feet of men (Bamberger, 1974). In our own society, the images are no less powerful nor the messages less clear. In hospital rituals, (usually) female nurses hand over the tools of the trade to (usually) male surgeons. Nurses and female doctors are often called by their first names, while male doctors are addressed by their professional titles, actions that not only symbolize but also confer authority and prestige. In many American families, men sit at the head of the table, are waited upon by the females in the family, are often served first, and are usually offered the choicest piece of meat.

Purity and Danger

A set of symbols common to many rituals throughout the world identifies women with notions of sexual pollution and danger. Women are, on the one hand, portrayed as virginal and pure and, on the other, as sexually dangerous and polluting. In this paradoxical position, women are identified with and seen as closer to "nature," while men are closer to "culture," a false but useful dichotomizing process in the world of sexual politics (Ortner, 1974). Women are the "other," a marked category in relation to the generic, unmarked category of "self," which is owned by the male.

In many societies, women undergo elaborate purification rites at particular times, such as after childbirth or menstruation. While such cleansing rites carry multiple layers of meaning, they can be used, according to anthropologist Mary Douglas (1966), to assert male superiority, to claim separate social spheres for men and women, or to blame male failure on women's transgressions. Purification rituals, argues Douglas, both mirror and reinforce existing cosmologies, social structures, and balances of power, binding men and women to their prescribed social roles. Where social systems are stable and well-articulated, such purification rites may be largely unnecessary, but where the social structure is poorly articulated, and gender roles and relationships are highly ambiguous or changing, those who would challenge the established hegemony represent danger and must be defined as polluting.

While few clearly defined purification rites exist in our society, we are subjected to a discourse and to a set of diffuse rituals that define women as unclean and as sexually dangerous. The onset of menstruation has often been a solitary, secretive, and shameful experience, marked only by a furtive trip to the drugstore and perhaps by the young girl's first pelvic examination, itself often a ritual of humiliation. The event is not, as Washburn (1977) says, *recognized* in a way that provides the young girl "with a symbolic framework within which to find resources for her questions of meaning" (pp. 12–13). She does not usually emerge from this crisis with an increased sense of pride in her own body or an enhanced sense of worth. Furthermore, the well-documented tabooing of sexual relations during menstruation, pregnancy, and in the postpartum period, in spite of an absence of evidence of health hazard, "clearly suggests that the widespread notion of sexual pollution is shared by Americans" (Paige & Paige, 1981, p. 276). In what seems to be an increasing number of televised exhortations, women are advised constantly to cleanse, douche, and perfume their private parts, presumably once again a reminder of their polluting propensities.

If menstruation is associated with impurity and uncleanliness, it is also linked with notions of power. Weigle (1982) accumulates a rich cross-cultural sample of ritual, myth, and folklore demonstrating that the menstruating woman is seen as dangerous, as emitting a *mana* or supernatural power. Not only must men protect themselves from contamination, but in some societies male rites symbolize the taking over of the reproductive powers that menstruation implies, as in *couvade* rituals or in the ritual cutting of male genitals in circumcision or supercision. If in traditional societies men must refrain from sex before a hunt or a raid, in our own society some athletes must observe similar sexual taboos. For example, "during summer training camp—a liminal period prior to the start of the football season—professional players are isolated from their wives or other women. Both college and professional players are also expected to abstain from sex on the night before a game" (Arens, 1976, quoted in Kottak, 1978, p. 513).

In this society, the menstruating female is defined as "sick," as suffering from a "syndrome," and as being in need of isolation or rest. As a woman so "cursed" or vulnerable to pregnancy, she is frequently defined as a less valuable or reliable worker. Despite the fact that our society seems to be moving toward sexual liberation and equality for women, many young women starve themselves and ritually gorge and emit food. Like the rituals of fasting or starving during menstruation seen in the mythologies of various traditional societies, eating disorders may express the female's shame over her own body image and bodily processes by denying her own sexuality and conforming to male-defined stereotypes of beauty— another way women are denied power over their own bodies.

Innovative Women

Women's lives, I am arguing, are poorly ritualized in this society. The words and actions in women's rituals frequently reinforce male domi- nance/female submission themes as well as women's assignment to men and to the domestic world, and warn of women's sexual power and pollu- tion potential. For women who reject heterosexual marriage, who are dissatisfied with it, who are victimized in it, or who, for other reasons, are unable to remain in it, or for women who choose a lesbian life-style, our society provides even less sanction or help in the form of cultural ritual. Such women's lives are largely unsung and unstoried; single and lesbian women are either denied a major role in the construction of social dis- course or are defined as deviant in the dominant discourses. Their knowl- edges are subjugated and, thus, lack sanction in the larger cultural context. As is the case with poor women, aging women, and women of color, single and lesbian women must write their own histories, claim their own power to story and ritualize their lives and, indeed, innovate their own rituals, often in relatively invisible and marginalized contexts.

Unmarried women, often treated like children or incomplete adults, are frequently peripheral in central family rituals and in family decision-making about rituals, are assigned important and sometimes dreary tasks, but have marginal roles in the family drama. Their lives, their time, their choices are typically seen as less important than the lives of their married sisters or their bachelor brothers. Women in lesbian families often find their choices unsanctioned and unmarked, if not held in contempt, in the community and larger social context; similarly, their life partners are excluded from family-of-origin and other social rituals. Such women are then left with a sense of anger, disappointment, incompletion, emptiness, and sometimes shame and guilt. How do these women draw upon the power of ritual to bring definition and order into their lives, to sanctify their knowledges, to story their experiences?

The connections among story, discourse, myth, what Foucault calls "knowledge," and ritual are very strong ones, since it is often through ritual that knowledges are awarded a special or "sacred" place and are communicated to all who participate. As we will see in the next section, women have become increasingly aware of the importance of creating new knowledges and affirming them through ritual.

RECLAIMING WOMEN'S RITUALS

Mastery of life events, the integration of transition, healing, celebration, and other phenomena that provide grist for the therapist's mill occur naturally over the life course as people seek to understand their worlds, consolidate their own identities, and empower themselves. Our friends, our clients, and the novelists, poets, dramatists, and other artists of our times are usually our best teachers as we name and shape into "models" and "interventions" the creative healing processes that surround us. It is frequently the person at the margins who leads the way.

Today, some women are claiming the right to participate more actively in, and indeed lead, public rituals. Women, albeit in small numbers, are sitting on the judge's bench. There are predictions that the 1990s will be the decade of women in politics. An increasing number of religious groups have admitted women to the clergy. The recent phenomenon of female stand-up comics, some of whom exclude men from their performances, marks a radical shift in our society's rules for the male domination of public humor and provides an opportunity for women to "joke" about their husbands, their male lovers, their fathers and fathers-in-law in a medium where women have been the usual targets of humor.

Other women are redefining old, outworn rituals that no longer represent their stories or their life experiences. For example, many women, with the help of men, are rewriting marriage ceremonies to symbolize more egalitarian expectations. Gender-conscious men and women, particularly in dual-career households, are reexamining their family rituals, pushing for more shared responsibility and more enactments symbolic of parity in the cycle of holiday celebrations that have traditionally reinforced women's domesticity and left them exhausted and depressed.

Additionally, there are signs that women are reexamining their own rites of transition and families are reshaping rituals for their daughters. For example, modern baby showers may mark for women their sexuality as well as their domestic skills, baby showers celebrate the pregnant woman as well as the expected progeny, and divorce celebrations may express and help women define their new status and the challenges they anticipate. Some women, perhaps to satirize the traditional male bachelor party rite, go to male strip shows to mark *their* movement from a world where women's friendships are primary to the constraints implicit in heterosexual marriage or, as in the film *Twice in a Lifetime*, to mark the divorced woman's emergence from a period of mourning to reintegration into life as a single woman open to new sexual and relational experiences. Some families have found creative ways to mark and celebrate the onset of menarche, while others are hosting "independence" parties for daughters leaving home whose destiny, in the near future at least, is something other than marriage.

In addition to reclaiming and reshaping rites of passage within such traditional social structures as church and family, some women have created alternative contexts for the celebration of womanhood. This is particularly the case regarding women's spirituality, a movement of women who have turned away from patriarchal religion where the role for women has been to decorate the church and raise funds, to serve refreshments and "swell the chorus of liturgical song, and still slavishly accept their second-class status as 'non-creative' pillars of the church" (Walker, 1990, p. 4). Walker, in her introduction to a sourcebook on the creation of women's rituals, points out:

For many centuries, men have been devising the religious rituals of our civilization. They have written formal prayers, invocations, and other liturgical speech. They have composed anthems, hymns, processions. . . . They have designed and built ritual spaces, utilizing every talent of the best available architects, artists, and craftspeople. They have set up vast, complex structures of hieratic action having no purpose except formal celebration of male-centered religious beliefs. . . . In our

Western culture, men alone have claimed the right to invent, teach, or lead religious rituals. Women have been almost totally excluded from the process. Even when patriarchal religious authorities took over older ceremonies that once celebrated the Goddess and were first created by her priestesses, men erased the signs of feminine authorship and changed the gender. . . .

When women continued their own ancient ceremonies privately, or outside of the framework of male orthodoxy, they were labeled witches and made legally subject to torture and murder by the male establishment. (1990, p. 3)

Some women have formed spirituality groups that practice witchcraft and Goddess worship, trance, magic, and other innovations. Others have been drawn to less radical groups that explore women's spirituality and provide new opportunities for adult identity consolidation. In a study of 10 women who participate in an adult creative ritual group, Shorin (1988) argues that the group serves as an alternative ritual structure for completing the transition into adulthood in a women-affirming environment. Still others strive to alter sexist rituals within existing patriarchal religious institutions.

If all women are oppressed in a patriarchal society, certain women are particularly subjugated. Their stories and rituals are denied and kept secret by the larger society in order to reinforce particular discourses. Subjugated groups themselves participate in the denial and secretiveness to avoid shame, harassment, or more violent forms of degradation. What is remarkable is the courage and invention such women demonstrate in their efforts to ritualize and story their lives and to create their own alternative celebrations and mythologies.

Elsewhere (Laird, 1989), I have described how women reconstruct themselves in the storying of their lives. For some women, the writing of their story and its public telling through the published word or the television talk show has become a ritual for our times. This phenomenon illustrates again the very intimate relationship between story and ritual. The writing, storying, or public telling of one's life may be thought of as an identity-making ritual which must follow the conventions for discourse-making so closely connected with issues of gender and power, as Heilbrun (1988) so brilliantly illuminates. Today, many women biographers and autobiographers are very consciously following a new set of rules for women's storying as they write their own lives and the lives of others in new ways that acknowledge women's ambitions and quests apart from the world of men (e.g., Conway, 1989).

Perhaps no story has been more suppressed in this century than that of the incest victim, that ultimate keeper of secrets whose very experiences were denied her, sometimes in her own consciousness. Some adult survivors of incest, in addition to or instead of formal therapies, have developed their own healing rituals. In a study of how incest survivors have used the ritual of autobiographical writing to heal from the wounds of traumatic sexual abuse, Winslow (1990) describes the inventiveness of many of these women in creating elaborate, heavily symbolic healing and expiation rituals. The writing itself marks a rite of passage, transporting the survivor from a world of private troubles to one of public expression and claiming, a form of linking the personal and the political. These women, often in the context of women's friendships and kinships, are also revising and celebrating more traditional family rituals that hold ambivalent and painful memories. As Winslow frames it, the reclaimed rituals are effective because they allow the incorporation of different emotions and memories within a protected, circumscribed time, place, and action, and because they allow the expression of "intense, difficult, and dissimilar emotions and events that are not readily integrated into everyday life" (p. 32).

Minority women have also been disempowered—their discourses, their rituals, and thus their sources of power are largely unknown and unrecognized. Barkley-Brown (1989), using quilt-making as an example of women's creative rituals, demonstrates how African-American women have "created their own lives, shaped their own meanings, and are the voices of authority on their own experiences" (p. 927). In a similar vein, Carpenter (1990) describes how African-American women, in their quilt-making rituals, and particularly in the making of narrative quilts, record and transform their lives. At one level, the group ritual of quilt-making joins women over the generations, celebrating connection and continuity. However, the quilts can also serve as powerful social documents in the case of these women whose "needles became their pens and quilts their eminently expressive texts . . . " (Ferraro, Hedges, & Silber, 1987, p. 11). For African-American women, who were denied education and discouraged from writing, story quilts communicated their experiences of oppression and marked their fights for freedom.

Lesbian women, both single and in life partnerships, are often forbidden participation in both public and domestic rituals and have become particularly sensitive to the need to develop rituals that will enrich and define their lives. Lesbian families are typically excluded from the usual public rituals that define and sanction couplehood and family life: engagement celebrations, weddings, anniversaries, or even acknowledgment of a lifetime together in their obituaries. They are denied a range of legal sanctions, such as mutual property rights, the right to adopt the child of their life partner, the right to certain health and other insurance benefits, and so on. Heterosexist society provides no language to define family relationships, particularly the relationship of the co-parent to the child, thereby depriving both adults and children of ways to proclaim, story, and thus empower their lives—a process so necessary to individual and family consolidation and identity. As Slater and Mencher (1989) point out, lesbian couples who do not have children are viewed as unconnected individuals, friends, roommates, or "girls" unable to find male partners. When the traditional, middle-class, heterosexual family life cycle does not fit the lesbian experience, how do lesbians "punctuate the long series of moments between the first and final words of life?" (Slater & Mencher, 1989).

Many lesbians, like other people at the margins, draw upon their own creativity, often with little help from the larger context, to affirm and validate their experiences. For some women, the rituals are very meaningful but very private, lacking the public witnessing so important to one's connection with the social context. In more tolerant communities, lesbian couples have found clergy who will marry them or who will bless their unions in individually designed ceremonies of commitment. The lesbian anniversary party, an affirmation of the tenacity of many such relationships in a hostile environment, is becoming a more common phenomenon in areas where there is a lesbian community. Many lesbian women insist that their partners be included in their own family-of-origin rituals and in the rituals of school, work, and other contexts in which families as units are recognized.

Many believe it is crucial, in the fight against homophobia, to begin to "tell" and ritualize their lives in public contexts. The gay and lesbian pride marches that have taken hold in many parts of the country demand public acknowledgment and offer a powerful, shared affirmation of gay and lesbian life-styles. Others, however, are understandably more cautious and more private in the ways they learn to enact their experiences and transitions in ritual.

WOMEN, RITUAL, AND FAMILY THERAPY

Family therapists need to be knowledgeable about and sensitive to the power and importance of ritual and its relationship with gender on at least two levels. The first concerns the rituals of the profession itself, those contexts and occasions during which we witness ourselves, define the profession and its values and rules, eulogize its leaders, and, indeed, create and reinforce our own heroes and heroines in a perpetual and circular process of mythmaking. The second level concerns the use of therapeutic ritual in a gender-sensitive and empowering way in our work with individuals and families.

The meetings of the professional organizations, the family therapy conferences, and our professional journals serve as the major contexts or repositories for the rituals of the family therapy profession. On these occasions and in these places, the field's hierarchy is proclaimed, interpersonal relationships of dominance are enacted, the prevailing discourse is reaffirmed, and its "knowledge" reinvested with renewed power. In public performances, stories are told and retold, and a very powerful mythmaking process unfolds, reminding us all of whom we are to admire, who are our gods and goddesses, and what legends will form the core of our family therapy folklore. The "history" (and it has been largely HIStory) of family therapy is constructed and reconstructed as we "dance attitudes."

While there has been some change as evidenced by an increase in women's leadership in family therapy's professional organizations and in the representation of women on conference programs and in the journals, over the years many women have found our professional rituals both sexist and demeaning. Close observation of the field's public enactments reveals blatant and subtle performances and professional interactions in which male dominance (or, at times, the illusion of male dominance) is reenacted, women are demeaned or ignored, and thus the proper social order of things is recanonized. Two examples might be drawn from the American Family Therapy Conference held in 1990.

In one panel presentation consisting of four editors of the field's journals, the first two (male) speakers (and especially the second) claimed three-quarters of the total time allowed for the session. The third speaker, also male, in an impressive and graceful performance, spoke very briefly, giving up his own time in order that the final presenter, the lone woman, might be allowed some time for her carefully prepared remarks. Men, by virtue of their claim to the public forum, tend to claim more airtime than is their due. (The gender-sensitive ethnographer will also note how much more frequently women, as number two, "try harder." That is, they frequently tend to be better prepared than many of the men, many of whom appear to have more sense of entitlement and whose publicly-recognized voices allow them to speak more informally and casually. Women, in contrast, seem to feel that they must continue demonstrating their right to stand in front of an audience.)

One might also note that often both men and women, but particularly men, respond to and apparently "hear" only the comments of male speakers. The words of a poorly prepared male speaker often seem to merit more discussion than the better prepared and more provocative female speaker. Although women as "other" do try harder and often are better prepared, more scholarly, and more innovative, it is frequently the casual comments of male speakers that form the core of any dialogue. Women themselves tend to cooperate in these powerful mythmaking, ritualized processes by failing to claim and story their own contributions or to credit the work of their women colleagues, thus following the gender rules implicit in the discourse and the history-making process.

A second rather dramatic example of how public rituals such as the annual AFTA conference are used to reaffirm dominance in gender relationships and to exclude women from their own history occurred during a 1990 panel session honoring four of family therapy's founding *fathers*. (Four or five other founders, all male except for Virginia Satir who had recently died, were invited but could not attend.) Ivan Boszormenyi-Nagy, James Framo, Salvador Minuchin, and Lyman Wynne were interviewed by Peggy Papp about their views of the beginnings of the field and their own contributions. As they painted a picture of the field's origins—family therapy's own creation myth—it became clear that no women had been involved in this "birthing" process; the birth of family therapy was, like human birth, a male medical miracle. In this version of Genesis, the field had, indeed, magically sprung from the heads of these Zeus-like figures.

When Papp asked the members of the panel what impact new developments such as the Women's Movement had had on their thinking, the answers were remarkable. Minuchin, the first to respond, said, "Well, for instance, I am looking here for a black woman and there is not one." After a rumble from the audience, he said "Two? I really think that is too few." After this troubling and divisive strategy, he changed the subject. His implication was, of course, that the Women's Movement must be blamed and therefore discredited for the poor representation of women of color at AFTA. One wonders if the Women's Movement is also responsible for the very small number of men of color in AFTA. Nagy returned the subject to gender and said that, among other things, he hoped that eventually there would be a creative dialogue in which *man* could learn from females. Presumably we are not there yet, although he acknowledged the work of Carol Gilligan. All of the men mentioned that they had learned (it is not clear what) from working with female co-therapists, whom one of the founders indicated were more "intuitive" and "ethical." Only Wynne credited any women for contributing to his *thinking*, women such as Margaret Mead, Florence Kluckhohn, and Margaret Singer. No "founder" cited any of the remarkable contributions to family therapy theory and practice made by women present in the room, including the moderator, or the radical changes feminist family thinking has already brought about in the family therapy field.

This example, while extreme, is representative of the ways in which the professional public ritual is used to promote and reinforce the myth that men are in charge of creativity and progress in the public world and to reinforce existing hierarchies of dominance of men over women. It illustrates the strong connection between myth and ritual, as the power of the professional ritual is used to reinforce a history/mythology in which women do not exist; they are not in charge of "birth." Interestingly, in the field of family therapy, perhaps Virginia Satir is the only genuine female folk heroine, although others are emerging. Her contributions, like those of many women who dare to become "larger than life," often go unremarked, at times have been ridiculed, and have gradually become identified as marginal, outside of the mainstream, less serious or scholarly than those of, for example, the "new epistemologists." Women's contributions to theory tend to be minimized, trivialized, and, worst of all, utterly overlooked in the construction of the field's history. Those courageous women who have taken enormous personal and professional risks in recent conferences by calling attention to and challenging the sexism in our professional rituals are frequently accused of creating divisiveness. They are designated the "witches/bitches" of this era.

Women and Ritual in Family-centered Practice

In other writing (Laird & Hartman, 1987; Laird, 1988), I have given a number of clinical examples of how women's ritual lives may be interpreted and women's self-images reconstructed through the use of ritual in family therapy. These examples include innovative rituals that mark the female's passage through the life course, including the onset of menstruation and midlife, the ritualizing of a previous, incompletely mastered transition, the recognition of lesbian couple relationships through family-of-origin ritual, and the "leaving home" of a Jewish woman in her thirties seeking to reclaim religious and spiritual meaning as a feminist in the context of the patriarchal Jewish church. Imber-Black (1989), in addition to her most useful edited volume on the theory and practice of ritual in family therapy (Imber-Black, Roberts, & Whiting, 1988), has provided a number of helpful examples of how women, in particular, can reclaim their rituals, deal with loss, and master life transitions through ritual.

These works provide numerous illustrations of *how* ritual theory may be incorporated into practice with women and with women in families. More importantly, however, therapists must become conscious of the relationship between power and ritual, the ways that the therapy ritual itself can be used to reinforce women's subjugation to a higher authority, the ways that women are systematically closed off from access to certain kinds of ritual power, the ways that ritual can be used to define too narrowly women's domain and, finally, the ways that ritual can be used to demean and degrade women in both their public and private lives. This consciousness, along with a commitment to a just distribution of power for men and women, will help therapists, in dialogue with their clients, to enhance the ritual dimensions of the therapeutic conversation.

REFERENCES

Arens, W. (1976). Professional football: An American symbol and ritual. In W. Arens & S. P. Montague (Eds.), *The American dimension: Cultural myths and social realities* (pp. 3–14). Port Washington, NY: Alfred.

Bamberger, J. (1974). The myth of matriarchy: Why men rule in primitive society. In M. Rosaldo & L. Lamphere (Eds.), *Women, culture, and society*. Stanford, CA: Stanford University Press.

Barkley-Brown, E. (1989). African-American women's quilting: A framework for conceptualizing and teaching African-American women's history. *Signs: Journal of Women in Culture and Society, 14,* 921–929.

Bateson, M. C. (1984). *With a daughter's eye: A memoir of Margaret Mead and Gregory Bateson*. New York: William Morrow.

Carpenter, F. (1990). *Piecing life together: Therapeutic dimensions of African-American quilt-making*. Unpublished master's thesis, Smith College School for Social Work, Northampton, MA.

Conway, J. (1989). *The road from Coorain*. New York: Knopf.

Douglas, M. (1966). *Purity and danger: An analysis of concepts of pollution and taboo*. New York: Praeger.

Ferraro, P., Hedges, E., & Silber, J. (1987). *Hearts and hands: The influence of women and quilts on American society*. San Francisco, CA: The Quilt Digest Press.

Foucault, M. (1980). *Power/knowledge: Selected interviews and other writings*. New York: Pantheon Books.

Freeman, D. (1983). *Margaret Mead and Samoa: The making and unmaking of an anthropological myth*. Cambridge, MA: Harvard University Press.

Heilbrun, C. G. (1989). *Writing a woman's life*. New York: Norton.

Imber-Black, E. (1989). Rituals of stabilization and change in women's lives. In M. McGoldrick, C. Anderson, & F. Walsh (Eds.), *Women in families: A framework for family therapy* (pp. 451–469). New York: Norton.

Imber-Black, E., Roberts, J., & Whiting, R. (1988). *Rituals in families and in family therapy*. New York: Norton.

Keesing, R. (1982). Introduction. In G. H. Herdt (Ed.), *Rituals of manhood: Male initiation in Papua New Guinea* (pp. 1–43). Berkeley: University of California Press.

Kottak, C. (1978). *Anthropology: The exploration of human diversity*. New York: Random House.

Laird, J. (1988). Women and ritual in family therapy. In E. Imber-Black, J. Roberts, & R. Whiting (Eds.), *Rituals in families and family therapy* (pp. 331–62). New York: Norton.

Laird, J. (1989). Women and stories: Restorying women's self-constructions. In M. McGoldrick, C. Anderson, & F. Walsh (Eds.), *Women in families: A framework for family therapy* (pp. 427–450). New York: Norton.

Laird, J., & Hartman, A. (1987). Women and ritual in family therapy. *Journal of Psychotherapy and the Family, 3*(4), 157–173.

Langness, L. L. (1974). Ritual power and male domination in the New Guinea Highlands. *Ethos, 2*, 189–212.

Levi-Strauss, C. (1969). *The elementary structures of kinship*. Boston: Beacon Press.

Moore, S., & Myerhoff, B. (1977). Introduction: Forms and meanings. In S. Moore & B. Myerhoff (Eds.), *Secular ritual* (pp. 3–24). Amsterdam, The Netherlands: Van Gorcum.

Myerhoff, B. (1983, November). *Rites of passage*. Plenary speech, National Symposium, National Association of Social Workers, Washington, DC.

Ortner, S. (1974). Is female to male as nature is to culture? In M. Rosaldo & L. Lamphere (Eds.), *Woman, culture, and society* (pp. 67–87). Stanford, CA: Stanford University Press.

Paige, K., & Paige, M. (1981). *The politics of reproductive ritual*. Berkeley: University of California Press.

Rich, A. (1986). *Of woman born: Motherhood as experience and institution*. (10th Anniversary Edition) New York: Norton.

Rosaldo, M. A. (1974). Woman, culture, and society: A theoretical overview. In M. A. Rosaldo & L. Lamphere (Eds.), *Woman, culture, and society* (pp. 17–42). Stanford, CA: Stanford University Press.

Rubin, G. (1975). The traffic in women: Notes on the "political economy." In R. Reiter (Ed.), *Toward an anthropology of women* (pp. 157–210). New York: Monthly Review Press.

Schwartz, P. (1987). *American couples: The intimate struggle for power*. Plenary paper presented at the annual meeting of the American Family Therapy Association, Chicago, IL.

Shorin, J. (1988). *Creative ritual practice and adult identity consolidation in women*. Unpublished master's thesis, Smith College School for Social Work, Northampton, MA.

Slater, S., & Mencher, J. (1989). *The lesbian family life-cycle: A contextual model*. Unpublished manuscript.

Starhawk (1987). Ritual to build community. *Utne Reader, 24*, 66–71.

Tuleha, T. (1987). *Curious customs: The stories behind 296 popular American rituals*. New York: Harmony Books.

Walker, B. (1990). *Women's rituals: A sourcebook*. San Francisco: Harper & Row.

Washburn, P. (1977). *Becoming woman: The quest for wholeness in female experience*. New York: Harper & Row.

Weick, A. (1990). Overturning oppression: An analysis of emancipatory change. Paper presented at University of Kansas School of Social Work Symposium, June 9, 1990. Lawrence, KS.

Weigle, M. (1982). *Spiders & spinsters: Women and mythology.* Albuquerque: University of New Mexico Press.

White, M., & Epston, D. (1990). *Narrative means to therapeutic ends.* New York: Norton.

Winslow, S. (1990). The use of ritual in incest healing. *Smith College Studies in Social Work, 61,* 27–41.

Wolf, E. (1990). Distinguished lecture: Facing power – Old insights, new questions. *American Anthropologist, 92,* 586–596.

IV
FAMILY THERAPY

8

WILLIAM J. DOHERTY

Can Male Therapists Empower Women in Therapy?

T
HE QUESTION POSED BY the title of this chapter would have been unthinkable a generation ago. For one thing, "empowerment" of women would have struck the reader as a curious notion. Even if that notion could have been made acceptable, why would one question the ability of male therapists to deliver optimal services to women clients? Since most therapists were men and most clients were women, the question would threaten the underpinnings of the therapeutic structures of the day.

The last three decades of the 20th century have brought an end to the age of the political innocence of psychotherapy. What was unquestioned has now become problematic. What was received wisdom has now become controversial. When women began to find and assert their voices in society, the traditional apolitical, value-free paradigm of psychotherapy of women by men began to totter. It is currently common (although I am not aware of reliable data on the topic) for women to request a female therapist both for their individual therapy and their couples therapy. In my own experience of moving to a new community in the late 1980s, my initial clients at a small group private practice were either men or a few women who preferred a female therapist but were "willing" to see a man if no woman was available. This is not how my therapy career started in the mid-1970s! Eventually, more women began to call voluntarily after my former female clients and current female colleagues vouched for me.

I conveniently tucked away these observations and experiences as an understandable by-product of the women's movement and of publicity about sexual abuse by male therapists of female clients—in other words, as "signs of the times"—until Thelma Jean Goodrich asked me to write this chapter. Then I decided to confront the issue more systematically. Let me begin by setting a context for the question of whether male therapists can empower women in therapy.

I assume, on the one hand, that therapists of both sexes can be competent therapists with a wide range of clients and client systems, and that personal qualities and professional skills are more important factors for therapists than their sex. Indeed, the large body of literature on the effectiveness of psychotherapy and the characteristics of effective therapists supports this generalization (Bergin & Garfield, 1986). On the other hand, research on therapy outcome has generally focused on improvement in symptoms or in measurable dysfunction, not on more subtle issues such as empowerment and personal autonomy. For example, a female client may recover from her depression equally well with a male or female therapist, but is she equally likely with each one to grow in her sense of control over her own life in this society? Such questions tend to fall outside the purview of traditional psychotherapy research.

An additional assumption I hold is that being a female therapist is no guarantee of empowering female clients. I have seen just as many female therapists as male therapists become over-responsible for female clients and not allow them to grow up as powerful adults. The fundamental issue for the therapist, in my opinion, is *consciousness of the issues of power that women and men face in therapy and in society*. This consciousness, of course, is gendered, thus requiring therapists to work within their own gendered experience to help a female client to find her own power. Feminist therapists have been working on this problem for over two decades. Male therapists have just begun to face it.

In this chapter, I examine whether and how men can empower women in therapy. My greatest fear in doing so is that I will misunderstand what women need from men in therapy and thus perpetuate the problems I am trying to alleviate. My next greatest fear is that I will inaccurately generalize from my own experience and observations about what men do as therapists and thus lose or offend male readers who do not connect personally with what I write. Other than having these small concerns about the wrath of the world's female and male therapists descending upon my head, I approach this chapter with complete confidence!

POWER: DEFINITIONS AND DISTINCTIONS

The term "empower" refers to helping a client develop power but begs the question about what "power" means. That term has been used in very broad ways, sometimes nearly synonymously with all desirable psychological qualities, and other times referring mainly to the ability to accomplish goals in social interactions. I will deal with power in terms of interpersonal relations, for three reasons. First, the idea of a strictly intrapsychic power seems highly abstract and perhaps best conveyed by other specific terms such as self-esteem, self-discipline, or impulse-control. Second, beneath most definitions of power lies the notion of "influencing" someone or something in the environment. Third, as a family therapist with a systems orientation, I am most interested in the individual in the social environment.

The term power, even in its interpersonal sense, has been used in a wide number of ways, including notions of authority, hierarchy, control, and dominance (Cromwell & Olson, 1975; Maddock, 1990). Power is defined by the Random House Unabridged Dictionary as the "ability to do or act; capability of doing something or accomplishing something." Maddock (1990) distinguishes between power and control. Control is defined by the dictionary as follows: "to exercise restraint or direction over." According to Maddock (1990), power and control are reciprocal aspects of social systems: Power refers to the ability to influence another, and control refers to the ability to limit or channel the influence of another.

Taken as characteristics of a person in a social system, power refers to the ability to take action to accomplish one's goals, and control refers to the ability to set limits or to channel the influence of another. Because semantically the terms power and control have such similar connotations to many people, I will substitute the following more descriptive terms: "assertive power" and "boundary-setting power." *Assertive power* refers to the ability to act effectively in behalf of one's goals in interpersonal situations. *Boundary-setting power* refers to the ability to contain, limit, or channel the influence of others in social situations. These two terms appear to capture the basic duality of the power/control dynamic described by Maddock (1990). Individuals need both assertive power and boundary-setting power to function well in life, and somewhat different skills are involved in each.

The second distinction I want to make is between *power processes* and *power structures*. According to Szinovacz (1987), this distinction has become widely viewed as important in family sociology. Power structures are the organizational aspects of relationships—role patterns, hierarchies, lines of authority—whereas power processes are interactional behaviors in the presence of overt or covert conflict. In parent-child relations, for example, parental hierarchical authority constitutes a power structure, and a disciplinary interaction is a power process. Power structures can vary in the extent of the imbalance of authority, permeability of the hierarchical boundaries, effectiveness in accomplishing goals of the social system, and consensual nature of the role arrangements. Power processes can vary according to the nature of the attempts to deal with conflict: dominating attempts, reactive attempts, or collaborative attempts (Doherty, Colangelo, & Hovander, 1990).

At the level of the individual, the structure versus process distinction can be conceptualized in two ways. The individual may have different levels of ability to use personal power in different kinds of social structures. In a traditional patriarchal marriage, the wife may be severely constricted by the power structures from engaging in anything more than certain reactive boundary-setting processes. In other words, one's place in the power hierarchy constrains one's ability to exercise both assertive power and boundary-setting power. In sum, it is necessary to examine the structures the client occupies as well as the conflict-management skills she has learned. This idea, of course, is quite consistent with feminist therapists' insistence that women's behavior be understood within the context of larger social systems (Goodrich, Rampage, Ellman, & Halstead, 1988).

MALE THERAPISTS AND POWER

Here I draw on the fascinating anthropological work of David Gilmore (1990). Gilmore analyzes dozens of disparate cultures, both premodern and modern, for their underlying notions of what a man is supposed to be. Gilmore draws some conclusions similar to those of feminist authors such as Eisler (1987) and French (1985). With Eisler, he believes that the problems associated with patriarchy are problems inherent not to the male sex but to troublesome social structures, and that a partnership model of social relations is inconsistent with traditional notions of manhood. With French, Gilmore emphasizes the cultural assumption that becoming a woman is a natural, biologically based process, but becoming a man involves learning to exercise "unnatural" levels of control over one's self, one's environment, and women. However, as a man and as the first scholar to focus specifically on manhood in currently existing cultures, Gilmore offers a perspective that I have found powerful and persuasive. Following are Gilmore's major conclusions:

1. With few exceptions, manhood or masculinity is culturally defined in terms of three functions for the family and society: protection, provision, and propagation.
2. With few exceptions, the development of manhood is experienced not as a naturally unfolding process, but as a difficult achievement requiring intensive preparation and continual vigilance. In nearly all cultures, a man is one face-losing mistake away from the charge that he is not a real man, that he has no "balls," that he is—worst of all— a woman.
3. In environments that involve danger from enemies and physical risks in providing food and sustenance, cultural concepts of manhood emphasize aggressiveness, bravery, competition, power assertion, and self-sacrifice. Since nearly every society's environment involves danger, men have been socialized to protect and provide and propagate for the good of their families and their society.
4. Protecting, providing, and propagating are how men nurture. Nearly every culture requires that men be willing to sacrifice their lives at a moment's notion in defense of their family or community and to engage in occupations of high risk—hunting large game, deep-sea fishing, mining, bridge-building. Gilmore writes that he expected to find a much stronger egoistic element to manhood, but he concluded that even Latin *machismo* has an important theme of dedication to the larger social order. The truly selfish man who does not sacrifice and does not give back to the society is despised in most cultures.
5. In two cultures that Gilmore reviewed, Tahiti and Semai, the environment does not present enemies or dangerous providing activities. In both, manhood is not emphasized, is not seen as an achievement, and is not experienced as continually threatened. In both societies, relations between men and women are relatively egalitarian.

Gilmore's observation shed light on a dynamic described by Hare-Mustin about men's conformity: "Men conform more than women because the violation of gender role requirements has more negative consequences for men. Traditionally, a man's greatest fear is to be thought to be like a woman" (1989, p. 71). Gilmore maintains that *both men and women* in nearly all (but not all) cultures enforce the mandates of "real" manhood. The fundamental reason, according to Gilmore, is that male power assertion and bravery are deemed necessary (rightly or wrongly) for the society's survival in a dangerous, competitive world.

Gilmore does not deal with the historical question of how the social world became so dangerous—perhaps because men have always been combative? But presumably the physical environment for most human societies has always involved dangers on land and at sea. French (1985) makes a similar point about the role of the physical environment when she suggests that hunting societies were more apt to become "male-supremist" because the hunt, primarily a male activity, involves more risks and uncertainties than gathering, primarily a female activity. Thus, it is the physical conditions of life, in addition to the social conditions, that creates and sustains the ideology of manhood.

In sum, Gilmore argues that the more dangerous the environment, the more the culture teaches men to be invulnerable, competitive, aggressive. The prized males have been those who would die at a moment's notice to slay big game, navigate dangerous fishing waters, or fight an enemy of the community. These are not just ego-trip activities for men; they are forms of male nurturance. Gilmore was surprised at his own conclusions:

When I started researching this book, I was prepared to rediscover the old saw that conventional femininity is nurturing and passive and that masculinity is self-serving, egotistical, and uncaring. But I did not find this. One of my findings here is that manhood ideologies always include a criterion of selfless generosity, even to the point of sacrifice. Again and again we find that "real" men are those who give more than they take; they serve others. . . . Men nurture their society by shedding their blood, their sweat, and their semen, by bringing home food for both child and mother, by producing children, and by dying if necessary in faraway places to provide a safe haven for their people. This, too, is nurturing in the sense of endowing or increasing. However, the necessary personal qualities for this male contribution are paradoxically the exact opposite of what we Westerners normally consider the nurturing personality. (1989, p. 229–230)

Naturally, this analysis raises important questions about whether we still need to raise boys to be fighters and hunters in the latter part of the 20th century.

What is the relevance of this discussion of manhood to how men can empower women in therapy? From the perspective of cultural notions of manhood, the risk is that male therapists will enact a manhood script with female clients who will, in turn, experience this male nurturing as both comforting and disempowering. If we consider the three forms of male nurturance, we find these dangers:

Protecting can involve a reflexive desire on the part of the male therapist to prevent the female client from experiencing emotional risk or pain. A classical example is the male psychiatrist who prescribes tranquilizers to the female patient who cannot "cope." Another example is the therapist who sees a female client for an indefinite period because he believes she needs his permanent guidance in order to be able to live in the world. I wonder how often family-of-origin work is *not* suggested or supported by therapists (male and female alike) out of a need for the therapist to protect (read: overprotect) the client from the pain of dealing with relatives. Men are conditioned to respond protectively when a woman cries; an unaware male therapist may pull back from a needed challenge to a female client when she begins to cry—thereby treating her as a young child instead of as an empowered adult woman who is entitled both to cry and to be challenged.

The *providing* dimension of masculinity can lead a male therapist to underplay the importance of economic self-sufficiency for female clients. By confining the domain of therapy to the psychological or relational factors in the woman's life, the male therapist may de-emphasize the employment and economic roles of women clients. With employment so central to the identity of most men in American culture, male therapists are not apt to ignore this issue with male clients. But with female clients, a male therapist who has not absorbed the feminist literature about the connection of societal roles and family life, may be tempted to focus exclusively on intrapsychic and intra-familial issues. Furthermore, a male therapist who has not been trained by gender-sensitive supervisors is apt to underplay the economic vulnerability of many women, particularly homemakers, in today's world (Holder & Anderson, 1989).

The *propagating* role of men in most cultures involves them in active, sometimes intrusive and boundary-invading sexual behaviors towards women. The other areas of traditional male nurturing—protecting and providing—do not involve intense face-to-face interactions with women. The one intense experience with women expected of men after childhood is sexual activity. The emotional intensity of individual therapy with a female client can prompt some men—particularly those who are experiencing a variety of psychological problems—to turn the encounter into a sexual one. For other men who have been socialized to view sexual "conquests" as demonstrations of their manhood, the main precipitating factor may be the opportunity created by the power imbalance in therapy. In either case, the cultural association of male sexuality with power (French, 1985), coupled with the intimacy of the therapeutic relationship, creates a special risk that male therapists will transform a clinical relationship into a sexual one.

An implication of this analysis is that male therapists must examine their own cultural training for manhood with a focus on how this training finds its way into therapy with women. The growing feminist literature about therapy offers extensive discussions of women's cultural training, but inevitably offers only a partial picture of men's experience. A literature on men in therapy is just beginning to emerge (e.g., Meth & Passick, 1990). My belief is that when men become more active in examining masculinity and its role in therapy, the image of men in therapy and in families will become fuller and more balanced. As a contribution to this effort towards balance, I offer the following ideas about how traditional male nurturing activities can be used as positive contributions to the therapy of women.

First, the role of protector can help men pay attention to the clear dangers that women experience in the family and in the community–the danger of physical attack and intimidation, of sexual abuse, of discrimination, and of other forms of disempowerment. An appropriately protective therapist alerts clients to risks they may be ignoring or underplaying. The challenge for the male therapist is to use his cultural training in protection within an expanded consciousness about what risks women experience to their safety and selfhood in contemporary families and society and within an expanded consciousness of women's ability to take charge of their self-protection.

Second, the role of provider that male therapists know well can be used to make an empathic link to women for whom paid employment is important to their identity and crucial to their economic viability. Men know about these issues and the intense fears and satisfactions that accompany them. Male therapists who can realize that for women the "work" part of Freud's "to love and to work" is just as important as for men will find themselves able to help women empower themselves in this area.

Third, the role of procreator makes men acutely aware of the sexual dimension of human life. Indeed, men are often accused by women of being controlled by their penises. While the downside of men's cultural script is preoccupation with sex, the upside for doing therapy with women clients is that a male therapist who perceives women as equally interested in the sexual domain of life (albeit with a different social script than men) can be highly supportive of her asserting her rights and needs in this area. As with the providing role, the challenge for the male therapist is to perceive the female client as being fully engaged with the same fundamental issues as men. Once this perception takes hold, then male therapists can call on their own cultural training about the importance of sexuality in order to support and encourage women clients in their sexuality.

In summary, cultural training for manhood offers both disadvantages and advantages for male therapists dealing with female clients. There is a positive opportunity for empowering female clients behind every gender-linked obstacle presented by our culture. The key is for male therapists to engage in personal exploration of how we became men in our society, and then to use the fruits of this learning to create an empowering style of therapy.

EMPOWERING VERSUS DISEMPOWERING WOMEN IN THERAPY: A GUIDE FOR MALE THERAPISTS

The male therapist/female client relationship can be used either to empower or to continue the disempowerment of women. This discussion is organized around three core dimensions of the therapist/client relationship: structure, connectedness, and shared meaning. These three dimensions are derived from the Family FIRO Model (Doherty & Colangelo, 1984) and are an attempt to delineate the core aspects of the inclusion phase of interpersonal relationships. Doherty, Colangelo, and Hovander (1990) have applied this model to therapist/client systems in the following way. The initial phase of therapy for the therapist/client system involves dealing with issues of inclusion, namely, how to structure the relationship, how to connect interpersonally, and how to develop a shared meaning about the goals and processes of therapy.

If these *inclusion* issues are adequately dealt with, then a working therapeutic alliance is formed. The therapist/client relationship can then proceed to the *control* phase in which the client can challenge the therapist in potentially healthful ways. If these control struggles are managed constructively and respectfully, then clinical relationships may experience periods of healthy mutual self-disclosure, which we call the *intimacy* phase. Often therapy is ready to terminate at this time. For the present chapter, I will organize the empowering/disempowering interactions in therapy around issues of inclusion (structure, connectedness, and shared meaning) and then around issues of control.

Empowering Women in the Inclusion Phase of Therapy

The *structuring* of therapy begins with the first phone call that a woman client makes to a therapist. (Conversations with Marilyn Petersen have alerted me to the subtleties of the gender dance in this phase of therapy.) The female client may be requesting either individual or relational therapy. Involved are issues of fees, insurance, scheduling, who will participate in therapy, and who is in charge of the first session. I believe that male therapists should be careful to avoid language that conveys a nonnegotiable decisiveness when discussing these issues with a female client. Women have been trained to give away structural power to men by not competing with them and not asserting their wants. My first guideline for men who wish to empower women in therapy—or at least to avoid disempowering them—is as follows: *Explain your practices and logistical arrangements rather than dictating the structural terms of therapy.* This suggestion does not mean that you agree to see her and her husband at 7:00 a.m. on Saturday morning, but rather that you noncoercively explain what hours you do therapy and what time slots you currently have available. I realize that this type of presentation appears to be simple courtesy, but I do not know how often it is used. A danger in the insensitive use of Whitaker's notion of the "battle for structure" (Whitaker & Keith, 1981) is that the therapist may overwhelm and disempower the client, who is simply trying to partici- pate in setting up the logistics of therapy.

An example of a structural issue is the question of who comes to the first session. When a woman says that she is having marital problems and wants to come in alone to discuss them, suppose the therapist says, "The only way I will see you is with your husband." I suggest that such a statement by a male therapist, at the outset of the discussion on the phone with a potential female client, may signal to her that she will have no power in the therapeutic relationship. She must either yield or withdraw. Consider the alternative: "Generally, when people tell me that they are having marriage problems, I ask to see both spouses. How would you feel about that?" The negotiation can continue from there, and the therapist can become firmer if he deems it appropriate. But he will bear in mind that the woman may have quite legitimate fears of having her husband involved (such as fear of abuse), and that the question of her inviting her husband may need to be an initial focus of therapy rather than a fiat by the therapist on the telephone.

Simultaneously with the structuring of therapy is the process of establishing *connectedness*. This process concerns issues of rapport, support, and establishing and respecting boundaries in the therapist/client system. Here I offer three guidelines:

Nurture but do not caretake. Men are particularly apt to caretake women by giving them advice rather than joining and staying with them emotionally. This is the cultural script male therapists have to overcome in therapy: When women are in emotional pain, either fix them or flee them. I have found it important, when seeing women for individual therapy, to focus from the outset both in connecting with their pain and on helping them gain access to their own nurturing supports outside of therapy. When a woman is in therapy with a partner or family members, the challenge for the therapist is to validate her experience of disjunction from her loved ones, while helping to rebuild those connections if possible—but in either case to avoid becoming a semipermanent substitute for family and friends.

Value her needs for connection and do not denigrate them. Feminist family therapists have argued convincingly that most family therapy models have emphasized the negative side of female connectedness (Luepnitz, 1988). Many men feel connected to their wives by providing for them and having sexual relations with them and being at home regularly. It is easy for male therapists to assume that women who want a different kind of connection than men do are being unreasonable. A woman client whose male partner is not offering the emotional connection she needs will feel empowered if a male therapist supports her efforts to ask for what she wants.

Value her needs for autonomy and do not overlook them. Hare-Mustin (1989) has argued convincingly that the dichotomy between connection and autonomy is misleading, that each is involved in the other. Male therapists must be especially alert to the assumption that men in families have greater autonomy needs than women. An example is the wife pursuer/husband distancer pattern. The most important issue for the woman to work on may be her own autonomy, not her need for intimacy. A male therapist who identifies with the distancing husband's needs for autonomy might miss the fact that the wife needs more autonomy as well.

Respect her physical and psychological boundaries rather than walking the edge. Boundary invasion by a therapist is the most extreme form of disempowerment of clients. Sexual contact is obviously abusive and unethical. However, more subtle boundary incursions can also be disempowering to women clients (to men clients as well, of course). In the physical domain, incursions can take the form of inappropriate touch at tender or challenging moments of therapy. I know a woman who was traumatized when her male therapist placed his shoe on her foot as he made a challenging point in a therapy session. Verbally, boundary invasion can take the form of regular compliments or remarks about the woman's appearance or attractiveness. On the positive side, a man who can engage in the emotionally close level of therapeutic conversation with a woman, with full respect for her boundaries, may help her realize that emotional closeness with men does not have to involve sexual contact.

The third component of the inclusion phase of the therapist/client relationship is *shared meaning*, the process by which the therapist and client(s) arrive at a common understanding of the goals and issues of therapy. Here the key issue is *negotiating meanings versus dictating them*. Given cultural scripts, male therapists might be particularly prone to take an expert stance on a woman's experience and, thereby, disempower her. For psychologically oriented therapists, a risk is that delivering a diagnosis or an MMPI evaluation can disempower a woman from her own sense of reality if delivered in a nonnegotiable, "objective truth" fashion. For therapists with a family system orientation, the disempowering might take the form of the therapist's "reframing" the woman's reality in a way that is not open to her input and her efforts to shape a consensual reality. Conversely, a male therapist who is always ready to explore the connection between his meaning and those of his female clients is offering them a new paradigm for dealing with men in an empowered way.

The Family FIRO Model proposes that, when issues of inclusion — structure, connectedness, and shared meaning — are adequately addressed in the therapeutic relationship, then it is possible to resolve in a healthy fashion a variety of control/conflict issues when they arise in the course of therapy. Indeed, it is only when a woman feels safe and connected with in a caring and respectful manner that she is likely to challenge a male therapist directly. The male therapist can view these challenges as opportunities *par excellence* for growth and empowerment for the female client. An example is a wife who confronted me after several sessions of therapy for paying so much attention to her husband's depression that I was neglecting her needs and her issues. I acknowledged that she was right, and I offered to discuss how to refocus the therapy. I also congratulated her on her willingness to confront me, something she had rarely done with her father or her husband. In sum, the first guideline in the control phase of therapy is to *view a female client's challenges to the therapist as an opportunity for empowerment as opposed to a form of resistance*.

The second guideline refers to helping the female client develop an ability that is of ultimate importance for healthy control in interpersonal relations by *supporting her boundary-setting power*. I believe that when women do not have boundary-maintaining rights and abilities in a relationship, this issue must take the first priority in therapy. Teaching her to assert power without the ability for self-protection would be foolish and dangerous. Many sexual issues in couples revolve around boundary-setting power for women. With female clients, the male therapist must be especially attuned to their rights over their own bodies, especially given cultural scripts that associate manhood with sexual access to women. Male therapists are not immune to such preconceptions about men's sexual rights. The starting point for discussion of sexual behavior, then, must be the boundary-setting power of both parties. As I point out to husbands, "If she can't say 'no,' then she can't really say 'yes.'"

The third guideline in the control domain refers to the reciprocal of boundary-setting power: *Use your experience in power assertion to support the woman's abilities to verbalize her needs and wants, to negotiate for them, and to insist on them, if necessary*. The manhood script teaches men to understand assertive power, its uses and management (although not all men learn constructive uses of assertive power). A male therapist can use his experience to work with women clients on how to enhance this form of interpersonal power. The key is that the therapist must identify assertive power with being *human*, not just with being male, and must appreciate that his client will exercise assertive power in her own gendered way. I am suggesting that this opportunity in therapy is akin to how women therapists use their cultural training in emotional sensitivity to teach men to identify and to express feelings. Male therapists can serve a parallel role for female clients in the area of power assertion. (Of course, male therapists can also teach men about feelings, and female therapists can teach women about power.) I once coached a professional woman on how to confront various elements of the power structure in her organization in order to create the leverage necessary to require her employer to fulfill his contractual obligations to her.

CONCLUSION

In this section, I will discuss several contextual issues involved with the empowerment of women by male therapists. One is the importance for male therapists to have female colleagues and supervisors to talk with about their female clients. (I think the same is true for women therapists about their male clients.) Such consultation is especially important in cases where the female client is not articulate about her needs and priorities and where the male therapist might miss larger, gender-based concerns such as her fear of her ex-husband, her fear of getting ill and not being able to support her children economically, or her feeling of low self-worth related to her weight. There also can be subtle forms of seductiveness occurring in the male therapist/female client relationship that can be revealed through a frank discussion with female colleagues. Similarly, when a male therapist is angry at an "aggressive" female client, female colleagues or supervisors are well positioned to question the possibility that a gender script is keeping the therapist from appreciating the important power assertion his client might be making. Alternatively, sometimes female colleagues can aptly point out that the male therapist is being misled by the woman's acting-out her anger at the therapist rather than working to take control of her own life.

My final comment pertains to what male therapists have to gain from working to empower female clients. I will be personal here. When women acquaintances have asked my wife over the years about the problems in having a family therapist for a husband, her typical response has been, "Mostly it's a plus, because when he can hear things from his female clients that I have been trying to get through to him, he comes home and lets me know that he is beginning to get it." When I think about what I have learned from female clients, it has generally been in the areas of power assertion and boundary-setting. In therapy, as opposed to the rest of my life, I am usually at my best in trying to understand people's experience. Many times I have struggled to understand the experience of a woman who was becoming empowered in her life. Every time I have come to understand her experience, I have felt my understanding of women and men and relationships enhanced. This new awareness helps me both with future clients and with women who are important to me in my personal life. I "get" one more piece of the world's most complex puzzle: how women and men feel about themselves, each other, and about life. To be willing to be changed by exposure to the struggles of women in therapy— and to let them know that we "got" it—is empowering to male therapists and their clients alike.

REFERENCES

Bergin, A., & Garfield, S. (1986). *Handbook of psychotherapy and behavior change*. New York: Wiley.
Cromwell, R., & Olson, D. (1975). *Power in families*. New York: Wiley.

Doherty, W. J., & Colangelo, N. (1984). The Family FIRO model: A modest proposal for organizing family treatment. *Journal of Marital and Family Therapy, 10*, 19–30.

Doherty, W. J., Colangelo, N., & Hovander, D. (in press). Priority setting in family change and clinical practice: The Family FIRO model. *Family Process* (In press).

Eisler, R. (1987). *The chalice and the blade: Our history, our future.* New York: Harper & Row.

French, M. (1985). *Beyond power: On women, men, and morals.* New York: Summit.

Gilmore, D. D. (1990). *Manhood in the making: Cultural concepts of masculinity.* New Haven, CT: Yale University Press.

Goodrich, T. J., Rampage, C., Ellman, B., & Halstead, K. (1988). *Feminist family therapy: A casebook.* New York: Norton.

Hare-Mustin, R. T. (1989). The problem of gender in family therapy theory. In M. McGoldrick, C. M. Anderson, & F. Walsh (Eds.), *Women in families: A framework for family therapy* (pp. 61–77). New York: Norton.

Holder, D. P., & Anderson, C. M. (1989). Women, work, and the family. In M. McGoldrick, C. M. Anderson, & F. Walsh (Eds.), *Women in families: A framework for family therapy* (pp. 357–380). New York: Norton.

Luepnitz, D. A. (1988). *The family interpreted: Feminist theory in clinical practice.* New York: Basic.

Maddock, J. W. (1990). Dialectical ecology: Foundations for family theory? Submitted for publication.

Meth, R., & Passick, R. (1990). *Men in therapy.* New York: Guilford.

Szinovacz, M. (1987). Family power. In M. B. Sussman & S. K. Steinmetz (Eds.), *Handbook of marriage and the family* (pp. 651–693). New York: Plenum.

Whitaker, C., & Keith, D. (1981). Symbolic-experiential family therapy. In A. S. Gurman & D. Kniskern (Eds.), *Handbook of family therapy* (pp. 187–225). New York: Brunner/Mazel.

9

NADINE J. KASLOW AND ALICE S. CARTER

Depressed Women in Families: The Search for Power and Intimacy

I S THE EXPERIENCE OF depression different for women than for men? We argue *yes*, and that these differences have important implications for marital and family treatment. Unfortunately, minimal attention has been paid to the need for gender-sensitive marital and family therapy with depressed women (Braverman, 1986). Even the recent National Task Force on Women and Depression (McGrath, Keita, Strickland, & Russo, 1990) fails to address the issues of marital and family therapy for this population. The purpose of this chapter is to provide the sociocultural context in which women's depression emerges and briefly discuss how depressed women's families function. Then, we will present our model of an object relational, gender-sensitive approach, which we have found to be effective for families in which a woman is depressed.

In our experience working with depressed women and their families, the central themes that emerge are the imbalance in power and the lack of intimacy. Thus, as family therapists we help the family work toward altering interactional patterns in order to develop a more adaptive balance

We would like to thank the members of the Family Therapy Study Group which the first author attends for their thoughtful comments on this material: Sandy Bialos, R.N., M.S.N., C.S., Davis Gammon, M.D., Chris Greene, M.S.W., Thelma Jean Goodrich, Ph.D., Bob Horowitz, Ph.D., Maria Tupper, M.S.W., and Janet Rooney, R.N., M.S., C.S.

of power and intimacy, in which the woman feels empowered, interpersonally connected, and affectively integrated. Some feminists have held that husbands are unwilling to relinquish their position of power over their wives in these marriages. Based upon our experience, when men gain awareness of their need for intimacy, they begin to understand how the coercive use of power interferes with closeness. Many are willing to "give up" power to "gain" intimacy in their marriage. Thus, we have found that many depressed women and their husbands can and, indeed, do benefit from gender-sensitive, object relational marital and family therapy.

SOCIOCULTURAL, FAMILIAL, AND DEVELOPMENTAL CONTEXT

In order to understand the increased risk, higher incidence, and greater frequency of recurrent episodes of unipolar disorders in women as compared to men (McGrath et al., 1990; Nolen-Hoeksema, 1990), we must view depression within the sociocultural, familial, and developmental contexts from which it emerges (Braverman, 1986; McGrath et al., 1990).

Socioeconomic and Political Context

The predominant cultural legacy has placed men in positions of power and dominance and women in positions of oppression and subservience. The disparity between men and women in salary level, promotion rates and possibilities, the stereotyped sex roles, and the fact that laws allow fathers to renege on child support are important variables in understanding why more women than men are depressed. High levels of depressive symptoms are also common in individuals of low socioeconomic status (McGrath et al., 1990), and thus the "feminization of poverty" puts women at greater risk for depression. We must take into account the ethnic and religious context in understanding women's depression, as many ethnic and religious cultures value dominant, powerful (e.g., machismo) men and submissive, passive, and respectful women.

Socialization

We agree with authors who assert that applying traditional theories of psychological development to women is problematic because these theories rely on a male model of development that emphasizes autonomy, achievement, and the utilization of intrapersonal and cognitive problem-solving methods (Chodorow, 1978; Gilligan, 1982; Miller, 1984). In contrast, women's orientation to relationships is a central, unifying, positive construct in their development; therefore they tend to develop primarily interpersonal problem-solving methods.

Unfortunately, our societal values have supported a type of relational development which predisposes women to depression. The inhibition of activity, the suppression of anger, the desire to please others, the need to accommodate to others' expectations, and the propensity to accept blame are characteristics encouraged in women. All of these characteristics are associated with depression (Kaplan, 1984).

Thus, it is not surprising that women often come to therapy reporting that interpersonal conflicts have precipitated their depressive episode. Also, women often report having difficulties in interpersonal and familial functioning when they are depressed (Weissman & Paykel, 1974). Typically, interpersonal experiences related to loss and unresolved mourning; physical, emotional, and sexual abuse; neglect; and rejection and abandonment are family of origin issues which depressed women either present with when they seek therapy or bring up during the therapy process (Stiver & Miller, 1988). It is our observation that women with these interpersonal histories are often involved in the recapitulation of these dynamics in their family of creation. Thus, they may be feeling oppressed and rejected by an alcoholic or abusive spouse, a troubled child, or a demanding parent.

The learned helplessness hypothesis (Abramson, Seligman, & Teasdale, 1978) is a potential explanation for the preponderance of depression in women. This hypothesis proposes that women who adopt a stereotypical, traditional sex role have a cognitive set against assertion and independence reinforced by societal roles. As a result, these women are prone to feeling and acting helpless and powerless in effecting change in their lives. While it is unlikely that the learned helplessness model fully accounts for women's increased vulnerability to depression, it does describe a powerful psychosocial factor.

Multiple Roles

Many life-stage transitions (e.g., transition to parenthood) are perceived as more stressful by women than by men; in addition, parenthood and marriage have different implications for men and women (Russo, 1990). Given that the subjective experience of stress is more predictive of depression than objective counts of life events, these differences in perception place women at greater risk for depression. This risk can be best understood as a function of sex-role stereotypes and traditional Western values, in which these transitions place greater demands on women than on men. This is especially true in terms of the social and caretaking demands placed upon them by family and community. In addition to the stress of child rearing, women are more likely to be expected to provide the bulk of caring for elderly parents and/or in-laws (McBride, 1990). It is often the case that when a woman's needs for power and intimacy come into conflict with societal expectations for performing the roles of "good woman," "good wife," and "good mother" (Jack, 1987), she becomes depressed and may seek therapy.

Reproductive-related Events

When a woman is in therapy, it is important for the therapist and the woman to consider the physiological and biological changes associated with the female reproductive system (e.g., menstrual cycle, pregnancy, childbirth, infertility, menopause) and those medical procedures undergone only by women (e.g., abortion, hysterectomy) that may be associated with the woman's presentation as depressed. It is important to remember, however, that while clinical depressions often occur in association with events in the female reproductive cycle, these reproductive-related events do not explain the overall gender difference in depression rates (e.g., McGrath et al., 1990).

Violence and Victimization

As women have felt more empowered to discuss the role of violence against them (physical and/or sexual abuse in childhood or adulthood; sexual harassment), it has become painfully evident that violence against women is a significant causal factor of depression in women. It is often the case that women who have suffered from various forms of interpersonal victimization present with depression as part of their post-traumatic stress disorder.

GENDER-SENSITIVE FAMILY THERAPY
FOR DEPRESSED WOMEN

While the sociopolitical context and the socialization processes described above are highly resistant to change, we have felt empowered as therapists and women by achieving success in changing the balance of power and intimacy in individual families. This is not, however, to minimize the importance we place upon continuing the struggle to effect change within those larger systems in order to empower women.

For enhancing the functioning of depressed women and their families, we recommend an object relational family therapy approach which emphasizes family and individual dynamics (e.g., Scharff, 1989). It is essential to conduct this treatment in a gender-sensitive manner (e.g., Kaslow and Carter, 1989; Luepnitz, 1988). Gender-sensitive family therapy for depressed women must build upon clinical and theoretical writings on feminist family therapy (e.g., Goodrich, Rampage, Ellman, & Halstead, 1988; Luepnitz, 1988; McGoldrick, Anderson, & Walsh, 1989; Walters, Carter, Papp, & Silverstein, 1988), object relations family therapy (e.g., Scharff, 1989; Slipp, 1988), and interpersonal and family theories and therapies for depression (e.g., Coyne, 1976, 1988; Feldman, 1976; Hogan & Hogan, 1978; Keitner, 1990; Klerman, Weissman, Rounsaville, & Chevron, 1984; Pollack, Kaslow, & Harvey, 1982; Rubenstein & Timmins, 1978).

In outlining our model of gender-sensitive, object relational family therapy for depressed women, we begin with a summary of the basic tenets of object relational family therapy in terms of their applicability for work with depressed women. We then discuss the need for multiple levels of assessment in order to devise an appropriate treatment plan, whether that be individual, marital, and/or family therapy. We briefly comment on those situations in which individual therapy is indicated. Marital therapy is discussed in detail, with particular emphasis on finding the balance between power and intimacy. Given the added demands placed upon women with children, we present family interventions that focus on enhancing parent-child interactions. In addition to methods associated with feminist and object relational family therapy, we have found the incorporation of therapeutic techniques from a variety of theoretical orientations to be quite helpful: strategic and systemic (e.g., Coyne, 1988), psychoeducational (e.g., Beardslee, 1990; Holder & Anderson, 1990), interpersonal (Foley et al., 1987), and cognitive-behavioral (Bedrosian, 1988; Coffman & Jacobson, 1990; Dobson, Jacobson, & Victor, 1988; Falloon et al., 1988).

Tenets of Object Relational Family Therapy

We agree with object relational family therapists who assert that experiencing satisfying interpersonal relationships is a fundamental motive of life. The drive for interpersonal connectedness is particularly strong for women in our culture. When women feel socially isolated and become self-focused, they are more vulnerable to depression. Intrapsychic conflicts regarding issues of power and intimacy, which are related to the expression of depression, derive from one's family of origin and continue to be enacted in current intimate relationships, especially within the family of creation. Both positive and negative aspects of relational experiences with one's parents are internalized and retained as introjects, the psychological representations of external objects. These introjects are re-projected onto current family members in the individual's effort to achieve gratification by compensating for unsatisfactory and depression-inducing relations in childhood.

We concur with object relational family therapists who place special value on the role of transference and countertransference in facilitating the therapeutic process. When, as therapists, we utilize our own empathy and reactions in response to the family's behavior (objective countertransference), we have greater access to the shared yet unspoken experiences of each family member regarding the interactional dynamics that characterize their family (unconscious family system of object relations). As therapists, we utilize our objective countertransference to interpret for family members patterns of interpersonal behavior in which one family member induces other family members to behave or respond in a circumscribed fashion (process of projective identification).

Interpretations permit new family interactional patterns, as well as alter the structures of individual's personalities. In doing this work, we should be mindful of potential countertransferential pitfalls which commonly emerge when working with families with a depressed woman. We find that these countertransference reactions may include becoming overprotective towards the depressed woman and thereby increasing her feelings of inadequacy and helplessness; mirroring the woman's feelings of dysphoria and despondency so closely that we fail to provide a sense of hopefulness or fail to act when indicated; or experiencing intense anger resonating with the covert or overt anger held consciously or unconsciously by either member of the marital dyad. As Luepnitz (1988) has asserted, gender-sensitive object relational family therapy requires that, in addition to making interpretations, the therapist lead the patient to action by making suggestions or giving advice. This active stance on the part of the therapist provides the depressed woman a model for being assertive as well as caring.

Consistent with this active stance, gender-sensitive object relational family therapists must focus on breaking the interactional cycle of collusion within the family system which maintains feelings of dysphoria, helplessness, anger, and emotional isolation on the part of all family members. The interventions should simultaneously address interpersonal processes and stressors, on the one hand, and individual dynamics and personality characteristics (e.g., self-esteem, cognitive patterns, affect regulation, and communication patterns), on the other.

Individual, Marital, and Family Assessment

It is important that the first stage of therapy involve a multimodal assessment to examine each family member's individual characteristics, the structure of the family, its communication and interaction patterns, and the environmental stressors affecting dysfunction in the family system (e.g., Freeman, Epstein, & Simon, 1986). Then, the clinician must choose where to intervene in the depressogenic interactional cycle in terms of major themes (power, intimacy, autonomy, regulation of negative affect, and cognition) and the level of the system (individual, marriage, parent-child, family, larger community). At this point, the clinician must also decide the sequence of therapeutic modalities (e.g., family, couples, parent-child, individual, psychopharmacological). Intervening at any point in the system will affect the entire system and may alter the depression-maintaining mechanisms and thus improve individual and family functioning.

Individual Treatment

We have found that individual treatment is indicated, and often necessary, when the level of negative expressed emotion in the marital dyad is high, when the depressed woman assumes an extremely passive and helpless stance in relation to her husband, when the depressed woman feels so threatened by the husband that she is unable to assert herself, and/or when the husband is highly resistant to treatment (i.e., is unwilling to relinquish power and/or undermines the woman's newfound power). Individual treatment may be conducted either prior to or concurrent with the marital therapy.

Marital Therapy

Marital therapy is often an appropriate treatment for depressed women (Jacobson, Holtzworth-Munroe, & Schmaling, 1989), given the strong association between marital difficulties and depression in women (Clarkin,

Haas, & Glick, 1988; Freeman et al., 1986; Gotlib & Colby, 1987). Indeed, marital therapy is efficacious in ameliorating depressive symptoms and is more effective than other treatments in increasing marital satisfaction and improving marital functioning (Beach, Sandeen, & O'Leary, 1990; Foley et al., 1987; Friedman, 1975; O'Leary & Beach, 1990). Further, depressed women involved in active marital disputes do not improve as much in individual therapy as those without partners or those with stable marriages (Rounsaville, Weissman, Prusoff, & Herceg-Baron, 1979). However, when choosing marital therapy, it is important to remember that the short- and long-term effectiveness for the treatment will be mediated by the level of support and criticism in the marital relationship. In other words, marital therapy is not a treatment of choice for couples who are highly critical and/or unsupportive of one another.

Marital therapists need to be aware of the cultural context, their own gender biases, and the gender perspectives of both members of the couple. To impose one's own values or to adopt blindly the biases of the couple renders the couple helpless in determining its own course and minimizes the possibility of adaptive change. For treatment to result in change, the therapist must offer a gender-sensitive perspective, which may include a different set of values from that held by the couple. When offering this different perspective, the therapist must frame these new ideas in a way that challenges the couple's values without alienating the couple.

Power in marriage. Traditional marital therapy has ignored the connection between marital conflicts and culture-wide gender prescriptions that reinforce inequitable power distributions in the family (Goodrich et al., 1988) and contribute to the higher incidence of depression in women. Therefore, in developing and implementing an effective treatment plan for depressed women and their husbands, the clinician needs to evaluate the power dynamics carefully. As noted above, an imbalance in power is characteristic of marital dyads in which the wife manifests depression. These women perceive their husbands as dominating (e.g., Hoover & Fitzgerald, 1981; Jack, 1987) and experience themselves as yielding after disagreements to their husband's position. Husbands appear to be unaware of their wives' experience of submission in the marital relationship (Hoover & Fitzgerald, 1981).

Intimacy in marriage. In addition to a focus on power dynamics, the clinician must attend to the couple's experience of marital intimacy. An intimate relationship is a strong buffer against depression; however, the marriages of depressed women are lacking in support, comfort, and other aspects of intimacy. Thus, these women are vulnerable to continuing and recurring depressive experiences (Haas & Clarkin, 1988). Marital interactions between depressed women and their spouses are characterized by excessive displays of hostility, discrepancies between verbal content and affective tone, distancing maneuvers, minimal self-disclosure, and a lack of task orientation or facilitative behavior, which often results in inadequate resolution of conflicts (e.g., Hinchliffe, Hooper, & Roberts, 1978; Kahn, Coyne, & Margolin, 1985). Needless to say, when these types of interactions dominate the marital relationship, genuine intimacy is impossible and marital satisfaction remains low.

Power and intimacy. With depressed women and their husbands, it is important to encourage exploration of needs for power, intimacy, and autonomy. They each need to find a balance between interpersonal connectedness and autonomous functioning. The goal of treatment is to empower the depressed woman in such a way that she feels effective and competent in social relationships and work roles.

Empowering these women involves creating a therapeutic holding environment in which they recognize, understand, and change their role in inequitable power relationships and coercive interactional processes in their marriage. This work must take into consideration the larger sociocultural context in which women and men are burdened by rigid sex-role stereotypes that equate femininity with dependence and masculinity with autonomy. However, the goal of treatment must be change within the marital dyad, not adjustment to prevailing conditions oppressive to women. Thus, marital therapy needs to focus on changing gender roles that maintain the family conflict and power imbalances that perpetuate women's depressions. For example, more equitable role-sharing regarding household chores (both those that require a hammer and those that require a sponge), caregiving, bread-winning, and money management can be encouraged by therapeutic intervention.

For the depressed woman, treatment involves validating the choices she makes regarding the importance and centrality of her role as nurturer, caregiver, and expresser of affects. Treatment must also underscore that she can continue to function as a member of the couple while simultaneously asserting her needs and feeling and behaving in a more autonomous fashion. This validation of the woman's needs for both power and intimacy enables her to shift flexibly between interpersonal stances requiring both a powerful and dominant manner and a well-differentiated sharing of intimacy, on the one hand, and a comfortable dependency in which she allows herself to be taken care of without losing her sense of self-efficacy, on the other.

To achieve the goal of empowering depressed women, treatment also involves legitimizing the husband's desire to feel greater self-control and more competence while underscoring the importance of expressing these feelings in an assertive and empathic fashion, rather than in an aggressive and domineering manner. Additionally, the husband must learn to recognize and express his own needs for intimacy and dependency. Expanding and then learning to share a wider range of affective experiences are other goals.

Treatment must address both partners' feelings of helplessness and powerlessness, which result from the pairing of the wife's submissive and depressed functioning with the husband's overprotective, dominant, and coercive functioning. It is frequently the case that each partner takes turns experiencing feelings of depression and helplessness (Rubenstein & Timmins, 1978). This process serves to regulate distance (Jessee & L'Abate, 1983), as true intimacy may be difficult to attain when one member of the dyad is depressed.

In those families in which the husband is unwilling to relinquish a dominant stance over the woman and/or is reluctant to work toward greater intimacy with his wife, marital therapy cannot improve the quality of the marriage or ameliorate the woman's depressive symptoms. In such cases, the woman is faced with a difficult choice. She may remain in an oppressive and depression-inducing marriage or work toward marital separation and divorce.

Empathy and intersubjectivity: Finding the balance between power and intimacy. As therapists, we must help the couple acquire increased empathy and intersubjectivity. In other words, we must facilitate the development of new interactional patterns in which both partners help one another to balance their needs for power and autonomy with their desires for intimacy and sharing. This process may be accomplished as each individual develops an understanding of the origin and adaptive nature of his/her own and his/her partner's intrapsychic dynamics and interpersonal behaviors. Each individual is supported in expressing respect for the partner's strengths and competencies, accepting weaknesses in an understanding manner, and providing support when both partners feel that support is indicated. When a relational reparation occurs, feelings of self-efficacy and self-esteem are enhanced for both partners. Thus, treatment facilitates the psychological maturation and expression of "true" self for each individual, as well as the growth of the partnership.

Family Therapy

Maternal depression. When treating a depressed woman who is also a mother, the therapist should be attentive to difficulties she may be having with parenting, as well as difficulties her children may be experiencing. Children of depressed mothers are at increased risk for a range of emotional and behavioral disorders and difficulties throughout the life-span (Downey & Coyne, 1990). In the past decade, the influence of maternal depression on children's development has received a great deal of attention (Beardslee, Bemporad, Keller, & Klerman, 1983), whereas the effects of paternal depression have been understudied. The paucity of research on paternal depression reflects a tendency to blame mothers for the origin of neurotic and psychotic ailments in children (Caplan & Hall-McCorquodale, 1985).

While the association between maternal depression and developmental difficulties in children may be attributable in part to direct genetic transmission of the disorder (Trad, 1987), considerable evidence suggests that environmental mechanisms such as parenting behaviors, family interaction patterns, and more general family dysfunction contribute to this association. All of these suggested causes have their basis in the family, which is *not* to say the mother is to blame.

Family intervention: Remembering the children. Often, depressed women come to the attention of the mental health community when their children are identified as having psychological difficulties. This presentation may reflect the tendency for depressed women to place their own needs below the needs of other family members. In such cases, it is often difficult to define the most appropriate level at which to intervene: family, marital, parent-child, or individual parent and/or individual child. Just as a woman's depression may be reflective of underlying family dysfunction, a child presented as the identified patient can also serve as the symptom-bearer of a family-wide depressive experience (Kaslow & Racusin, 1990). It has been our experience that when a family presents a child as patient along with a depressed mother, and the family is not amenable to family therapy, a brief course of family-sensitive individual therapy with the child may serve as an entry into more direct family interventions.

Husbands and children of depressed women are more likely to evidence depressive symptomatology and a range of psychological difficulties. The causal direction of this association remains unclear. Typically there are reciprocal interactions that perpetuate and exacerbate dysfunction in the family. Given this association, family therapy is often particularly effective in addressing the psychological symptomatology and the cognitive, affective, and interpersonal functioning of each individual and of the family unit as a whole (Kaslow & Racusin, 1990). Indeed, with depressed outpatients, family therapy is effective (Bernal, Konjevich, & Deegan, 1987). Further, with depressed inpatients, family therapy concurrent with individual and pharmacologic interventions is more effective than individual and pharmacologic interventions alone (Haas et al., 1988). This is particularly true for female patients (Haas et al., 1988).

It is our belief that family therapy should focus, in part, on helping depressed women and their husbands develop and utilize adaptive parenting skills. Adopting new skills and increasing feelings of competence in the parenting role serves to empower women. Interventions aimed at improving parental functioning must take into account the special needs of the children, the developmental stage of each family member and the family unit as a whole, the dynamics in the marital dyad that interfere with parenting, and the unique parenting styles of each adult.

In devising family interventions for depressed women, the central focus of the work must be the reciprocal nature of the problematic power dynamics that maintain the woman's depression. In this work, family members are viewed as partners, colluding to maintain the woman's depression (Rubenstein & Timmins, 1978). Thus, a major task of therapy is to help the family identify instances in which the woman's dysphoric mood, dependency, and lack of assertiveness maintain her state of powerlessness in relation to other family members (e.g., husband, children, parents) and when other family members' dominance over her and aggression towards her serve to maintain her depression (Bedrosian, 1988; Hogan & Hogan, 1978). The therapist may help the family to interpret this interactional cycle.

For example, the family may come to understand that the woman's dependency behaviors protect the husband from expressing his own dependency needs or feelings of powerlessness, as he is assured of her continued involvement in the relationship in a one-down or powerless position. Similarly, the therapist can help the family to understand how problematic interactional cycles within the family are sequenced. Thus, the husband, in his one-up position, may act in an overprotective and omnipotent manner and express oversolicitous thoughts, feelings, and behaviors. These overprotective behaviors, which often include excessive displays of sympathy, interest, concern, and practical help, often undermine the woman's resourcefulness and reinforce her role as the weak and helpless family member (Teichman & Teichman, 1990). We have observed two responses on the part of the woman to being placed in this helpless state. Consistent with the learned helplessness model (Abramson et al., 1978), many women who feel that they are helpless and lack control over their own life situations become depressed and more passive. Other women become angry about feeling powerless and respond by becoming passive-aggressive or overtly hostile. In both cases, the woman is likely to reject family members' efforts to "help" her. In those cases in which the woman responds by becoming depressed, rejection of "help" reflects her feelings of hopelessness and lack of a sense of efficacy regarding change. Where the woman responds with anger, rejecting others' "help" is an indirect way of expressing anger, rather than a direct expression of anger, which is inhibited due to cultural prohibitions (Bernardez, 1988). Sometimes it is the case that the woman's rejection of "help" may reflect her efforts to project her own feelings of helplessness onto other family members in order that they may share her experience (projective identification). Whether she responds with depression or anger, her behavior only serves to further distance her husband and other family members. These distancing maneuvers will further fuel her depression, as the level of intimacy in the family decreases. The depressive interactional cycle is thus perpetuated and intensified (Feldman, 1976).

After helping family members to identify these dysfunctional interaction patterns, the treatment must help them to interact in a more adaptive fashion. Family intervention needs to focus on empowering each family member to feel more efficacious, to experience more positive attachments, and to promote an age-appropriate process of separation and individuation. The intervention must also emphasize issues related to the regulation and expression of negative feelings and thoughts (Cole & Kaslow, 1988; Kaslow & Racusin, 1990; Rutter, Izard, & Read, 1986). Family therapists can help each family member to express appropriately his or her negative feelings (e.g., sadness, anger, shame, guilt, grief), to validate affective experiences for one another, to discuss reactions to these negative feelings, and to develop more adaptive modes of emotional communication. Further, these negative feelings and thoughts can be reframed as the fuel for positive change within the family system (Bedrosian, 1988).

We believe that the provision of a holding or facilitating environment (Winnicott, 1965) is of utmost importance in conducting this work. A "good enough" holding environment is one in which the therapist enables family members to feel safe and secure so that they can learn how to be both authentic individuals and members of the family group. That is, the goal is for them to be able to experience meaningful shared intimacy and still maintain selfhood. Each family member is empowered to experience and express a full range of emotions and to establish individual boundaries while being sensitive to the feelings and needs of other family members.

When identifying and interpreting current problematic interaction patterns and their functions in the context of a solid holding environment does not lead to an amelioration in depressive symptoms and dysfunctional patterns, we have found two additional avenues of exploration to be helpful and informative. First, empathy and intersubjectivity among family members are heightened when the therapist helps the adults to uncover and disclose the intergenerational origins of their maladaptive patterns. Second, we have found that sharing our countertransference feelings can be particularly helpful in elucidating for the family each person's role in maintaining dysfunctional interactions and in helping family members to identify more adaptive and gratifying ways of relating.

CONCLUDING COMMENTS

In our clinical experience, we have been led to conclude that dysfunctional family interaction patterns involving themes of power and intimacy are associated with the development, maintenance, and course of depression in women. These interactional cycles, combined with prevailing sociopolitical and cultural conditions, place women in subservient roles in which they feel powerless in relation to the men in their family and in society. The men in their interpersonal world are likely to assume a dominant, aggressive role and/or a compliant, overresponsible caretaking role (Bedrosian, 1988; Rubenstein & Timmins, 1978). In addition, depressed women tend to experience the parenting role as burdensome and thus feel powerless and ineffectual as parents. This self-perception is consistent with the mother-blaming ethos in our society.

Gender-sensitive, object relational family therapy provides clinicians with a vehicle for addressing interpersonal and intrapsychic issues in the families of depressed women, as well as the larger familial and sociocultural contexts from which they have emerged. We must place primary emphasis on empowering all family members, particularly the women. Feeling empowered is associated with increased feelings of self-efficacy, a more satisfying balance between intimacy and autonomy, and the development of more adaptive strategies for experiencing and expressing thoughts and feelings.

REFERENCES

Abramson, L. Y., Seligman, M. E. P., & Teasdale, J. (1978). Learned helplessness in humans. *Journal of Abnormal Psychology, 87*, 49–74.

Beach, S. R. H., Sandeen, E. E., & O'Leary, K. D. (1990). *Depression in marriage: A model for etiology and treatment*. New York: Guilford.

Beardslee, W. R. (1990). Development of a preventive intervention for families in which parents have a serious affective disorder. In G. I. Keitner (Ed.), *Depression and families: Impact and treatment* (pp. 121–136). Washington, DC: American Psychiatric Press.

Beardslee, W. R., Bemporad, J., Keller, M. B., & Klerman, G. L. (1983). Children of parents with major affective disorder: A review. *American Journal of Psychiatry, 140*, 825–832.

Bedrosian, R. C. (1988). Treating depression and suicidal wishes within the family context. In N. Epstein, S. E. Schlesinger, & W. Dryden (Eds.), *Cognitive-behavioral therapy with families* (pp. 292–324). New York: Brunner/Mazel.

Bernardez, T. (1988). Women and anger – Cultural prohibitions and the feminine ideal. *Work in progress, 31*. Wellesley, MA: Stone Center Working Papers Series.

Bernal, G., Konjevich, C., & Deegan, E. (1987). Families with depression, school, marital, family and situational problems: A research note. *American Journal of Family Therapy, 15*, 44–51.

Braverman, L. (1986). The depressed woman in context: A feminist family therapist's analysis. *Family Therapy Collections, 16*, 90–101. Rockville: Aspen Publication.

Caplan, P., & Hall-McCorquodale, I. (1985). Mother-blaming in major clinical journals. *American Journal of Orthopsychiatry, 55*, 345–353.

Chodorow, N. (1978). *The reproduction of mothering*. Berkeley: University of California Press.

Clarkin, J. F., Haas, G. L., & Glick, I. D. (Eds.) (1988). *Affective disorders and the family: Assessment and treatment*. New York: Guilford.

Coffman, S. J., & Jacobson, N. S. (1990). Social learning-based marital therapy and cognitive therapy as a combined treatment for depression. In G. I. Keitner (Ed.), *Depression and families: Impact and treatment* (pp. 137–156). Washington, DC: American Psychiatric Press.

Cole, P. M., & Kaslow, N. J. (1988). Interactional and cognitive strategies for affect regulation: A developmental perspective on childhood depression. In L. B. Alloy (Ed.), *Cognitive processes in depression* (pp. 310–343). New York: Guilford.

Coyne, J. C. (1988). Strategic therapy. In J. F. Clarkin, G. L. Haas, & I. D. Glick (Eds.), *Affective disorders and the family: Assessment and treatment* (pp. 89–114). New York: Guilford.

Coyne, J. C. (1976). Toward an interactional description of depression. *Psychiatry, 39*, 28–40.

Dobson, K. S., Jacobson, N. S., & Victor, J. (1988). Integration of cognitive therapy and behavioral marital therapy. In J. F. Clarkin, G. L. Haas, & I. D. Glick (Eds.), *Affective disorders and the family: Assessment and treatment* (pp. 51–88). New York: Guilford.

Downey, G., & Coyne, J. C. (1990). Children of depressed parents: An integrative review. *Psychological Bulletin, 108*, 50–76.

Falloon, I. R. H., Hole, V., Mulroy, L., Norris, L. J., & Pembleton, T. (1988). Behavioral family therapy: In J. F. Clarkin, G. L. Haas, & I. D. Glick (Eds.), *Affective disorders and the family: Assessment and treatment* (pp. 117–133). New York: Guilford.

Feldman, L. B. (1976). Depression and marital interaction. *Family Process, 15*, 389–395.

Foley, S. H., Rounsaville, B. J., Weissman, M. M., Sholomskas, D., & Chevron, E. (May 1987). *Individual vs. conjoint interpersonal psychotherapy for depressed patients with marital disputes.* Paper presented at the annual meeting of the American Psychiatric Association, Chicago, Illinois.

Freeman, A., Epstein, N., & Simon, K. M. (Eds.) (1986). Depression in the family. *Journal of Psychotherapy and the Family, 2.*

Friedman, A. S. (1975). Interaction of drug therapy with marital therapy in depressive patients. *Archives of General Psychiatry, 32*, 619–637.

Gilligan, C. (1982). *In a different voice.* Cambridge: Harvard University Press.

Goodrich, T. J., Rampage, C., Ellman, B., & Halstead, K. (1988). *Feminist family therapy: A casebook.* New York: Norton.

Gotlib, I. H., & Colby, C. A. (1987). *Treatment of depression: An interpersonal systems approach.* New York: Pergamon.

Haas, G. L., & Clarkin, J. F. (1988). Affective disorders and the family context. In J. F. Clarkin, G. L. Haas, & I. D. Glick (Eds.), *Affective disorders and the family* (pp. 3–28). New York: Guilford.

Haas, G. L., Glick, I. D., Clarkin, J. F., Spencer, J. H., Lewis, A. B., Peyser, J., DeMane, N., Good-Ellis, M., Harris, E., & Lestell, V. (1988). Inpatient family intervention: A randomized clinical trial. II. Results at hospital discharge. *Archives of General Psychiatry, 45*, 217–224.

Hinchliffe, M., Hooper, D., & Roberts, F. J. (1978). *The melancholy marriage.* New York: Wiley.

Hogan, P., & Hogan, B. K. (1978). The family treatment of depression. In F. F. Flach & S. C. Draghi (Eds.), *The nature and treatment of depression* (pp. 197–228). New York: Wiley.

Holder, D., & Anderson, C. M. (1990). Psychoeducational family intervention for depressed patients and their families. In G. I. Keitner (Ed.), *Depression and families: Impact and treatment* (pp. 157–184). Washington, DC: American Psychiatric Press.

Hoover, C. F., & Fitzgerald, R. G. (1981). Dominance in the marriages of affective patients. *Journal of Nervous and Mental Disease, 169*, 624–628.

Jack, D. (1987). Silencing the self: The power of social imperatives in female depression. In R. Formanek & A. Gurian (Eds.), *Women and depression: A lifespan perspective* (pp. 161–181). New York: Springer.

Jacobson, N. S., Holtzworth-Munroe, A., & Schmaling, K. B. (1989). Marital therapy and husband involvement in the treatment of depression, agoraphobia, and alcoholism. *Journal of Consulting and Clinical Psychology, 57*, 5–10.

Jessee, E., & L'Abate, L. (1983). Intimacy and marital depression: Interactional patterns. *Journal of Family Therapy, 5*, 39–53.

Kahn, J., Coyne, J. C., & Margolin, G. (1985). Depression and marital conflict: The social construction of despair. *Journal of Social and Personal Relationships, 2*, 447–462.

Kaplan, A. (1984). The "self-in-relation": Implications for depression in women. *Work in Progress 14.* Wellseley, MA: Stone Center Working Papers Series.

Kaslow, N. J., & Carter, A. S. (August 1989). *Treatment of depressed women.* Paper presented in a symposium entitled Depression in Women: Childhood to Adulthood, M. O'Hara (Chairperson). American Psychological Association, New Orleans, Louisiana.

Kaslow, N. J., & Racusin, G. R. (1990). Depressed children and their families: Toward an integrationist approach. In F. W. Kaslow (Ed.), *Voices in family psychology* (pp. 194–216). Newbury Park, CA: Sage.

Keitner, G. I. (Ed.) (1990). *Depression and families: Impact and treatment.* Washington, DC: American Psychiatric Press.

Klerman, G. L., Weissman, M. M., Rounsaville, B. J., & Chevron, E. S. (1984). *Interpersonal psychotherapy of depression.* New York: Basic Books.

Luepnitz, D. A. (1988). *The family interpreted: Feminist theory in clinical practice.* New York: Basic Books.

McBride, A. B. (1990). Mental health effects of women's multiple roles. *American Psychologist, 45,* 381–384.

McGrath, E., Keita, G. P., Strickland, B. R., & Russo, N. F. (Eds.) (1990). *Women and depression: Risk factors and treatment issues.* Washington, DC: American Psychological Association.

McGoldrick, M., Anderson, C. M., & Walsh, F. (Eds.) (1989). *Women in families: A framework for family therapy.* New York: Norton.

Miller, J. B. (1984). The development of women's sense of self. *Work in progress No. 3.* Wellesley, MA: Stone Center Working Papers Series.

Nolen-Hoeksema, S. (1990). *Sex differences in unipolar depression.* Stanford: Stanford University Press.

O'Leary, K. D., & Beach, S. R. H. (1990). Marital therapy: A viable treatment for depression and marital discord. *American Journal of Psychiatry, 147,* 183–186.

Pollack, S. L., Kaslow, N. J., & Harvey, D. M. (1982). Symmetry, complementarity, and depression: The evolution of an hypothesis. In F. W. Kaslow (Ed.), *The international book of family therapy* (pp. 170–183). New York: Brunner/Mazel.

Rounsaville, B. J., Weissman, M. M., Prusoff, B. A., & Herceg-Baron, R. L. (1979). Marital disputes and treatment outcome in depressed women. *Comprehensive Psychiatry, 20,* 483–490.

Rubenstein, D., & Timmins, J. G. (1978). Depressive dyadic and triadic relationships. *Journal of Marriage and Family Counseling, 4,* 13–24.

Russo, N. F. (1990). Overview: Forging research priorities for women's mental health. *American Psychologist, 45,* 368–373.

Rutter, M., Izard, C. E., & Read, P. B. (Eds.) (1986). *Depression in young people: Developmental and clinical perspectives.* New York: Guilford.

Scharff, J. S. (1989). *Foundations of object relations family therapy.* Northvale, NJ: Jason Aronson.

Slipp, S. (1988). *The technique and practice of object relations family therapy.* Northvale, NJ: Jason Aronson.

Stiver, I. P., & Miller, J. B. (1988). From depression to sadness in women's psychotherapy. *Work in Progress, 36.* Wellesley, MA: Stone Center Working Papers Series.

Teichman, Y., & Teichman, M. (1990). Interpersonal view of depression: Review and integration. *Journal of Family Psychology, 3,* 349–367.

Trad, D. V. (1987). *Infant and childhood depression.* New York: Wiley.

Walters, M., Carter, B., Papp, P., & Silverstein, O. (1988). *The invisible web: Gender patterns in family relationships.* New York: Guilford.

Weissman, M. M., & Paykel, E. S. (1974). *The depressed woman: A study of social relationships.* Chicago: University of Chicago Press.

Winnicott, D. W. (1965). *The maturational processes and the facilitating environment.* London: Hogarth Press and the Institute of Psychoanalysis.

10

JUDITH MYERS AVIS

Power Politics in Therapy With Women

W HEN WE TALK ABOUT empowering women in therapy, it is important to note that there is a critical distinction between feeling powerful and having power; we must not confuse the process of helping women to claim and exercise a greater degree of personal choice with the process of helping them to actually *have* power either in their family relationships or in the outside world. As Butler (1990) has pointed out, although feeling powerful is a useful first step in *preparing* women for power, it is not the same thing as actually *having* it. When we "empower" a woman therapeutically, we frequently help her to exercise choices that still occur within the fundamental context of oppression and that do not change the context or remove her from it. A woman may choose to separate from her abusive partner, for example, but she may then experience poverty, inadequate housing, and a lack of police protection from her former partner's continued, and sometimes life-threatening, harassment. Similarly, the recent move to recriminalize abortion in Canada has made it painfully clear that a Canadian woman does not have real power

I am grateful to the numerous colleagues, students, workshop participants, and clients who have shared their ideas and experiences with me, challenged my thinking, and helped me in a variety of ways to expand and integrate my work with women.

over her reproductive choices, no matter how clear she is about what is best for her or how assertive she is on her own behalf.

I find it imperative to examine my work with women within the context of a patriarchal society and to not confuse therapy with changing that context or delude either myself or my clients into thinking that therapy makes any dent in that oppressive superstructure. If I want to change the patriarchal context so that women actually *have* power, and not simply help women to cope and live with their oppression, then I must be politically active outside the therapy room. Political action may involve various forms of social and political activism, feminist research, community or professional education, writing, fundraising, and so on. Although it is not the subject of this chapter, political action is an essential backdrop to any discussion of the empowerment of women in therapy.

THERAPY AS A POLITICAL PROCESS

An exploration of therapeutic empowerment must begin with a recognition of the power dynamics embedded in the therapy process itself. Therapy is not a neutral endeavour. There is a hierarchical relationship between a therapist who is paid for her or his expert knowledge, and clients who are seeking the benefit of that expertise. The therapist is in a more powerful position than the client by virtue of her or his expertise, position, status, and the fact that the client is paying for what the therapist offers. As a consequence, the therapist's words, directives, questions, interpretations, etc., are weighted by the client as possessing far more power than her own. Only by recognizing our power and privileged position in therapeutic relationships can we be fully cognizant of using this power in ethical and empowering ways. Jacobson (1983) and Avis (1985) both address the fallacy of believing that therapy can ever be a neutral, value-free process. Just as it is impossible not to communicate, it is equally impossible not to express our values. As therapists, we constantly attend to, reinforce, and highlight the importance of some behaviors and attitudes, while ignoring and challenging others. In this process, we not only express our own beliefs and values about what is important, functional, problematic, and so on, but we also use our power to influence our clients.

Once we recognize the political influence we exercise in therapy, we can scrutinize our practice to ensure that we exercise this power with judgment and integrity. In my own practice, I find that such exercise of power involves walking the fine line of deliberately reducing hierarchy by demystifying therapy, using self-disclosure, and putting as much information and control as possible in a woman's hands, while at the same time not denying or undermining my own personal authority and competence. I also endeavour to be as aware as possible of the values I am expressing, either directly or indirectly, and to be open with clients about what I believe. As I clarify for clients my personal beliefs (e.g., "I believe that relationships work best when there is an equitable balance of power."), I also make clear the client's freedom and responsibility for determining her own values and beliefs. (This applies, of course, to male clients as well as female; however, the focus in this chapter is on work with women.)

THE THERAPEUTIC RELATIONSHIP

Within the therapeutic relationship, it is essential to remember several major power-related transference and countertransference issues. First, the woman client is reworking old material in the new (therapeutic) context where the therapist is in a position of power. In this context, the client will demonstrate to the therapist how she has learned to deal with power in the past (Butler, 1988). If she has learned to deal with powerful figures by pleasing and overvaluing them, she will do the same with the therapist. If she has learned to deal with a power figure by "resisting" or by passive-aggressive behavior, she will do that with the therapist. If she has learned to cope with power by triangulating others, she will do so with the therapist. We can learn a great deal about the client's beliefs and experience simply by observing her behavior with us and by not getting "hooked" by it. It is important to remember that most women have grown up in situations in which women in general, and themselves in particular, have very little power and have had to find indirect, often "manipulative" ways to protect themselves from the power of others.

In working with women clients, countertransference issues often revolve around working through our relationships with and ambivalences about our own mothers. Whatever is still unresolved for us in this primary relationship will continue to be worked out in every therapy hour. For women therapists, a particular pitfall is overidentification with the woman client, resulting in our becoming overly enmeshed in her feelings of power-lessness and hopelessness. Another frequent pattern is rescuing and overworking, followed by anger and frustration. When caught in this pattern, we may make the error of giving advice, telling a woman what to do, or encouraging her to take a particular direction which reflects our agenda rather than her own (e.g., leaving an abusive relationship). Another common countertransference pattern is for the therapist to attempt to be the all-powerful, nurturing, wise mother. In this case, the therapist's power will disempower the woman client. If the therapist is *too* powerful and too nurturing, then the woman client will be unable to find strength and power in herself. By being human and imperfect, by setting boundaries and limits, and by not being perfectly available or all-giving, we can allow the client to search within and find her own strength rather than rely on ours. When I take a needed break and am unavailable for several weeks, I find that my women clients surprise themselves with their resourcefulness and competence in caring for themselves in my absence. This pattern points to the necessity of our continually working on our own issues so that therapy is directed not by our needs to be needed, valued, and important, but rather by the client's need to find power in herself. Healing truly begins with the health of the therapist.

For the male therapist working with women clients, countertransference issues often result in tendencies either to be an overprotective and overindulgent father, trying to prove that he is not like other men (Butler, 1988), or to have a highly exaggerated idea of a woman's control or power. These patterns simply reinforce old learning and reenact past situations where a male authority figure knew what was best for the woman. The former pattern infantalizes the client and reinforces her helplessness and powerlessness, while the latter pattern reinforces experiences of male hostility and domination. Again, it is critically important for therapists to work on their own issues so that they do not unwittingly act them out against less powerful clients in the therapeutic relationship.

THERAPEUTIC SKILLS

Perceptual and Conceptual Skills

There are numerous perceptual and conceptual skills necessary for a feminist approach to systems therapy. A detailed listing of these skills can be found in Wheeler, Avis, Miller, and Chaney (1989). This chapter will focus only on those directly related to power and empowerment.

Understanding Women in Social Context

Only a thorough understanding of the economic, political, social, and biological constraints that shape women's lives and behavior will allow the therapist to be truly empowering. This understanding includes knowledge of how women's lives are dominated and controlled by poverty, minimum wage, inadequate day-care, violence, sexual abuse, cultural biases against women, the culturally supported male domination of women and children, gender socialization, and guilt. It also includes knowledge of the impact of women's biological life cycle on their symptoms, options, and relationships. To attempt to do therapy with women *without* this knowledge is, as Weiner and Boss (1985) have pointed out, akin to a surgeon's operating with outdated knowledge.

Evaluating Women Positively

In order that we not misuse our therapeutic power in working with women, we must honestly examine anti-woman biases we may have internalized from the culture. I agree with Schaef (1981) who suggests that it is impossible to grow up in North America without absorbing both racist and sexist attitudes. We are nurtured on these beliefs from infancy, and we absorb them along with the air we breathe and the food we eat. Eventually, they become part of the ever-present lens through which we perceive reality. If left unexamined, these beliefs will result in an unconscious tendency to evaluate women negatively and to think about them in stereotypically blaming ways. This blaming includes holding women responsible for whatever difficulties occur in marital and family relationships as well as viewing them through any of the images that express the cultural hatred and distrust of women: masochistic, castrating, aggressive, bitchy, angry, passive, nonprotective, suffocating, cold, rejecting, hysterical, nagging, etc.

To counter these cultural images of women, many of which may have taken up residence in our own heads, we must first allow ourselves to be aware of our beliefs and then to focus on evaluating women positively. This positive evaluation includes recognizing women's strengths and competencies (including the strength it takes simply to survive in oppressive situations), recognizing and valuing the essential reproductive, nurturing, and physical work women do in families, and valuing women's relational skills. It also involves vigilance in monitoring our own internal process, observing our stereotypical perceptions, and countering them with a consistent effort to understand women's behavior in the larger context of the oppression of women.

Recognizing Power Inequities between Women and Men as a Major Dynamic in Individual, Marital, and Family Problems

I am using the word "power" here to refer to control over one's own life choices as well as to the ability to influence others and to influence the outcome of decisions that affect one's life. Before being able to empower women effectively, we must first recognize the impact of gender-based power inequities on both individual and relationship well-being. We must then be able to analyze marital relationships in terms of equality of access to influence, control, choice, resources, and opportunity, as well as in terms of equality of responsibility. Without such a firm grasp of the dynamics of gender-based power, the marital or family therapist will become hopelessly mired in the convolutions of systems thinking and of such systemic notions as "the power of powerlessness." What is required is not a total negation of systems theory, but the ability to view interactions through both a systemic lens and a feminist one simultaneously (Goldner, 1985).

Recognizing Power Issues as Power Issues

It is common for family therapists to confuse power issues with communication issues and to focus therapeutic attention on helping women to ask more nicely for what they want or helping men to express their feelings. These therapists completely miss the point—if a woman could have obtained what she wanted from her mate (e.g., his greater involvement in parenting and housekeeping) by asking nicely, she undoubtedly would have. The issue is one of power, with the man having the power to refuse and the woman not having the power to persuade him to share responsibility. A woman's "nagging" behavior in these situations must be understood as a behavior of the powerless—those with power to make things happen do not have to nag. Similarly, in working with couples, it is essential to recognize power issues when we see them and to not focus on helping a man express his feelings as a substitute for challenging his tactics of power and domination.

Intervention Skills

At one time I conceptualized my therapeutic work with power and gender as involving the empowering of·women and the challenging of men, until I realized that each action is a part of the other. I cannot empower without challenging, and respectful challenging empowers. A great deal of my work with women involves challenging their beliefs, expectations of themselves and others, and their socialized behaviors, thus enabling them to expand their range of choices and take greater conscious control of those aspects of their lives over which they do have some power. For me, this process of empowering women therapeutically involves four major components:

1. Providing a conducive *context* within which the empowering process can occur;
2. communicating an empowering *attitude and belief system* regarding women;
3. challenging a woman's *internalized belief system*, absorbed from the dominant culture, which blinds her to her subordination and keeps her in place;
4. helping a woman to *take action* in her own life, on her own behalf, according to what she deems best for herself.

The following list of interventions is organized within the framework of these four components. Although far from exhaustive, it includes those interventions that I use most frequently and have found most effective for empowering women.

Providing a Conducive Context for Empowering Women

One of the most effective means I have found for empowering a woman within the context of couple or family therapy is to spend some time working with her alone. I use individual sessions for the following purposes:

1. To assess, on a routine basis, for any history of physical, sexual, or emotional violence in the couple relationship;
2. to provide a forum for a woman to convey her needs and concerns without worrying about protecting her mate from them;

3. to communicate a view of the woman as a separate individual as well as a member of her relationship systems;

4. to know and experience the client *out* of her relationship context as well as within it;

5. to provide a context where I can challenge a woman's internalized beliefs about gender and coach her in more assertive, powerful behaviors without her partner interfering and without her feeling she must protect, defend, or please him. In his absence, she is free to explore new ideas and behaviors without worrying about how they will affect him, and without the magnetic pull of his reactivity in the session.

6. to balance the marital power imbalance in preparation for couple work. The more unequal the marital power balance, the more essential are individual sessions. When there is physical abuse in a relationship, I refuse to do marital work until both partners have been engaged in individual and/or group therapy, and the violence has stopped for a period of six months. However, even when they are not physically abused, many women experience some degree of emotional abuse, psychological intimidation, economic control, coercion, or any one of the more "minor" everyday patterns of subordination and inequality with which women's lives are riddled.

When the power balance in the relationship is highly skewed, even though there may be no physical violence, I usually work with a woman alone for a number of sessions, sometimes for a number of months, in order to help her to reexamine and alter her socialized beliefs and behaviors sufficiently so that marital therapy is possible. Without such preparatory work with the disempowered woman, therapy is usually doomed to a maintenance of the marital status quo as a result of one of two nonproductive processes: Either therapeutic challenges to the present power arrangements are met with objections from the wife as well as from the husband, or the wife is unable to know and affirm her own position on marital issues under the stress of her husband's disapproval and/or emotional control.

After I have worked with a woman alone for a period of time, I always have several individual sessions with her partner prior to beginning couple work so as to join with him and understand his beliefs both about gender relationships in general and about the problems in his marriage in particular. I also make it very clear to both partners that my individual work with the woman is necessary to help her to stop assuming the burden of the marriage, not because she is responsible for it.

Communicating an Empowering Belief System Regarding Women

Perhaps the most important and empowering belief the therapist can have is that the client is competent and is the best expert on herself. I hold this belief deeply and communicate it to my clients in numerous ways.

I use a variety of metaphors with a woman to refer to and invoke her personal expertise: her inner voice, her guide, her inner wisdom, her self-knowledge, her unconscious, her wise teacher. I constantly refer to this expertise, ask her to consult and trust it, and use various means, including guided imagery, to help her gain access to it.

In order to develop an *informed* inner wisdom, uncontaminated by the constricting beliefs embedded in gender socialization, a woman may need new information which provides alternative ways of constructing reality. Approaches to offering this information will be suggested in the following section.

Listening to her own voice. Having been socialized throughout her life to focus on and respond to others' needs rather than her own, a woman may begin therapy totally out of touch with her own needs and with her own knowledge of herself. One of the first goals of therapy, then, is to help her to develop a relationship with herself and to begin to listen to, validate, and articulate her own needs. When a woman tells me that she does not know what her needs are or what direction she should take, I usually observe: "I believe that you know what to do, and what is best for you; you just don't know yet that you know. So the first thing we have to do is help you start listening to yourself again." I emphasize the importance of her own voice, of being heard first by herself and then by others, and often ask when she lost her voice or who took it away. I then use a variety of means to help her make connections with her inner self.

1. *Inner Guide exercise.* I frequently use an adaptation of Butler's Guide exercise (1988) to help a woman connect with her own wisdom. Using guided fantasy, I lead her through a process of meeting and talking with a Guide figure who knows and understands all that has happened in her life and who is wise, compassionate, and loving towards her. I then ask her to consult her Guide whenever she is

unsure of what to do, whenever she feels afraid, or whenever she is in need of reassurance, comfort, or a loving voice. I have used this exercise with remarkably positive results both for individual women and for groups of sexual abuse survivors.

2. *Listening to symptoms.* Another method for helping a woman to tune in to her own voice and self wisdom is to direct her to listen to her symptoms and to what they are telling her. I suggest to her that her symptoms are actually healthy reactions of her self-system to situations of inequality, powerlessness, coercion, fear, anger. Headaches, overeating, fatigue, and depression can all be listened to as powerful and helpful messages from her inner self.

3. *Writing exercises.* I also draw on a variety of writing exercises to help women to find, express, and listen to their own voices. Writing is a major tool for helping a woman develop a relationship with herself, for in the process she often discovers new and powerful self-awareness, self-appreciation, and self-connections. Drawing is another avenue to facilitate a woman's expression of her inner self, so that she may begin to observe and engage in a dialogue with parts of herself previously invisible, unheard, and unknown.

4. *Ericksonian hypnotherapy.* Erickson's deep respect for the benevolent power of the unconscious makes his approach to hypnotherapy easily integrated into feminist work. I find it particularly useful for helping women to center on their inner selves and to gain access to their own knowledge and wisdom. It can be effectively used with incest survivors to anchor them in the present, to reduce fear and anxiety, and to gain access to unconscious knowledge which is helpful for healing (Dolan, 1991).

Affirming the client's reality. I affirm a woman's perceptions, feelings, ideas, experiences, and reality, particularly those aspects of her reality that are related to being female in a patriarchal system and that have been negated or ignored by others, her husband, her family, and/or the society. Such experiences include, for example, her feeling exhausted by or resentful of the "double shift" of an outside job plus housekeeping, feeling abused and depressed as a result of her partner's verbal attacks, feeling angry and yet guilty about her anger, feeling burdened, and feeling powerless.

Avoiding over-helping. I communicate to a woman my belief in her competence and expertise by avoiding the urge to help too much, to take over for her, or to be the all-giving, idealized mother. At times, I empower by doing nothing, reminding myself to "Don't just do something—stand there."

Listening to the client's fears and going slowly. I positively connote the part of a woman that is reluctant, fearful, ambivalent, or procrastinating, pointing out the importance of paying attention and listening to what this part of her is saying. In this process, a woman often begins to listen to and validate a part of her wisdom she has previously ignored. I typically join with the part of her that is reluctant, affirm the importance of going slowly, of listening to all of herself, and of waiting until she is ready to make any change. At the same time, I continually affirm that when the time is right (for a decision, change, move, etc.), she will know it. I also affirm that change *will* occur, when she is ready, using terms such as "when" and "as" rather than "if."

Redefining normality to highlight women's strengths. I reframe and relabel as strengths what a woman regards as deficits or deviance or pathology. Thus, I redefine depression as a healthy, normal, adaptive reaction to depressing circumstances and ask her to pay attention to what the depression is telling her. With an abused woman, I marvel at the incredible strength she must have had to survive—and to help her children survive—under such devastating circumstances.

Challenging the Client's Internalized Belief System

I consider this area of intervention to be the *sine qua non* of the therapeutic empowerment of women. Sometimes called "social analysis," it is the set of interventions that allows us to connect the personal and the political and, in so doing, to free a woman from the coercive control of internalized oppression. As someone has so aptly observed, "It is hard to fight an enemy who has outposts in your own head."

Cognitive restructuring. Most women coming to therapy believe their problems are personal, of their own making, a result of their inadequacy, ineptitude, unworthiness, badness, stupidity, impatience, or ignorance, and they feel great guilt and shame. Even when a woman appears to be angrily blaming her partner for difficulties in the relationship, this position most often is a defense against her underlying belief that the blame and guilt actually belong to her. I use cognitive restructuring to disassemble these beliefs in a gentle way and to explore their foundations. Much of this process involves questioning: "Where did you learn that you are responsible for making other people happy?" "Who told you that you shouldn't ask directly for what you want?" "Where does this belief come from?" "Does it still make sense to you?" "What were the expectations for women/men in your family of origin?" "How were you taught to look after men?" Cognitive restructuring also involves pointing out underlying beliefs of which the client may be totally unaware: "You seem to be assuming that it is your responsibility to see that the children get their homework done." "You seem to believe that your husband is fragile/can't change." "You act as though your needs are completely unimportant." "It sounds as though you believe your anger is bad." I also ask more open-ended questions to explore various beliefs: "What do you believe would happen if you said 'No'?" "What do you believe a woman's responsibilities are in a marriage? . . . for her children? . . . for herself?"

Providing new information. Since information is power, it is important to find as many ways as possible to put this power in women's hands. After exploring and identifying her beliefs, I find it essential to provide each woman with new information which will challenge these beliefs and support alternative constructions of reality. I do so in several major ways.

The first way is by discussing and elaborating the whole process of gender socialization and helping her to understand that her beliefs are just that—beliefs—which have been *taught* to her; they are not absolutes or reality. "I'm not surprised that you feel guilty when you leave your children—most women are taught that their children's well-being depends almost exclusively on them." "Of course you believe that your husband's needs are more important than yours. Everything in your life from birth on—family, school, media—has told you this is so."

Another way of providing new information is by helping a woman to see and understand the power imbalance between men and women, as well as the ways in which she has been socialized to accept, not see, and not challenge this imbalance. This understanding provides a new lens through which to examine the difficulties she experiences in her marital and family relationships, and allows her to begin to separate her own voice from the multitude of voices in her head that repeat the powerful messages of female gender socialization.

A third way of providing a woman with information is by *addressing power issues directly*. Most couples present for therapy with some variation of what they define as marital conflict or difficulties in communication, and it is relatively rare that either partner has recognized or articulated the power imbalance underlying their problems. If the problem is to be resolved in a way that actually redistributes power in the marital system rather than further disempowering the wife, it is essential that the therapist directly address the underlying power issues masquerading as communication issues. This involves raising for discussion such questions as:

1. What is the division of childcare and housekeeping responsibilities? Note that it is how *responsibilities*, not tasks, are divided that gives us the most information about the division of power and responsibility in the system. Watch, for example, for fathers who refer to spending time with their children as "baby-sitting," as well as for who plans the menus, and who knows when the milk is low or when the children need new shoes.
2. How is money earned, handled, shared, and thought about? Do they think of it as "their" income, or as "his" and "hers?" Do they have a joint bank account or separate accounts? Does each have an equal personal allowance for which she or he is not accountable to the other? Does each have equal accessibility to the couple's financial resources and equal accountability to the other for how she or he spends those resources?
3. *How* are decisions made? Note that how *many* decisions is not as important as the *kinds* of decisions. She may make hundreds, such as what food to buy, how to organize day-care, what clothes the children need, etc., while he may make relatively few, such as when to move, what car to buy, etc. How decisions are made includes who has the power to delegate, who has veto power, and who has the power to abdicate from involvement in particular decisions.
4. Does any form of intimidation (overt or covert) exist in the relationship?

In the process of exploring such issues, the underlying power structure of the couple relationship is revealed. When the division of power and responsibility is unbalanced (as it almost always is, to at least some degree), I comment on the imbalance, I ask about how they came to decide on this particular division, and I link the imbalance to their presenting difficulties. I then challenge the beliefs underlying this division and encourage both partners to move towards a restructuring that involves a genuine redistribution of power. As we move through this process, most women feel empowered as they recognize the socialized assumptions that have imprisoned them. In my experience, the majority of men resist, to a greater or lesser degree, the loss of privilege and power such restructuring entails. A discussion of interventions for effectively challenging men to make such change is beyond the scope of this paper (see Dienhart, 1989). However, simply raising the issues is highly empowering to women, raises their consciousness, and is helpful to them in asserting their needs, wants, and demands for more equitable relationships with their partners.

I also provide new information by simply stating facts that challenge a woman's beliefs: "It is only by nurturing ourselves that we are able really to nurture others." "You are responsible for your own needs." "By standing up to your husband and by caring for yourself, you are teaching your daughters how to respect and care for themselves and teaching your sons to respect women." I also find it effective to report research findings that challenge a client's beliefs: "Almost 40% of all women have some experience of sexual abuse before the age of 18." The research adds weight to my message, while at the same time expanding the client's information base.

Finally, I provide new information through bibliotherapy. I have found this to be a particularly effective way to share the power of information directly with women. Although I use this means constantly and extensively, I also use it judiciously, since it is *disempowering* to give a woman something to read that is too difficult, too long, or too academic for her to understand easily. I keep a variety of materials on hand—poems, cartoons, newspaper articles, book chapters, and books of all descriptions—from which I carefully make a selection to match the client's level of literacy, awareness, and type of problem, and then I give or loan the material to her. For clients who are eager to read, I usually suggest that they buy some of their own books, and I have an arrangement with the local bookstore to keep a good stock of the books I most frequently recommend.

"We" statements. I have found this type of statement to be a simple and powerful way to connect the personal and the political, to decrease hierarchy between myself and the client, and to connect the client with the sisterhood of women. "We" statements can take a number of forms, but they all bring in the larger context: "As women we have been taught that . . . (it is not OK to be angry)"; "Many women feel . . . (guilty, depressed)"; "Most of us have learned . . . (that when things go wrong we are responsible)"; "Most of the women I see have had similar struggles with this issue . . ."; "As women, many of us have experienced . . . (harassment, intimidation)." This intervention can also be used by male therapists in their work with women by presenting these messages in terms of what his wife, women colleagues, friends, or students have taught him about women's common experiences. For example, "My women colleagues have told me that many women struggle with. . . . "

Helping Women to Take Action in Their Own Lives

Clarity regarding responsibility. Since most women come into therapy feeling and believing that they are to blame for their own and their children's problems, I have found it empowering to clarify for what a woman is and is not responsible. I am guided here by Wykoff's (1977) very helpful framework. The first step is to help a woman to realize that she is *not* the cause of her own problems and to understand how the patriarchal context and her gender socialization have shaped her life. The second step is to help her to take responsibility, as an adult, for what she *can* change. This process frees her from the burdens of both guilt and helplessness and affirms her ability, and responsibility, to take action on her own behalf as an adult woman.

Dealing with anger. Helping women to claim, to feel, and to express their anger, and use it for their own benefit, is one of the most empowering things I do in therapy. I regard anger as a vital part of becoming more conscious and of making change, and deliberately try to mobilize it by predicting it, reaching for it, and affirming it as highly positive and helpful to the client.

I use social analysis to point out how we, as women, have been robbed of our anger and have been taught to be docile and out of touch with our power and strength. I discuss the high cost to us, as women, of anger substitutes, whether directed inward and resulting in depression and psychosomatic illness, or directed outward where it seeps into our relationships and may result in bitterness, attack, and hostility.

I often use the metaphor of white light in describing the benefits of anger, pointing out that it is a clear, strong emotion which has the potential for energizing the client and focusing her energy on her own behalf. I normalize the experience of intense anger at various points in the processes both of becoming aware and of healing and change. I encourage women to feel their anger and to experiment with various means of physical expression such as yelling, pounding a pillow, stomping, and physical exercise. I also encourage writing and imagery as other safe means for releasing anger. Lerner's (1985) *The Dance of Anger* is an enormously useful book to share with clients, and I have found that it often speeds up the client's work in this area.

Helping women to exercise direct forms of personal power. The most empowering word a woman can learn is "No", and its power is directly proportional to the difficulty most women have in uttering it. I give permission and coach women to say "No", to assert, and to do. The idea of "going on strike" is completely new for most women, but it is also freeing and deliciously satisfying. I coach women on how to say "No" firmly, deliberately, and without guilt, to all demands, requests, expectations, etc., that they are not willing to meet, whether these come from partners, children, friends, bosses, or colleagues.

Psychodramatic work. I frequently use modified psychodramatic interventions to help a woman identify, listen to, and validate different parts of herself; for example, between the part of herself that wants to be in constant contact with others and the part that wants time and space alone. As I double for her and repeat her words, she is able to hear her words spoken back to her and recognize her own wisdom. I work with her toward collaboration between her different parts or voices, and, in so doing, I help her to move toward inner validation and harmony. As one part of her informs another part, a woman is able to listen to her own wisdom and find her own resolution.

Working with women in groups. The potential for empowering women is so much greater in groups than in individual work that it always surprises me that we do not use them more often. I have developed groups in two different ways. When I have had several women clients with similar issues, I have invited them to form a group. This approach has been extremely successful in counteracting the individualization of women's problems, in providing both support and challenge, and in empowering through connection with other women. One such group continued to meet together as a support group long after I had left the city where it began. I have also found groups an essential adjunct to individual work for many women who are adult survivors of child sexual abuse. For these women, group therapy breaks down isolation and shame and provides the connection and validation necessary for healing. To protect both clients and myself, I have firm rules for such groups about screening, about working with a co-therapist, and about not working with the same clients in both individual and group therapy. See Courtois (1988) for helpful guidelines. Groups also have great impact with abused women, and although I have not led such groups myself, I consider them to be an essential part of good therapy with these women.

Preparing women for "change-back" messages. One of the simplest yet most potent things I do to empower women in carrying through with their change efforts is to predict and warn them about change-back messages from their various systems. I explain the normality of change-back messages, how to recognize them, and how to respond. I tell women that such messages are signs of their success, that is, that they have made such significant changes that members of their system feel threatened and are trying to push them back into their previous role. One woman told me that the single most helpful thing I had done for her in a three-month period of intensive therapy was to tell her about change-back messages. That knowledge had enabled her to make sense of, and deal with, her husband's seemingly mysterious negative response to her making the very changes he had been encouraging her to make for years.

CONCLUSION

This chapter has examined a number of dimensions related to power politics in therapeutic work with women. The process of empowering women therapeutically cannot adequately be summarized with a list of interventions such as that above. Empowerment is a holistic process which involves our comprehensive integration of (1) a political understanding of the oppression of women, including its embeddedness in the culture, its maintenance in family relationships, and its internalization with individual women; with (2) a high degree of respect for women, their strengths, and their self wisdom; and (3) an understanding of change at individual, family, and larger systems levels. Thus, none of the dimensions or interventions discussed stands alone; each is connected with the others, and all are important at different times in the therapeutic process. I share my thinking about them with you in the hope that it may support, affirm, and stimulate your own thinking about this work.

REFERENCES

Avis, J. M. (1985). The politics of functional family therapy: A feminist critique. *Journal of Marital and Family Therapy, 11,* 127–138.

Butler, S. (1988, May). Group therapy with survivors of child sexual abuse. Workshop presented at the No More Secrets Conference, Ontario Institute for Studies in Education, Toronto.

Butler, S. (1990, May). Speaking in tongues: Finding the language of healing. Plenary address delivered to the Woman and Therapy Conference, Guelph, Ontario.

Courtois, C. (1988). *Healing the incest wound: Adult survivors in therapy.* New York: Norton.

Dienhart, A. (1989). Engaging men in family change: An exploratory Delphi study. Unpublished master's thesis, University of Guelph, Guelph, Ontario.

Dolan, Y. (1991). *Resolving sexual abuse.* New York: Norton.

Goldner, V. (1985). Warning: Family therapy may be dangerous to your health. *The Family Therapy Networker, 9,* 19–23.

Jacobson, N. S. (1983). Beyond empiricism: The politics of marital therapy. *American Journal of Family Therapy, 11*, 11–24.

Lerner, H. G. (1985). *The dance of anger: A woman's guide to changing the patterns of intimate relationships*. New York: Harper & Row.

Schaef, A. W. (1981). *Women's reality*. Minneapolis, MN: Winston.

Weiner, J. P., & Boss, P. (1985). Exploring gender bias against women: Ethics for marriage and family therapy. *Counseling and Values, 30*, 9–23.

Wheeler, D., Avis, J., Miller, L., & Chaney, S. (1988). Rethinking family therapy training and supervision: A feminist model. In M. McGoldrick, C. Anderson, & F. Walsh (Eds.), *Women in families: A framework for family therapy* (pp. 135–151). New York: Norton.

Wykoff, H. (1977). *Solving women's problems: Through awareness, action and contact*. New York: Grove.

V
CLINICAL PRACTICE

11

MICHELE BOGRAD

The Color of Money: Pink or Blue?

W HEN WOMEN TALK ABOUT POWER, we usually address interpersonal dynamics, gender politics, and self-esteem issues. We discuss male vs. female power tactics, whether there is really a power of the weak, how we can be strong, clear-spirited selves, and the costs of such a stance. But, amidst important theoretical clarification and equally important self-discovery, we hardly mention the dirty word: money. Although, as the song says, money makes the world go 'round, we rarely examine how we as women mental health professionals orient ourselves to family therapy as our business, as our means to financial self-sufficiency, and as the economic clout to our professional and personal authority.

After six years in private practice, I was stiffed by a client whom I had seen for several months. After a year of gentle monthly bills, some phone calls, and several somewhat stronger letters, I finally took him to small claims court. In my last phone call with him, which I initiated in the secret hopes that he would finally pay me as he had repeatedly promised, he threatened to countersue me and bade me adieu with yet another heartfelt promise that a check was in the mail. On the day of the court date, I awoke with trepidation, anxiety, and images of him physically hurting me in the courtroom. To my relief, he did not appear. With the help of the courts, I received a check several months later—signed by his wife!

My anxiety and confusion about how to handle the financial issues, and my discomfort with directly confronting this man about his failure to honor the contractual nature of our relationship inspired me to talk with other women family therapists. I was surprised and somewhat dismayed at what I discovered: Almost every one had a story about one or more clients whom they allowed to disempower them over money issues. Several had permitted client balances to reach a thousand or more dollars, which the clients never paid. One had not billed her clients for six months, but felt sure that her clients would be responsible for their debts. Another had initiated a policy of having her clients pay each session, yet found it difficult to deal with those clients who walked out without paying her.

Several themes were common to our stories. Fundamentally, no woman therapist felt comfortable addressing money issues with clients. Most of us had struggled with how much to charge, and even some highly experienced therapists still charged well below the going rate. The decision to charge less was not always a political one to enable clients of limited means access to sophisticated clinicians. Instead, it was based on personal doubts these women therapists had about whether their work was worth $75 to $100 an hour.

Second, although all had received ample training in how to interpret a client's acting-out about money, few of us felt skilled to deal with the nuts and bolts of money exchange. For example, when I decided finally to ask clients to pay weekly to reduce my bookkeeping costs, I wrote the new policy in a letter—fueled more by cowardice than clinical wisdom, I fear. I just did not want to deal with it directly.

Third, many of us erred on the side of being too flexible (some could say, too easy) with financially irresponsible clients. That is, clients were always given the benefit of the doubt—even when they had repeatedly broken promises of payment. We often absorbed the long wait for insurance to reimburse us, although we knew other professionals who asked to be paid up front by the client and let the client be paid by the insurance company. Large balances accrued from clients who had enough money for vacations or leisure activities.

What was even more fascinating and surprising was that most of the male colleagues I talked to did not share these same concerns. Even relatively inexperienced clinicians more easily charged the average fee; most insisted on weekly payments and asked for checks at the end of the hour without awkwardness or hesitation. None felt any fear at the thought of court action against wayward clients.

How to account for some of these very general gender differences? I suggest they relate to (1) issues of personal entitlement; (2) dilemmas of money, status, and power; (3) the relational aspects of psychotherapy; (4) connections between money and caring.

PERSONAL ENTITLEMENT

Asserting their legitimacy, expertise, savvy, or smarts is still difficult for many women—especially in the professional domain. Getting paid for these heightens the dilemma. The financial component of psychotherapy, by definition, highlights that money is exchanged for wisdom, guidance, or answers. Many women therapists, in our private and personal lives, still struggle with what it means to speak clearly and loudly, to value our own ideas and perceptions, and to accept public recognition for our skills. Because of this conflict, we often feel uncomfortable seeking remuneration for ideas that feel incomplete to us. For example, I have felt uneasy accepting money for presentations of ideas that are still in the working stages. I feel grateful for the opportunity instead of believing that I should be financially supported for the development of my ideas. Most of my male colleagues refuse to volunteer time in similar situations. The healthy self-confidence that enables us to collect appropriate fees for hours of work and years of training is not part and parcel of our socialization as women. On the contrary, we were often taught to minimize our capabilities, to dim our brilliance, and to embed any ideas or suggestions in a web of qualifications and apologies.

I must add that this is not simply a personal failure of individual women, but is supported and promoted by institutional and professional contexts. Several years ago, I was invited to present at a day-long conference out of state. The male administrator asked what I charged. Anxiously, I set a moderate fee—since I denigrate my own abilities through my belief that *other* women family therapists are more recognized, prolific, or powerful than I am. To my amazement, the administrator later told me that my fee had been extremely low and that the university would have been willing to pay more. Willing—as if it were all my fault? It is clear that the institutional context made it difficult to me to receive the compensation that, in retrospect, I obviously deserved.

DILEMMAS OF MONEY, STATUS, AND POWER

In my early training, I was apprenticed to another psychologist. After several years, I resented that he was profiting from my labors, but I did not feel prepared to address the situation with him. We had an arrangement that I would pay him after my clients paid me. Eventually, I permitted one client to owe me a lot of money, which thus was owed to my colleague. He eventually demanded that I pay him and let the client pay me in the future. I, in turn, finally demanded that my client reconcile his bill. I recognized that I had been trying to get back at my colleague through money for the dependence upon him that I resented but felt powerless to change. I was left thoughtful about how often women therapists feel exploited by the systems in which they work, and how that feeling shapes our willingness to collect money. An unwillingness signifies passive resistance to exploitation. In addition, it signifies how hard it is to feel deserving of payment when we feel denigrated and devalued by a system.

Yet another element is that we are not accustomed to having power. I still find it difficult to charge full fees and to ask for ample payment for workshops in spite of my expertise and increased recognition in the field. I have wondered if I am fearful of too much visibility or accountability for my ideas. I still feel that others are doing me a favor if they pay me. If I am paid well, should not that mean that I am an expert, that I am deserving, that I am legitimate? Sometimes it seems easier to work for free. I have tended to view this as my problem. I am just starting to realize how deeply I have internalized beliefs about my proper place as a woman. It is one thing for me to be powerful intellectually, another to be powerful economically. The latter says: Take me seriously. For women to have financial self-sufficiency and clout threatens something very basic in everyone's notions about women.

THE RELATIONAL ASPECTS OF PSYCHOTHERAPY

While male therapists stereotypically view therapy as a product, as the provision of advice, insight, or strategies, female therapists stereotypically view relationship as the central component of therapy. Negotiations or struggles about money interfere with the relationship or at least make it temporarily awkward, uncomfortable, or angry. We would rather avoid this circumstance. Most of us have also been taught a lot about self-sacrifice. That is, we can sustain a relationship for a long period of time, even if the other person is not responsible or responsive. I have found that some women therapists do not even experience that they are being financially exploited by a client until their colleagues react with anger or shock at the outstanding balance. Even then, some therapists continue to berate *themselves* for feeling angry with the client.

Perhaps because relationship is so central to the conception of therapy itself, it seems hard for women therapists to acknowledge the unabashed selfishness, carelessness, or sociopathy of certain clients. Many of us believe in the inherent goodness of the people we treat and adhere to the clinical belief that remaining steady and nurturing in the face of clients' acting-out is healing. For myself, it took me longer than I like to admit to face that my client was lying to me over and over. Even when his lying became obvious, I still felt guilty for confronting him — as if *I* could jeopardize the therapeutic relationship that he had already severely compromised.

THE CONNECTIONS BETWEEN CARING AND MONEY

Given how widespread these patterns are, it is useful to seek explanation in the culture at large rather than in the personal histories of individual women. My sense is that, in our society, there are different cultural images of the connections between money and caring for men and women. Women are expected to care "naturally": Witness the beliefs that maternal skills and capacities are instinctual or ready-made. Furthermore, our culture does not define caring as a highly sophisticated, complex ability. In this context, women have also learned to take for granted or to devalue their abilities to understand and connect with others. As a male colleague said, "One way I think people think about it is that 'Women care, and men are taught to care.'" In other words, an underlying attitude is that women should not be paid for something that comes easily to them and is devalued by the culture at large. But we tend to appreciate and reimburse men who have made an effort to learn something different and are valued as having gained important skills and ways of being that distinguish them from other men. Furthermore, we look askance at women who exchange money for caring. We feel uncomfortable with women who are blunt about economic motivation being part of the relational bargain. Contrast our visions of prostitutes with that of selfless Mother Theresa. Our culture still holds a different opinion about men who, as expert doctors, psychiatrists, or gurus, charge large (if not exorbitant) rates for their knowledge and care.

VALUING OURSELVES

As women family therapists struggle with internal and external messages that devalue our capacity for caring, how can we begin to transform our ways of valuing ourselves, as well as the ways we are valued by others?

Most essentially, we need to value more deeply that our relationship skills are just that: highly evolved, practiced, fine-tuned, and important capacities. We tend to minimize not only our academic training, but the lifelong practice that we have engaged in to learn to care well for others, to tolerate strong and contradictory feelings, to move powerfully in the emotional domain, to sense others' pain and to give comfort, and to use ourselves in deep ways as instruments of change. Somehow, when we think of expertise, we tend to think of the production of ideas, information, and strategies—not of creating a close relationship. Clearly, a good therapist—male or female—has great expertise in both domains, which our culture splits apart and differentially values.

Women therapists need to gain greater comfort in setting the conditions of a treatment relationship. At times, we seem uneasy acknowledging that our relationships with our clients are contractual, that our availability is contingent upon their meeting our conditions for treatment. We sometimes fear that raising such sticky and uncomfortable issues will confuse the treatment relationship. If we ignore those issues, however, we send powerful messages to our clients that the therapeutic relationship is like many personal relationships in which the woman's care is taken for granted, her availability exploited, and her nurturance expected regardless of broken bargains. We are trying to change that social expectation; our consulting rooms and client relationships give us the opportunity to enact that change.

These changes will not be easily accomplished. Although individual women therapists struggle with money issues and with self-doubts, the problem is social, not personal. When we do not charge full fees, do not request remuneration for our caretaking services, do not demand mutual accountability in our relationships, we are being "good" women. When we take seriously our value—financially and in other ways—some clients and colleagues of both sexes will react in ways that push us back to our previous status. We are threatening something deep in the social order by not working for less.

This task is not an easy one. We struggle with our own beliefs and those of others around us about the value of our caring and our professional identities. The goal here is not for us all to charge high rates for services. Many of us politically question fees that exclude many women from receiving expert care by private practitioners. We also relish the collaboration that results from informal, unpaid, and time-consuming meetings with colleagues and intellectual comrades. Instead, my hope is that we can learn to make real choices about what we want to charge and how we want to handle financial agreements with our clients—rather than allowing discomfort or anxiety to shape our decisions. In this way, economic, personal, and professional empowerment will follow the same path.

12

LOIS BRAVERMAN

It's Bigger Than Both of Us

"**N**OT EVERY WORD A THERAPIST speaks or permits should be politically correct; and no interview should be 'scored' according to how many sexist or egalitarian thoughts are voiced. This kind of vulgar reductionism has no place in the clinical milieu, a setting far too dense with possibility and ambiguity" (Goldner, 1989, p. 58). Although I agree wholeheartedly with Goldner, there are times when the politics and the economics of patriarchy loudly intrude into family therapy. When I am confronted with a case where the economic disparity of earning power between the husband and wife is extreme, I am painfully reminded of how ineffective therapy really is in creating a serious shift in the balance of power in the marital relationship. The wife's options and possibilities, her leverage as a partner in the marriage, are overpowered by the husband's economic strength, which seems to undergird the marital relationship and to define the character of the family life which surrounds it. In such situations, therapy seems inadequate to the task of change. Goldner again puts the case well: "Gender and the gendering of power are not secondary mediating variables *affecting* family life; they construct family life in the deepest sense" (1989, p. 56). The following case illustrates this point.

THE CASE

The husband initiated therapy because his wife of four years was withdrawn and threatening divorce. This was his second marriage and her first marriage; he had three grown children from the first. They had a three-year-old son who was born about nine months after they married. The husband was 15 years older than the wife and was the president of a very successful family business. The wife had endured so many disappointments in the marriage that she hardly wanted to speak of them; she said that she was trying to forget the past. Meanwhile, she was withdrawn, noticeably angry, and depressed. She was very skeptical about marital therapy because she did not believe that "anything could really change. He'll just keep doing what he wants and justifying it."

The husband's claim is that he wants her to be happy. He explains that his work is very important and that she does not understand that he cannot take time out to have lunch with her or to be home with her and their son at four or five o'clock in the afternoon. He argues that he is home every weekend and that even when he goes into the office each Saturday morning, he takes his three-year-old son with him. He tells me that he rarely has to go in to the office on Sundays. He finds his wife's complaints about his absence irrational and ridiculous. He has hired a cleaning woman to come twice a week for her, his son goes to the best day-care facility in town five days a week, and they have "great" baby-sitters for the evening. He believes that his wife simply does not understand the pressures of work and its inherent responsibilities. He claims that he has given her substantial support by "generously allowing" her to have lots of household help. He believes that if she just felt better about herself and improved her self-esteem, everything would be better. He worries that she feels inferior to him because he is college educated and she is not.

I implore her to tell me about the pain she has experienced in the marriage. Overcoming her reluctance, she tells the following story. Trouble began on the honeymoon when, at the last minute, her husband was too busy to leave and she had to fly out alone. He followed her two days later. The birth of their son was very difficult and medically complicated. Her husband was not present during much of the labor because of business, and even when he was there, he spent most of the time on the phone talking to his office. When it was time for her to leave the hospital, he could not be there to pick her up and sent a limousine in his place to take her to her mother's house. He finally showed up 10 hours later. As an infection resulting from the birth progressed and she became sicker and sicker, he continued to go to work and felt she was asking for too much help and indulgence. She was soon hospitalized as the infection progressed to a life-threatening level. He came to visit her only twice during the entire week she was hospitalized.

The husband agrees that these are true and not exaggerated accounts of his behavior. He admits that he has made a few mistakes in judgment and in managing his priorities, but he has apologized and he believes she "just can't let these drop." She is not able to move beyond them. But the problem these incidents represent continues to recur in their life together, even though the current stories are less dramatic. The issue of how he spends his time and the apparently low priority she has in his life continues to plague her. He does not take vacations nor have they gone away for weekends. His involvement with work, he agrees, is excessive; but he loves it, and his customers have come to expect the kind of service he gives them.

THERAPEUTIC INTERVENTION

The therapy focused at one level on his examining the consequences for the relationship of his continuing to place work first and his wife second. His philosophy is that she can wait "because I have provided her with such a luxurious material life free of so many burdens the average gal has to do," and this is central in shaping his behavior. He has a strong and loud voice which seems to take up most of the space in my office. She seems to have given up on making her point. He finds a way of out-arguing her and she quickly becomes quiet and shrugs in resignation. I work with her in his presence to help her validate her rage and anger at his neglect in those critical years and to reclaim her voice. I encourage her to see the legitimacy of her position so that rather than asking just to have lunch with him once in a while, she will ask for far more significant amounts of time—such as a vacation together without their son.

I work with him on the only opening he offers—he does not want another marital failure. I suggest that just as he built a successful business with his devotion of time and energy, he would have to make the time for a successful marriage—another kind of "business" which needs the same attention to detail. He was not easily moved. He frequently cancelled sessions because he had to leave town or visit with important clients. These missed sessions were discussed and their meaning to his wife examined. Eventually, he began to get the message and made some minor changes in his time commitments. But the situation remained basically the same.

The problem, as I see it, is that the wife's lack of leverage inside the marriage is due in large part to her lack of economic power outside the marriage. If she did leave the marriage, what positions and salaries would be open to her, given her lack of education and limited work experience?

She would not even be able to earn a middle-class income, let along support herself and child in a way that approached her current standard of living. Her moodiness and withdrawal appear to be all she has left.

Despite the obvious problems, I need to try to help her increase her leverage interpersonally in the marriage by lessening her economic dependence on her husband. I broach the idea of her working outside the home and suggest plans for continuing her education. He responds strongly that she should remain at home. She, for her part, is reluctant to try these options, given that her work would be so menial in comparison to his, and her pay would be of little consequence to the family budget. If she really wanted to work, he claims, she could work for him and have more flexibility and free time. (His need for her to have more flexibility and free time, of course, argues that she give him precisely what he is unwilling to give her.) They both agree that at least one person should have the sort of open time necessary to make a family work. Of course, the "most logical person" is the wife. After all, he makes so much more money than she ever could.

What then about her going to school to get a degree that could increase her economic viability? First, she is not interested in a degree. Second, she thinks that because he would be happier with a wife who has a college degree, the idea is more reflective of his agenda than hers. Paradoxically, not getting the degree for her is a way to hold on to her sense of self against how he would like her to be.

Unfortunately, my attempt to help her become more economically self-sufficient, and thus to give her more leverage in the marriage and to protect her from continued economic dependence on her husband, failed. It seems that the higher the husband's income, the more difficult it is to effect a change in the relational power dynamics of a marriage. His economic power organizes not only his time and sense of self-worth, but her behavior and sense of self as well. She sees herself identified in some way with his economic worth and so participates indirectly and directly in creating a reality that is both enriched by his money and simultaneously constrained by it. Despite all their arguments, it is interesting that on the issue of her not working outside the home, they were united. This unity reflects the force of the economic framework of their shared reality.

The case was not a total failure, however; I feel good about my encouragement and support of the wife—the help I was able to give her in regaining her voice and getting her position heard. She came to see that her complaints were not the ravings of a hysterical, spoiled little girl, but legitimate concerns about the quality of their marital life together. Therapy was effective in getting the husband to take more seriously the wife's concerns about the quality and quantity of their marital time. The husband agreed to set time aside for a vacation together—beginning with a weekend and eventually agreeing to a week's vacation. Uninterrupted by work, the couple felt closer. The time symbolized for her his commitment to her and helped her feel that she was an important priority in his life. Some of her rage dissipated. There were no dramatic or fancy interventions here.

CONCLUSION

In marriages where there is considerable disparity of earning power between husband and wife, my efforts to move the wife in the direction of greater economic independence often fail. In this case, the couple left with more recreational time together, more understanding of the impact of their family-of-origin and sibling position on their styles in the marriage, some mild changes in the way money was managed, humorous ways of thinking about his workaholism, and some real appreciation of their differences, but no *significant* change in her power in the relationship. His work continues to come first. We negotiated for greater control over the household budget and hiring and firing of the people who work for them, but he can alter her decisions at any time, and she has no choice but to go along with him. Even his agreement to her having more say over the spending of money means little, for he will still ultimately decide the legitimacy of her requests, her desires, her dreams. Her leverage in the marriage is permanently limited by her lack of economic power. I leave the case feeling powerless myself. The change that needs to occur is bigger than both of us.

REFERENCE

Goldner, V. (1989). Generation and gender: Normative and covert hierarchies. In M. McGoldrick, C. M. Anderson, & F. Walsh (Eds.), *Women in families: A framework for family therapy* (pp. 42–60). New York: Norton.

13

BETTY CARTER

"Everything I Do Is for the Family"

THE MOST DIFFICULT marital cases are those in which both husband and wife are intensely afraid of the consequences of change. The husband, typically, does not readily embrace change that seems to, and probably *does*, cause him to lose privilege or his primary focus on his career goals. The wife may fear, quite correctly, that pushing for such a change may cost her her marriage. If his eye wanders from time to time, he may be comparing her to other women—while she compares him to solitude. Much will depend, too, on her age, her income, and the number and ages of her children. As Taffel (Taffel & Masters, 1989) has observed, these variables may strongly influence the degree of risk a woman is willing to take to promote change in her marriage.

Gene and Sally McKeon came to see me because Sally's depression had become so intense that she did not want to go away with Gene for a weekend. As she put it, going away was "too much trouble." They were both about 35 years old, he pale, rigid, all briefcase and three-piece suit; she red-eyed, weepy, and tense.

Within the first half hour, I asked each of them what kind of work they did and how much income they earned. Gene sputtered and looked embarrassed, then said angrily that he worked at an investment firm and earned over $150,000. I understood his anger to mean that this was none of my business, and I ignored it. Sally told me that she had a social work degree and worked part-time as an adoption counselor, earning about

$10,000 a year. She explained that her main job was running the house and raising their children — a seven-year-old boy and twin three-year-old girls.

I asked what impact their earning disparity had on their decision-making process. He snapped, "None!" She said, "Well, of course, I don't really feel I can insist on anything that costs money — or even fight for it very strongly. I really feel I have to defer to his wishes most of the time." Gene immediately assured her that such a position was not necessary. "Everything I make is yours, too," he said.

It took about another half-hour for her to connect her depression to the loneliness and resentment she felt night after night, after a day and evening with the children, waiting for Gene to come home at eight or nine o'clock. Because she felt unable to ask for herself, she asked for the children: "Gene, they need you. You never see them all week. They're growing up without you." Gene's jaw set and he said firmly, "Don't try to guilt-trip me, Sally. You know that everything I do is for the family. Don't you see how exhausted *I* am from this schedule? It can't be helped." She dropped her confronting manner and reassured him. We returned to this stone wall many times in the next few sessions, and, each time, Sally backed away.

Sally came alone to the fourth session, saying that Gene did not want to come anymore because the sessions were not helpful and only "stirred things up." I asked what she wanted, and she said she would like to make some changes in her own life and felt she could do that on her own, without coming to therapy "and upsetting Gene."

A year later, the couple came to see me again because of marital conflict. Gene looked the same, but Sally was "dressed for success" and looked quite cheerful. She had switched to a higher paying job and increased her professional hours significantly. She made twice as much money but was only half as tired, she said, because *over Gene's objections*, she had insisted on a live-in housekeeper. "And, furthermore, I don't think we're ready for therapy yet. Gene still won't change his work schedule, and I know I can't make him do it. But he's here today to try to change me back." She turned out to be right, so no further appointment was made.

I have not seen Gene and Sally in six months. Sometimes I wonder: Is Sally waiting for the children to get older or for her own income to reach the place where she can afford to escalate her confrontations with Gene, even though she will risk divorce? Has she already decided to divorce him? Is she having an affair or looking for one? In any case, I know she is on the move and I expect to see her again.

REFERENCE

Taffel, R., & Masters, R. (1989). An evolutionary approach to revolutionary change: The impact of gender arrangements on family therapy. In M. McGoldrick, C. M. Anderson, & F. Walsh (Eds.), *Women in families: A framework for family therapy* (pp. 117–134). New York: Norton.

14

BARBARA ELLMAN

Sleeping Beauty

IT IS DIFFICULT TO IMAGINE a time in history when women were faced with a more challenging set of paradoxes in their relationships with men than our time. Clinically, it is a gross simplification to say that what women want today is only equality, power, and respect. Although these are certainly the goals of our time, they are not inclusive of all that women desire. Sometimes these same goals are experienced by women as conflicting with other goals and desires, particularly the desire to be taken care of, to be looked after. One could argue that, *ideally*, having equality, power, and respect need not negate the experience of feeling cared for. In *reality*, women experience one or the other, or they live in a state of ambivalence and confusion. When women are conflicted in this way, their desire to feel powerful is often compromised.

In my office, I rarely see women come in with that look of malaise and confusion so well described by Friedan in *The Feminine Mystique* a generation ago. My clients (all white, predominantly professional) are women who, for the most part, know that their dilemma has a name—inequality, lack of status, disrespect, powerlessness—but they find it difficult to view themselves as the agents of change. They have claimed just enough from the feminist critique to be able to voice their anger and hurt; however, most are unable to go any further.

Why is it that these articulate women can be so clear about what ails them and yet be immobilized? Through feminism, we have learned that women are unable to see themselves as agents of change because they have been systematically denied the important opportunities—opportunities that are critical for coming to see oneself as powerful, as an agent, as an author, or as a hero/protagonist of one's own story. The feminist position points out that widespread prejudices in the culture continue to distort for women any capacity to see themselves as active agents, as powerful, self-determining actors throughout the life cycle.

The story of femininity, which is the classic story for women, is about waiting, lying in repose, being fragile, and being a victim seeking rescue. All the heroines waited for powerful heroes who had control, authority, and influence over others to make things happen. With this as our paradigmatic myth—women as helpless/powerless while men exert power over others—it is remarkable that women have been able to have the vision, and then summon the courage, to assert their desire for power at all! We all need to experience ourselves as powerful—not as having "power over others," but as having "the ability to act or produce an effect" on our own behalf. When we are able to experience ourselves as powerful, we are at our best, our most creative. We are most alive.

Waiting and acting are difficult to reconcile. With stories of waiting as women's collective mythology, in addition to the real denial to women of opportunities to experience themselves as powerful, it is no wonder that women are unclear about the acceptability of being powerful. Women are ill at ease and inexperienced in seeing themselves as powerful, often demonstrating a confusing mixture of assertion on the one hand and marked passivity on the other. Their general ambivalence regarding power (and even recognition) in their intimate relationships with men makes women's side of the heterosexual dilemma particularly painful. Add to this the husband's attitude and behaviors towards his wife's power, and the problems increase exponentially. The husband may feel threatened by his wife's developing sense of personal power and may attempt to intimidate his wife by tactics meant to "put her in her place." He may become hostile, turn away from her through work or another woman, or he may become seriously depressed. Tragically, neither the husband nor the wife realizes that it is precisely the wife's lack of power that contributes to the relationship's lack of authenticity and energy. Assisting the couple to see that it is in *both* their interests that the wife find her power should be the goal of the family therapist.

NICOLE AND STEVEN

Nicole and Steven have been married 10 years. Steven is seven years older than Nicole, is professionally respected, and provides their entire income. Nicole, a student without a source of income, feels her lower status whenever she is with him, even at home. Nicole reports that she never experiences this level of inferiority when Steven is not present. This observation, along with her experience of Steven's tendency to insist that all attention be on him (a tendency he acknowledges), leads Nicole to conclude that she is overwhelmed in this relationship by a much too powerful partner. To her credit, Nicole has little problem pointing out to Steven when she feels overwhelmed; she tells him when she experiences his needs as unfairly overshadowing hers, and she confronts Steven each time that his verbal remarks make her feel disrespected or dismissed. However, as they both acknowledge, their marriage is deadlocked, lacking vitality and intimacy.

Typically, Steven either begins the sessions or attempts to steer a session towards his agenda, while Nicole impressively holds her reality, comments on the attempted maneuver, and appropriately describes her feelings about what has occurred. When I asked Nicole what is preventing her from setting the agenda or taking the lead, Nicole remarked, "Do you know how well I'm doing just to stay with my experience, not to rescue Steven when he starts talking about his hurt, not to try to fix it, take his stuff on, feel guilty, leave the room, or worse—deny that I have feelings, too? This takes a tremendous amount of energy, and I cannot do anything more than this."

For six years Nicole had made Steven's needs and desires center stage, believing that Steven was the more important person in their relationship. Following a two-year depression, Nicole started taking courses at the local college and joined a women's study group. Nicole began to steadfastly refuse to be affected by this man and focused virtually all of her emotional energy in keeping him away. All his attempts at connection were experienced by Nicole as intrusion or excessive neediness.

I agreed with Nicole that working hard not to fall into the many mine traps drained a great deal of energy; staying clear of feeling responsible for Steven's feelings was particularly difficult since, in this culture, women are taught to feel responsible for the feelings of those they love. I added that she may be equally correct about her inability "to do anything more." However, the system they were now participating in still maintained Steven in his position of power and as the one in the relationship who feels entitled to set the agenda, speak his opinion, and change the subject.

Although Nicole had learned how to protect herself in her relationship, the development of her own sense of power was severely curtailed. I informed Nicole that I would like to help her get in touch with her wants, needs, and desires, in addition to holding her boundaries. In this way, she could experience more of her self, and then, secondarily, energize the relationship.

It was essential that the order of priorities be heard by both Nicole and Steven and that Nicole's finding her feelings, her dreams, and her voice be the first order of business. It was also essential that I point out to Steven the reason for this priority: Until Nicole had more of herself, Steven would not have her either. Nicole admitted that the idea that she might say something that would hurt Steven was stopping her from finding her voice, that it was intolerable for her to think of herself as someone who could hurt another individual. I told her that I was committed to helping her discover her needs as well as helping her tolerate whatever might come up for her as she let Steven know her truth. I also encouraged Nicole to begin the next session – not merely as a superficial structural change – but to help her start experiencing herself in a more assertive capacity. I told Steven that I would support him as he began the difficult and potentially painful process of listening to Nicole's feelings.

Over a number of sessions, when Steven was able to trust that I was equally committed to his well-being, he acknowledged that he would prefer to have Nicole be an active partner rather than the passive object that he had regrettably helped to create. (Steven was helped to see his role through our explorations of his family of origin and by drawing on the cultural prescriptions and social expectations that he, as a man, had been taught.) I suggested to Steven that he would forever be seen as the manipulative and controlling partner if Nicole did not have a strong and clear voice in this relationship, regardless of his best intentions. I pointed out to both of them that Nicole was now faced with the very difficult task of finding what had meaning for her and that this was the only hope for Nicole as well as for the relationship.

There was nothing in her experience to encourage Nicole to explore this direction. All her training, as a daughter in her home and as a good girl in the world, had oriented her towards experiencing herself in relation to how successful she was in nurturing and supporting her husband. Although Nicole may have been prepared by our early sessions for balancing her old role as caretaker with attention to self, what she was not prepared for was the challenge of the responsibility of creating a more vital and authentic place for herself in this marriage. There were several times when Nicole didn't like my turning the attention on her; yet, throughout, she was always able to communicate that she understood that I was nudging her to take herself seriously. She admitted to me that she found the entire prospect terrifying. We talked about how social constraints on women make taking ourselves seriously a bold act, and we explored her family of origin for clues as to why Nicole would find becoming powerful particularly terrifying. Nicole was eventually able to develop greater self-compassion, as well as receive genuine understanding and empathy from Steven. In return, Steven experienced a more authentic and responsive partner. Certainly, this was a substantial bonus for their relationship.

JANE AND PHILIP

A related component for women in their dilemma regarding power is their confusion, as well as that of their partner, about what is real and what is a role. An example of such confusion can be seen in my work with Jane and Philip. They came to see me after 11 years of marriage. Jane initiated the therapy because her attorney had suggested that before seeking a divorce she should attempt marital therapy regarding issues of distrust, intense disappointment, and emotional distance. Even though they had reported several traumas in the course of their marriage, and a recent incident suggesting possible infidelity, Jane came to most sessions sounding like a cheerleader for family values and revealing very little about her own needs and disappointments.

It was not until the sixth session, after much encouragement and prodding by me, that Jane let out a steady stream of anger: she had sacrificed friendships and ties by moving so many times; she had not been able to have more children; she had grown weary of struggling to keep the family together, etc. When she was finished, Philip looked dumbfounded. I told him that I could appreciate how shocked he was since he had never heard the list at one sitting. I asked him to hold on while I went back to Jane. I told Jane that I appreciated how hard it was for her to say out loud what her experience had been, since she had been taught that what she did through the years as Philip's wife was simply to be expected. I listed all her losses and pointed out how she had been taught to believe that she must accept every single one without complaint and without a thought about herself. I added, "This is your tragedy—the tragic error of believing that you had to do all of this without any thought, feelings, or need for yourself." I pointed out that this error was born of being a woman, that she had been taught not to think of herself, and that, in complying, she had been left with the choice of denial (her cheerleading) or resentment and rage at her spouse for giving her so little in return. For his part, Philip certainly knew that Jane had had a difficult time throughout the marriage, but rarely gave Jane a thought regarding how upset she might be personally. Philip had come to believe that Jane and her role were one and the same. So had she. Neither Philip nor Jane had ever considered that Jane would need to become stronger, more powerful, if anything in the marriage was going to get appreciably better.

Jane had found her most fulfilling role in cheerleading, while her husband made the touchdowns and the fumbles, and her son was in training. It was here that she thought she was her most powerful—seeing to the welfare of her charges. However, experience had taught her how fundamentally powerless she was over her husband's successes or failures. Placing all her energy and ambition outside herself had left her dependent on her husband's accomplishments to make her feel that her effort was worthwhile. When he failed to acknowledge her, or failed outright, Jane found herself susceptible to resentment, jealousy, and strains of paranoia. Jane was doing all the things she had been taught to do, and all the while getting further away from herself.

It was not difficult for Jane to realize how she had come to choose the particular path she was on. She had given her love and admiration to her stay-at-home mother who was married to a relatively high-ranking corporate executive, whom Jane also admired. As Jane began to trust me, she allowed me to challenge her with present and future choices that would acknowledge her intelligence and power. It became very exciting to her to begin to imagine herself with other choices. She elected to go back to teaching, found an evening in the week for herself, and began hanging up her pom-poms.

It is interesting to note that Philip sent Jane flowers the afternoon that I confronted her. He said that my telling Jane that she had made an error in her life was terribly strong stuff and that Jane needed some love and cheer. In spite of his possible hidden agenda, I told Philip that I thought his response was wonderful and encouraged him to keep cheering her on as she discovered more and more of herself.

WIVES AND POWER

These two women that I have described are not unusual in my practice. I am blessed with being able to work with some wonderful women who are attempting to change themselves in spite of their rather stereotypical marriages. The men are generally mystified, often threatened, and usually terrified that their marriages will end before they figure out what went wrong. It is one of my jobs to help the men understand their past role in hindering the women from becoming more powerful, and to assist them in developing a more empathic and supportive position to their wives' changes. It is also my job to show the wives how their actions contribute to their sense of powerlessness and feed "the system." Obviously, not all cases turn out like the two discussed here. Some men choose to leave rather than share the limelight and the power, and some women get scared and retreat back to their old roles. However, the level of change in the couples that push through this challenge convinces me that to hold out a lesser goal is to again ask the women to be less than themselves in the interest of keeping their marriages together. Concomitantly, to back away from challenging the men is to have the men settle for less than they can be.

Many women have been taught to believe that being powerful was for boys only, and they enter therapy with tremendous ambivalence about being seen as powerful. In the course of marital therapy, I provide an atmosphere and a way of thinking about power in relationships that I hope makes it compelling for women to claim their power. I believe the following contributes to this goal:

1. The husbands are in the therapy room with their wives, listening to their wives' fears and doubts about becoming themselves. This tur- moil is often a surprise to the men, since they have virtually never had such difficulty themselves. Additionally, being in the room and hearing their wives' stories evoke deeper understanding and empathy in many men who truly care about their wives.

2. The women are receiving precisely what they have needed but have been unable to orchestrate themselves: someone (the therapist) who cares about their welfare and wants them to become more of them- selves. With their husbands in the room as they struggle to find their more authentic voice, the journey, though terrifying, does not have to signal abandonment.

3. Counter to a wife's fear that power means "power to dominate another," in the feminist family therapy context, power is experi- enced as meaning strength, as individuals being able to summon up the best in themselves and share it with each other.

REFERENCE

Friedan, B. (1963). *The feminine mystique*. New York: Norton.

15

KRIS HALSTEAD

Bell, Book, and Candle

"WHY WOMEN'S GROUPS? We live in a world with men and women, so why not mixed groups?" These are questions often asked by colleagues. Because my answer has to do with women and power, I will present here my rationale for providing women's therapy groups and a particular method I use that developed as a result of my beliefs about group work.

Undeniably, isolation is a powerful factor contributing to the experience of powerlessness. When people are isolated from one another and also systematically pathologized with dehumanizing labels, they feel psychologically powerless and ashamed. Powerlessness and shame, in turn, prevent people from exposing themselves to one another and cause them to isolate all the more. This vicious cycle is a primary result of oppression. When people feel powerless and ashamed, they invalidate their own bodies, minds, spirits, culture, rituals, history, perceptions, conceptions. Since they need all of these aspects of identity to thrive in any system and their own identities have been invalidated, they borrow approved identities from the people in power.

One of the most blatant examples of this cycle of invalidation was evident during the enslavement of Africans in America. For example, in order to promote isolation, theories held that it was dangerous for slaves to be allowed to interact with their families. In fact it was believed that they would rather not do so and that women slaves would rather be sexually involved with their "beloved" owners than with their own husbands. To promote cooperation, there were theories that slaves who wished to escape suffered from a mental disease known as drapetomania. The treatment for slaves with drapetomania was "whipping the devil out of them." Any desire on the part of the slaves to band together or to flee the oppression of their enslavement was considered an aberration. These notions were integrated by many slaves into their own self-concept. Slavery, in all forms, can be so effectively maintained through isolation and diminishment that force and punishment are rarely necessary.

What has this example to do with psychotherapy? Psychotherapy, when done well, increases self-esteem by increasing a sense of self and by working specifically against isolation and diminishment. To experience the self, I believe, we must be able to experience ourselves in a context over which we have ownership. Slaves have no ownership over anything; on the contrary, they are owned. I must experience myself in *my* body, *my* mind, *my* house, *my* family, *my* belief system, *my* spirituality. I must know as mine the patterns and tendencies that motivate me, and I must experience ownership over the plans and proposals I make. Many women come into my office without a sense of this ownership of themselves. They feel isolated, diminished, and enslaved. The powerlessness and shame resulting from loss of ownership of self cause women today, as it did the slaves of yesterday, to adopt the theories, rituals, customs, attitudes, belief systems, and behaviors of the people who have the power.

One of the greatest benefits of women's groups happens when a woman looks into the eyes of another woman and says, "I know what you mean." The validation is transforming. Women come into therapy needing to be validated and strengthened enough so that they can begin to experience competency about creating their own theories, customs, attitudes, beliefs, and behaviors. Thus, group therapy is consciousness-raising with the added opportunity of changing old patterns and trying out new ones.

A group focus on spirituality is particularly empowering. Spiritual rituals and customs are traditionally used to celebrate important passages and transitions in life. One of the first things that an oppressive force does in order to subjugate a people is to attack their spiritual customs. The next thing this oppressive force does is to impose its own spiritual customs on the people to be subjugated. Spirituality under the rule of "God the Father" has estranged women throughout history from spiritual power and, as a result, from all power.

In women's therapy groups, women can, together, remember and help each other remember what the important transitions of their own lives have been. Many women have forgotten. As women begin tentatively to identify their important experiences, they speak about these to one another: childbirth, menstruation, coming out, ending a marriage, forming a healthy marriage, changing a name, finding a job, confronting an abuser, remembering abuse and relinquishing responsibility for it, recovering from an addiction, and so on.

Once remembered, these transitions and passages call out to be celebrated. In group therapy, women can learn to put aside the rubrics and rules of someone else's celebrations and create their own. As women begin to identify the materials to which they have access, they take them as materials of celebration. In other words, they learn that these materials are not mystical, magical substances belonging only to the elect. They are things like flowers, rocks, candles, water, salt, music, fabric, bread, herbs; these are the stuff of the universe taken from fire, air, earth, and water.

Women also begin to identify their own creativity, and this recognition enables them to create a simple ritual with the stuff around them for the transitions they experience—a ritual to cleanse or to empower or to grieve or to share joy. As the group matures, rituals, initially done only occasionally, also mature and become specific to the needs and personality of a particular group. It has been enriching for me to see the women in my therapy groups reclaim a sense of themselves as they learn to celebrate themselves and to see them celebrate themselves with authority and competence as they reclaim themselves.

Healing rituals are particularly poignant and enriching. I encourage my women clients to make a home altar. Women throughout history have been the makers and keepers of home altars. In many cultures, women of color create a space where they place candles, flowers, pictures (the child who died, the hero, the freedom fighter). It seems natural to women to build altars. I encourage my women clients to create a space where they can honor their strength and growth with symbols. Women choose such symbols as a picture of a favorite grandmother, a picture of themselves as children, seashells, crystals, recovery literature, candles, incense. These altars are living, changing altars. They change with fresh flowers, a newly discovered stone, a shell found while walking on the beach, a new picture of the forgiven and reclaimed self, the recent work of one's hands.

On occasion, I have asked women to bring something from their altar into group. These symbols of growth are placed on a table or on the floor, in the center of the circle along with candles, incense, flowers, any of the elements of celebration. In silence, we look at the elements, honoring each others' stories as we do. Each woman then speaks a few words about the meaning of her symbol, and we all hear, in a new way, about her work in therapy. The best rituals are simple, quiet, including time for reflection, emanating from the women in the group and ending with an "Amen" statement in the form of "That was great," "I feel so good," "I'm not sure what that was all about," "Thanks," "Wow."

I highly recommend this kind of work. It adds joy to freedom-seeking.

16

JO-ANN KRESTAN

The Baby and the Bathwater

I HAVE SPENT THE MAJORITY of my career trying to facilitate the inter-
face between systems thinking and alcoholism counseling. I have been
an apologist for AA (Alcoholics Anonymous) within family therapy circles
and an apologist and a spokesperson for family therapy within the "recovery" movement. Currently, I have been thinking about the notions of
power and powerlessness within AA. Some of this thought has been
prompted by the feminist critique of "codependency," a critique that I
have been part of since 1986. A consultation with a feminist colleague
challenged me further. Her client seemed unable to stay sober without
AA but her feminism limited her comfort within AA. Our talk underlined
my need to think through my emerging ideas about powerlessness and
feminism. These thoughts are very much in process. Here, however, I
want to share a few reflections on the current 12-step self-help movements
and then address the necessity of experiencing powerlessness in order to
free oneself from addiction.

In recent years, the concept of Adult Children of Alcoholics has led to
the more general Adult Children of Dysfunctional Families. The concept
grew because thousands of people identified themselves as having the
characteristics listed in Woititz' *Adult Children of Alcoholics* (1981). The
characteristics included statements such as, "I don't know what normal
is" and "I have a fear of abandonment." So many people found themselves
in Woititz' descriptions, even though they, in fact, had no alcoholism
in their families of origin, that a new term was born: Adult Children of

Dysfunctional Families. Subsequently, codependency all but replaced both earlier phrases as a catchword for traits such as controlling others or overly focusing on the lives of others. *Codependent No More* by Beattie (1987) became such a successful book that it spawned innumerable imitations and derivatives. An entirely new health care industry has come into being which includes, among other elements, inpatient treatment programs for "codependency" that are insurance reimbursable.

What is it about these movements that elicits such profound recognition from the public? People recognize that something is wrong with the family. Women recognize themselves in the descriptions of codependency that outline the ways in which they focus on everyone but themselves. These recognitions are only partial, however, because people attribute these problems to personal rather than political origins. It is the institution of family—the "normal" American family—that is and has always been dysfunctional because it is a patriarchal structure, and the codependency now ascribed almost exclusively to the women in that family is a natural outgrowth of women's socialization under that patriarchy. Of course, women focus more on everyone else's lives than on their own—they have been trained to do so. Family structures that maintain and institutionalize an inequality of relational, emotional, and functional responsibility are dysfunctional for all members of the family. Nonetheless, in ignorance and denial of the social roots of family dysfunction or "codependency," women embrace the term codependent as a self-descriptive label and thus pathologize themselves.

Recently, there has been much feminist criticism of the concept of codependency and, at the same time, criticism of Alcoholics Anonymous, the prototypical self-help movement (Bepko & Krestan, 1990; Haney, 1989; Johnson, 1989; Krestan & Bepko, 1990). Feminists charge that codependency is a woman-blaming label in that much of the behavior included in the concept is culturally prescribed as proper behavior for women. Women are then pathologized with this "diagnosis" for following these cultural prescriptions. As feminists see it, the problem with the behavior is not personal in its source, but cultural; yet people—primarily women—still receive the label. As for Alcoholics Anonymous and the other programs following its model, feminists raise concerns about the implications for women of the male and patriarchal origins of the male language (e.g., God, His), and the focus on the disease concept of alcoholism. Specifically regarding the latter, critics charge that these programs direct women's anger at their "disease" without embedding this "disease" in the larger context of women's place in an oppressive society—the proper target of women's anger. Most relevant for our purposes here is the criticism regarding the concept of powerlessness, a concept that is a central part of self-help dogma. With variations in wording, admission that "we are powerless over alcohol and because of it our lives are unmanageable" is the first step of all of the 12-step programs.

As should be clear, I agree with most of the feminist criticism of the concept of codependency and much of the criticism of AA and its derivatives. But while we are draining the bathtub of water, there is one baby I would like to save. I want to defend the usefulness and importance of the concept of powerlessness. The question is whether a feminist can, in good conscience, encourage a woman to accept the idea of powerlessness of any sort. All of the 12-step programs have steps stating that recovery includes "admission of powerlessness" over alcohol, codependency, food, and so on, and acceptance of "turning our will and life over to the care of God, as we understand Him or a Higher Power." Within AA, some groups are replacing the term God with Goddess; others are struggling to find gender-neutral language.

Can a feminist embrace powerlessness? I believe that the problem of addiction is, at its heart, a problem of power, the replacement of rightful "power to" with a misguided and exceedingly male idea of "power over." Other feminist critics of AA believe that women need to have power as responsibility, power to control their own lives, autonomy, and the power of choice. I agree that women need this power. Addiction unfortunately robs women, as it does men, of precisely that kind of power. My colleague, Claudia Bepko, has written about "alcoholism *as* oppression" (Bepko, 1989).

The use of "power" and "powerlessness" within AA is actually very specific. Admission of powerlessness over the chemical is the requisite admission that is part of "recovery." The serenity prayer that is recited at many meetings illustrates another use of "powerlessness." "God grant me the serenity to accept the things I cannot change, courage to change the things I can, and wisdom to know the difference." In the parlance of the program, acceptance of what one "cannot change" refers to an inability to have power over the chemical. It does not refer to a generalized powerlessness over one's life. Another lesson at meetings is that one is powerless to change other people, places, and things. Does not our empowerment as women start from changing our own beliefs about entitlement?

Frequently clients are uncomfortable with the idea of a Higher Power. I say to them, "I don't even care if you accept a Higher Power; I only care that you get it that you're not it." Women or men in the grip of an addiction often feel that they can control or change what they cannot change. Understanding that you are not the Higher Power, that you are one part of a system, addresses false ideas of control. In addiction, the failure to accept what Kurtz refers to as "essential limitation" leads to what Bateson called an incorrect epistemology, the belief that one *is* God (Bateson, 1972; Kurtz, 1982). The failure to accept limitation is at the heart of the problem of all addiction. It is a failure to answer the question, "How much is enough?" It is a failure to understand that the attempt to have power-over is not empowerment, but rather it is a flight from related-ness, actually a flight from the female. Surrendering what Sartre called the "project to be God," the project to have power-over, is the necessary, although paradoxical, precondition of power-to. Power-to is the power of choice unconstrained by addiction. I believe that surrender of the need for power-over can lead to empowerment for women.

I have a final word about the structure of AA and its relationship to feminist criticism. Although AA is indeed patriarchal in origin, I believe that it is feminine, if not feminist, in its structure. AA is governed by 12 traditions, unlike its myriad offshoots. The 12 traditions ensure a method of governing that is collective. Each group proceeds by consensus, and the traditions clearly state that anonymity is the spiritual foundation of the program and that members must always place "principles above personali-ties." Personal ambition has no place in AA. It is nonhierarchical, mutual, celebratory of community. Rather than encouraging the kind of false autonomy that represents the pursuit of conventional male ends, AA validates interdependence.

The recognition of interdependence is one of the only possible solu-tions to the problems of our planet. It is power-over that has been our addiction—power-over, and willful ignorance of limitation. These lead naturally to a focus on the other and thereby undermine our appropriate focus on ourselves. Moreover, the illusions that support the addiction to power must in turn be maintained by self-medication and abuse of a chemical. The personal and interpersonal solutions to the addiction to power are the foundation for the societal fight to change oppressive struc-tures without disqualifying oneself by the distorted judgment rendered by alcohol.

REFERENCES

Bateson, G. (1972). *Steps to an ecology of mind*. New York: Chandler.

Beattie, M. (1987). *Codependent no more*. New York: Harper/Hazelden.

Bepko, C. (1989). Disorders of power: Women and addiction in the family. In M. McGoldrick, C. Anderson, & F. Walsh (Eds.), *Women in families: A framework for family therapy* (pp. 406–426). New York: Norton.

Bepko, C., & Krestan, J. (1990). *Too good for her own good: Breaking free from the burden of female responsibility* (pp. 406–426). New York: Harper & Row.

Haney, E. (1989). *Vision and struggle: Meditations on feminist spirituality and politics*. Portland, ME: Astarte Shell Press.

Johnson, S. (1989). *Wildfire: Igniting the she/volution*. Albuquerque, NM: Wildfire Books.

Krestan, J., & Bepko, C. (1990). Codependency: The social reconstruction of female experience. *Smith College Studies in Social Work, 60*, 216–232.

Kurtz, E. (1982). Why AA works: The intellectual significance of Alcoholics Anonymous. *Journal of Studies on Alcohol, 41*(1), 38–80.

Woititz, J. (1981). *Adult children of alcoholics*. Pompano Beach, FL: Health Communications.

17

DEBORAH ANNA LUEPNITZ

Foucault, Feminism, and Prosecuting Daddies

Every woman adores a Fascist, The boot in the face, the brute Brute heart of a brute like you. <div align="right">S. Plath "Daddy"</div>	Power is everywhere not because it embraces everything but because it comes from everywhere. <div align="right">M. Foucault *The History of Sexuality*</div>

IN *THE FAMILY INTERPRETED* (1988), I described the clinical attempt to reconcile a contrite father with the adolescent daughter he had once abused sexually. Here I will describe a case in which I helped a mother use the power of the state against her husband and then discuss the issues raised in the terms of French philosopher Michel Foucault, one of this century's principal theorists of power.

CASE

Eve Linden, a homemaker in her late 40s, phoned me about a week after walking in on her husband, Kenneth, who was having sex with their 14-year-old daughter, Sandra. She learned that it had been going on for two years and that he had also fondled the 10-year-old daughter, Pam, who had refused after the third time. Kenneth, a successful engineer, was regarded highly in the community but was a bully at home.

Eve, emotionally shattered by the discovery, sought advice from a number of sources. The family doctor advised her to tell the girls that the sexual activity was not their fault and to let Kenneth "cool off" before coming back. Eve asked about taking legal action, but the doctor was against it. "That," he said, "would be too hard on the girls." Eve phoned a psychiatrist who advised her to reassure the girls that she still loved them. But an arrest? "Imagine their guilt if he went to jail. Prosecuting daddies is too hard on children." Eve decided to make one more call, "wondering if a woman might see it differently." I told her that I agreed with the point made by the other professionals to the extent that the girls might well feel guilty if they helped send their Daddy to jail. However, what worried me – and worries me more – is what we say to daughters – and fathers and sons – when arrests are not made. If he had had sex with the children next door, the act would be called criminal. By what logic does blood relation diminish the transgression?

Eve was waiting for someone to encourage her. Kenneth was arrested, although quickly released on bail. During the months before trial, he threatened Eve and refused professional help, just as he had throughout the marriage. Eve's lawyer supported her decision to press charges, but to her chagrin, *not* because he was confident of a conviction. Said the lawyer, "Your case is strong because you caught him in the act, but everything still depends on what kind of judge you get. However, if you *don't* press charges, the whole thing could disappear from history, and Ken could get joint custody of the girls."

Every day brought new advice, new threats from Ken. He took Eve's car and most of her money. Kenneth left warnings on Eve's answering machine to drop the charges, and she played them for me. I was glad to hear his voice and searched it for clues about him. I am interested in his story, but he has chosen not to tell it. All I know is that Eve and Kenneth met when they were young, and she admired him greatly; he seemed "charismatic and sure of himself." She had waited on him for many years, did as he said, and had frequent sex with him in the unusual ways he liked it. She had never been employed in her life and had certainly never spoken with a lawyer.

Eve has done superbly well – working two jobs, taking good care of her daughters and son, and writing copiously in a journal from which she reads to me occasionally.

Kenneth plea-bargained and was sentenced to four years in prison. He agreed to enter a guilty plea on condition that the girls remain present while he was sentenced. Eve accepted the plea-bargain, thus eliminating the need for a jury trial, and sparing the girls the embarrassment of testifying.

Kenneth was taken directly to jail. Both Sandra and Pam said that they had slept well that night for the first time. They sent word to me that I should help more mothers press charges against abusive fathers.

I have said little about the daughters because in the first year I worked primarily with their mother. Both girls were doing well in school and with peers. Although both girls had some somatic symptoms, they refused to attend more than a few sessions, saying they were sick of being made to talk. Eve asked if she should insist on their compliance, but together we decided that such a course was out of the question. The door would remain open, and, in the meantime, Eve would begin psychoanalytic psychotherapy with me. Through exploring her personal history and the transference/countertransference relationships, we have worked on the problem of her diminished sense of agency, her search for an overpowering authority, her dealings with the older daughter who is constantly testing her love. I have treated the daughters through my work with Eve. When the younger one started hearing a man walking around upstairs, Eve had the idea of asking a priest to come and bless each room of the house. This visit seemed to help.

A year has passed since the sentencing, and Sandra has become physically aggressive towards her sister. Sandra, who says she hates her father, seems to embody his brutishness at times. Despite their problems, Sandra and Pam are doing better than my sexually abused patients whose fathers were not apprehended.

What type of power analysis can be brought to bear in this case? I appreciate Foucault's work (1978) because it does not locate power in one place—i.e., in the father alone or in the family alone. A Foucauldian approach would analyze the distinct discourses of the physician, the psychiatrist, the lawyer, the judge, and the feminist therapist, and would look for the technologies of domination and the possibilities for resistance in each of them.

In a similar, but feebler way, family systems theorists, in rejecting a binary notion of power (daughter = victim, father = victimizer), have endeavored to spread the problem around a bit. This effort to move beyond the binary, however, has led to a facile switch in which the mother becomes the "co-abuser" or the "real" problem (see the critique of Boscolo et al. in Luepnitz, 1988). In any case, family systems theorists have placed beyond critique the institution of the family itself and the knowledge bases of which that institution is mutually constitutive. In contrast, Foucault's method is a searching and critical investigation of those structures and shows how the modern state rules through them.

What would such analysis tell clinicians regarding when to jail fathers and when to support rapprochement? Philosophers do not address such points. For practical notions, I recommend the guidelines of Judith Herman's brilliant book, *Father-Daughter Incest* (1981, p. 160). In fact, Foucault offers no easy answers about anything, but his writing provokes the farthest reaching questions. I will give one small example. While preparing to write this piece, I read a comment by a feminist attorney who prosecutes incest perpetrators (in Bass & Davis, 1988, p. 309). Damages, she says, can be won not only in cases where fathers are wealthy. It seems that *homeowners insurance policies* have paid claims to molested minors. "Hooray for those kids," we say. They can pay college tuition and psychotherapy bills. But a Foucauldian reading would require some deconstruction of this business. What exactly does it say about the culture we inhabit, and which inhabits us—specifically, what does it say about our notions of "home" and "ownership"? One implication is that property owners are guaranteed sexual access to the persons within their home. Incest enters that category of accidents and misfortunes that happen to occur on the premises (e.g., falling down icy steps) but that result in injuries the owner did not "intend." (How unsettling it is to think that both mothers and fathers pay into these policies all their lives!)

Now that we have reached the "end of history" and capitalism has triumphed, it is easy to scoff at Proudhon's old dictum that "property is theft." But studying Foucault has made me think again about the exchanges of power in our world, for example among property, knowledge, and the body.

The responsibility for sex crimes must lie only with the criminal. But, the perpetrator's *power* lies not only with the person—usually male—but also "everywhere"—in our monetary structures, our helping professions, our very notions of domesticity. Foucault is certainly right to assert that without the ability to analyze this "everywhere," we generally add our voices to one of the dominant discourses.

I have said too little about desire. Did Eve Linden, in the words of the poet, "adore a Fascist"? Will her daughters? Who will listen to these women without making them the culprits and also without trying to purify their minds and motives? The fact that Sandra did not refuse her father as her sister did, the fact that she was once "very close" to him, cannot be exhausted with the notion of "loyalty" that has been made to work so hard in family therapy. What is the relationship between loyalty and eros, between filial and physical love, between normal and incestuous families?

I have learned much from working with Eve and her daughters, and I hope to continue for a long time. What, then, is the place of my desire in this economy of desires?

This therapeutic work has also been costly to me; it is draining and even dangerous to try and help such families. In the face of this difficulty, we can ask what empowers the *therapist*, if not a community of people with shared values and a set of ideas rigorous and manifold enough to bear their moral weight? For me, the empowering community is the community of feminists. The ideas are the feminist reconstructions of psychoanalysis and of postmodern philosophies such as Foucault's.[1]

REFERENCES

Bass, E., & Davis, L. (1988). *The courage to heal: A guide for women survivors of child sexual abuse*. New York: Harper & Row.

Boscolo, L., Cecchin, G., Hoffman, L., & Penn, P. (1987). *Milan systemic therapy*. New York: Basic Books.

Foucault, M. (1978). *The history of sexuality. Volume I: An introduction* (R. Hurley, Trans.). New York: Random House. (Original work published 1976)

Herman, J. (1981). *Father-daughter incest*. Cambridge, MA: Harvard University Press.

Luepnitz, D. A. (1988). *The family interpreted: Feminist theory in clinical practice*. New York: Basic Books.

Plath, S. (1961). *Ariel*. New York: Harper & Row.

---

[1]Foucault's work has been subject to a number of feminist commentaries. See, for example, Diamond, I. & Quinby, L. (Eds.). (1988). *Feminism and Foucault: Reflections on resistance*. Boston: Northeastern University Press.

18

MONICA MCGOLDRICK

For Love or Money

UNLESS MARITAL THERAPY addresses the economic and power context of marriage, it ignores a crucial aspect of marriage that defines the freedom partners have to negotiate all issues in their relationship, and the freedom they have to leave. Blumstein and Schwartz (1983) and others have demonstrated clearly that the economic balance determines the power balance in most couple relationships. What is the point of addressing the details of a couple's communication if we have not addressed this fact?

Just as I would not consider making an assessment of a couple without knowing something about their ethnic background and family-of-origin experiences, I cannot understand marital problems without knowing the economic viability of each partner, which defines his or her options. I have come to the conclusion that marital therapy is virtually impossible unless the partners are both economically viable.

A specific demonstration of this belief is that on my genograms, above the name and birth date of each partner, I include their personal income and a notation of any inheritance they are likely to receive. I also include the education and employment history of each spouse. Without these facts I believe it is impossible to understand the stance partners take in the therapy room, because without this information we cannot possibly know the reality base from which each partner is operating in the relationship.

Just as I believe that being cut off from family is not good for mental health and so I strive to get people to reconnect with their families, I also strive to get them to be economically viable. I believe it is dangerous not to be economically viable; especially in the face of abuse, divorce, and old age, it is a risk women cannot afford.

Even economic viability does not equalize the power of the partners in a marriage, however, because we are so deeply influenced by the values we absorb from our society about appropriate roles for men and women. The cultural rule is that men marry women who are younger (by three years for first marriages and by six years for second marriages) (Glick, 1979). As a result, men have an ever-increasing pool of women to choose from, and women have an ever-diminishing pool of men to choose from.

We cannot ignore these social facts. We cannot teach women to be more effective in asserting themselves and their needs without considering the real-life consequences that are likely to follow. Generally speaking, unless a woman has someone else waiting in the wings, she cannot use the line: "If you don't change, I'll leave." Things have to be very bad for a woman to decide on such action, because her options after a marital breakup are so limited. Any woman over 40, before putting her marriage on the line—an action that might be necessary to change the relationship— must face the fact that the odds are heavily against her finding another husband.

THE PARADOX OF POWER

There is something paradoxical about the issues of power in marriage. When we try to explore them, we quickly discover some confusing incongruities which seem to stem from the different realms of experience. What makes exploring power issues so complex is that our emotional experience of power on an interpersonal level so often does not fit with what we can see so clearly about power imbalances at a social and cultural level.

Consider parent/child relationships. We can say rather easily that parents have more power than children. Yet we are all familiar with personal situations in which we felt totally controlled by the screams of an infant, the tantrum of a three-year-old, or the sullen, withholding contempt of a teenager.

The power relationship of adult men and women is even more complex, and there is a strong taboo against commenting on it. While men are almost always physically stronger, and we know statistically that real and threatened intimidation of women is a common factor in couple relationships, there is something deep within us (perhaps the will to preserve the species) that resists an emotional awareness of the power imbalance between men and women. The experience of being "in love," for example, grants an emotional power to the one who is loved over the one who loves, regardless of gender or physical, economic, or intellectual power. The general state of emotional dependence also obscures the power relationship between partners. We know, too, that even men who are extremely successful and powerful in politics, business, or the world of ideas, often experience themselves as impotent and unable to handle their family relationships. Furthermore, the abuses of power—sexual and other physical violence, bullying, intimidation, arrogance, and racism and other forms of bigotry—all reflect, paradoxically, a sense of powerlessness, not one of power.

So, our emotional, everyday experience in male/female relationships rarely fits with an analysis of relationships at a social level, e.g., that women have less power to affect the course of their lives and are disqualified in the dominant value system. For example, in the following clinical excerpt, the husband talks about the need for women's liberation as a joke.

HUSBAND   The biggest joke ever foisted on the American people is the idea of women's liberation. Women are the head of most families—I don't know about the Latin family, but I see it myself. If I'm sitting and want to watch a ball game and my wife and daughters come in and want to watch some skier who fell off a cliff and is going to sit in an iron lung for an hour and a half, they'll be watching it, and I'll be sitting out in the kitchen listening to the ball game on the radio.

MM   So you think women dominate men?

HUSBAND   Absolutely. And you know I've never told this to another person in my whole life.

MM   You think your mother dominated your father?

HUSBAND   Totally.

MM   And you think if you were to marry again, you'd fall right into the same thing?

HUSBAND   Certainly.

MM   You know, it's funny, because I think your wife's experience is that you dominate.

HUSBAND   Really? I don't know. This whole thing is so confusing.

I believe that this is this man's experience of women. Men do experience women as powerful. Yet, this husband was physically violent toward his wife and his children for 23 years. In one crisis during therapy, he almost beat the dog to death. When his daughter became enraged at him for the beating, he told her he could beat the dog if he wanted or beat her if he wanted. He could kill the dog if he wanted or kill her if he wanted. He handled the experience of his violence in a way men typically do—he dissociated from it. When he describes being intimidated by his wife, he is not thinking of his behavior when he beat her and his children and left them all intimidated by him. Dissociation, isolation of affect, and splitting are a normal part of the adult male identity. Men are expected to split off their feelings, and, of course, they learn to do it well. Therapy with this man was about helping him overcome his ability to dissociate. He learned over time not to block out the pain of what he did to his family. It became a part of his consciousness that he could no longer forget. He also moved to a position where he no longer saw his wife as being in control.

ADDRESSING THE PROBLEM

So what do we need to do besides becoming more direct about the societal context in which marriages exist? The therapeutic dilemma is how to intervene without alienating the husband or the wife. How do we introduce the political issues without becoming polemical? We cannot respond to people only on the basis of the power imbalance of economics, because they do not live at that level emotionally and therefore often cannot connect to that issue. We meet a similar situation when we work with adolescents whose parents pay the bills for therapy. We do not refuse them therapy because they are not paying for it themselves, but neither can we ignore their dependence.

We need to intervene in ways that empower all family members. We must deal with men's sense of entitlement, their tendency to find women's complaints trivial or boring. Often, the only problem husbands are aware of is wanting their wives to stop complaining. Women are typically overwhelmed by men's apparent reasonableness and their pragmatically oriented question: "What do you want me to *do* to make it better?" What women want is not a quick fix at the behavioral level, but rather subtle changes at the emotional level of feeling, connectedness, and relationship. They want their husbands to share their feelings, their doubts, their hurts, and their dreams.

RULES OF THUMB FOR THERAPISTS

I would like to offer a short list of rules of thumb for therapists. (The term rule of thumb, by the way, originated in the law that a husband could beat his wife only with a stick that was no thicker than a thumb!)

1. Pay attention to the income and work potential of the husband and wife and the implications for the balance of power in their relationship.
2. Pay attention to the relative physical strength of men and women in a family and to the impact of any incident of physical abuse or physical intimidation, however long ago, as a regulator of the balance of power between spouses. Well over 40% of women experience violence by their husbands at some point in the marriage.
3. Help the couple clarify the rules by which male and female roles are chosen and rewarded in their family and on their jobs: who makes decisions, who handles finances, who handles legal matters, who handles emotional matters, who makes the dentist appointments, who buys and wraps birthday presents, who cleans the toilet, and at a meta-level, who determines who makes the rules.
4. Place the couple's attitudes toward male and female roles in context by clarifying the broader political, social, and economic issues of divorce, aging, and child rearing, and encourage each to learn about these matters.
5. Validate the wife in her focus on relationships, yet, at the same time, empower her in the areas of work, money, and participating in the job market. We need to validate *her* ways of being in the world, not just help her accept the "male" value system. We need to help her find more effective ways of dealing with her anger than by blaming herself. Often these tasks will require help other than psychotherapy, such as a Dale Carnegie course or a seminar in money management.
6. Be sensitive to the price husbands have to pay in losing job advancement and, in addition, in being discounted and invalidated by other men if they change their "male" success orientation to give higher priority to relationships, caretaking, and emotional expressiveness. I believe therapy with men is primarily about helping them learn to connect—to overcome their typical dissociation of experiences and feelings.

7. Recognize the importance of sibling relationships and other family relationships as the emotional network of the marriage. It makes no sense to limit our focus to the couple alone simply because the couple presented the problem that way.

8. Urge family members to nurture their friendship systems. For women, close female friendships have been reported as second in importance only to good health for life satisfaction. Men often have no close friends. Yet friendship is an extremely important resource for all of us throughout life.

9. Encourage attention to spiritual values. We need to help couples ask themselves questions about what really matters in life in the long run—the very long run. It is absurd to persist in seeking purely technical, pragmatic, here-and-now solutions to the complex human problem of how to connect with each other and why it matters.

CONCLUSION

I do not accept the cynical view asserted by some that the relational and emotionally expressive aspect of development is intrinsic to women. We need to redefine human development as an evolution toward a mature ability for interdependence, connectedness, and intimacy, as well as for great individual accomplishments. I hope that family therapy can become a force that fosters more latitude for both men and women in their ways of relating to their mates and peers, their work, their community, and their intergenerational connectedness.

REFERENCES

Blumstein, P., & Schwartz, P. (1983). *American couples: Money, work, sex*. New York: William Morrow.

Glick, P. C. (1979). Future American families. *Cofo Memo II, 3*, 1–3.

19

LUCY PAPILLON

Heart to Heart

"I DESPISE MYSELF," Jane said. "I don't just dislike or not care about myself; I actually detest everything about who I am." These words were the first ones spoken by this 35-year-old woman during the latter part of my first session with her and her husband. She had been emotionally and physically abused repeatedly by her husband over the past six years. Throughout most of her childhood, she had been molested by several relatives. She said she felt so damaged that there was nothing redeemable about her.

During the session, her 40-year-old husband, Joe, had talked about her depression and his inability to comprehend why she had such "useless" feelings. He had also voiced his disbelief that she could end up in this "inpatient ward for psychos." (The session was taking place in a highly respected facility specializing in women's issues.) Joe seemed oblivious to the fact that his abusive behavior continually reinforced his wife's low self-image. "She gets out of hand," he stated matter-of-factly, "and I have no choice but to get her back in line, to motivate her to get out of that damned bed and take care of those kids she said she wanted."

It became clear to me that Joe adhered to strict role stratification that was defined entirely by his view of the way things should be. He ruled, she obeyed, or else she received massive doses of "emotionally poisonous" treatment, as Porterfield calls it (1989). Jane never uttered a statement questioning his definition of her. I was not sure whether she believed his view or endured her private agony in silence.

Moments before the session ended, I looked at Jane and said, "I want to tell you something. I want you to listen very carefully, and I want you to believe what I say. Of all the things I ever say to you, this one thing is absolutely true. You know how we can know things without questioning where the knowledge came from? We just know that we know?" She nodded an affirmative answer while staring directly at me. Joe was fidgeting nervously with his keys, looking very uncomfortable and impatient with the interaction taking place without his full inclusion. "What I am going to tell you is one of those kinds of knowing statements—not to be analyzed, just taken in and believed. And I do know what I know because I trust that intuitive part of me. There's a part of you that has never been tainted, never been touched by all the harm done to you—an essence that is as pure, as whole, perfect, and complete as the day you were born. It is there; we only have to uncover it from all the debris put on it/you by those who have tried to tell you who you are, tried to take from you what you are. They cannot succeed. That essence is there, just as innocent, just as invincible as it ever was, Jane."

Jane was speechless but very intense as she searched my eyes for any signs that might show doubt about what I was saying. Since she found none, she sat in silence. Given no space to talk, her husband remained crouched motionless against the side of the couch.

As suddenly as it had begun, the silence was broken by Jane's soft, yet firm voice, "I felt what you said; I mean, there was a quickening in my stomach—an actual physical response, as if I were feeling the first movements of new life inside me." There was as much wonder and awe in her look as in her statement. It was clear that she had assimilated on a deep, deep level the words I had spoken.

After the couple left my office, I began to assess how my "intervention" seemed to have affected the marriage. Jane was coming home again, home to herself, maybe for the first time since early childhood. Even though "home" had negative connotations for Jane, I thought of that metaphor because of the framing T. S. Eliot gives to the word "home":

> We shall not cease from exploration
> And at the end of all our exploring
> Will be to arrive where we started
> And know the place for the first time.

(1970, p. 129)

The shift I sensed and saw in Jane—the new power—came from the connection we had made with one another and she had made with herself. I believed this would alter the impact Joe had on her—this man she believed had irreparably damaged her. Joe seemed altered also. He looked less certain that he could regularly annihilate her in order to feel like "the boss," "the strength," "the major force in the marriage." After I made an empathetic statement to Joe, he stayed silent, continuing to stare at the wall. I eventually said, "Joe, you know this session can result in opening up many options in the relationship. In a sense you both can now take steps you were unable to make before this moment. I imagine that both you and Jane felt imprisoned by the roles each of you felt you had to play." I hoped that my invitation toward freedom would reassure the "jailer" as much as the "prisoner." I knew that both roles are indeed imprisoning.

My interventions with my clients are almost always instinctual on my part, just as this one was. I lead from my intuition and go from my heart into their hearts. I believe that we must teach ourselves to hear with our hearts. We must learn to understand with our intuition, with our higher wisdom, not with our minds, or with our necessarily biased intellect.

In my earliest training to be a therapist, I remember audiotaping a session for a class in graduate school. I was then asked to go back to each interaction and justify why I had said each thing I had said. I discovered that there was a logical progression stemming from the belief that I must enable patients to discover within themselves that light that no amount of darkness can eradicate. They must make this discovery if they are going to make any lasting changes. Evidently, during my journey in therapy, someone had helped me know (trust) that I also had a light that never failed me, and that I must allow it to shine.

My theoretical foundation stems from my spiritually based understanding of the universe: We are here to re-member who we are. I believe that life's purpose is for us to know that we belong to and are part of God. Thus, our essence is as pure, as innocent, and as free of illusion as it was when we were born. Whatever attacks we sustain from another being in human form, it is really another child of God crying out for love, for help, albeit in a very distorted way.

Just how much the intervention affected Jane showed in a symbolic way two days later in an individual session. That day she brought in with her a trivet she had made during occupational therapy. She said that, until now, she had always broken every piece of art she had made. It was quite frightening to her to keep this piece intact and to show it to me. She held it tightly to her chest for the first 15 minutes of the session as she gave this report about how she had previously dealt with her creativity. Finally, she slowly pulled the trivet down to her lap and allowed me to see it. It was perfectly balanced, with two major colors and a central piece of a third color—one small tile. She said, "You know, I thought a lot about what you said, and I must tell you that I had a very difficult time putting that piece in the center. I'd take it out and put it in and take it out. Finally, I just took the glue and placed the piece into its spot."

I said, "Jane, that is an incredible statement of your belief in what I told you." The tiny piece of tile she had placed in the center of this perfectly balanced trivet was a brilliant red heart, showing up so brightly that it looked as if it might beat as she again placed it near her chest in silence.

Indeed, Jane had come home again, but now with all the power and new life she needed within her to begin to heal.

REFERENCES

Eliot, T. S. (1970). *Collected poems 1909–1962*. New York: Harcourt, Brace, Jovanovich.
Porterfield, K. (1989). *Violent voices*. Deerfield Beach, FL: Health Communications.

20

PEGGY PAPP

It's the Same All Over

A T THE International Family Therapy Conference in Prague in 1988, I stood before hundreds of people from the East and from the West and began to speak about gender inequality. Afraid that my talk would be met both by the official denial of gender inequality in the East and by pat rationalizations in the West, I was stunned at the applause when I said, "There is one issue that cuts across all national boundaries, indeed, all boundaries of race, color, and creed—that is the issue of gender which exists in every country in the world where there are families. It is impossible to talk about love, marriage, sex, intimacy, and childrearing without taking into account gender inequalities."

Because I thought the applause must have come mainly from the women in the audience, I asked a group of husbands from both the East and the West if anything I had said seemed at all relevant to their lives or work. Their replies were remarkably similar to those of the women and related primarily to the domestic arena: "What do you think we hear from our wives the minute we open the door at night? 'I have two jobs while you only have one,' 'I have to take responsibility for everything,' 'You never help me with the baby, the laundry, the cooking.' And we hear the same complaints from the wives in the therapy we do."

Despite the rapid changes taking place in the world, this age-old problem never seems to change. One wonders, did Eve complain about Adam's lack of responsibility in the Garden of Eden?

The unfairness of double duty is such a common complaint from women in therapy that most therapists are bored with it and would prefer to tangle with "deeper," more "meaningful" issues. Therefore, they give it short shrift or get bogged in superficial details as to whose turn it is to do the dishes rather than address the basic attitudes and beliefs about gender that each husband and wife brings to the situation. Both men and women still think of the home as the wife's domain. Like the Little Red Hen, the wife finds it easier to do things herself than to try and change her husband's attitude. But her abiding resentment of the unfair burden reverberates throughout the marriage and colors every aspect of their relationship. Women need the support of therapists in validating the importance of this issue, and men need to become aware of the disparity between the lip service they pay to equality and what they actually do.

The following case deals with this universal problem. The therapy focuses on challenging the basic beliefs and assumptions of a couple on several different levels. (Evan Imber-Black served as my consultant, observing from behind the one-way mirror.)

A MATTER OF LIFE AND DEATH

The B. couple came to therapy in the midst of a crisis in which parity in the domestic area had quite literally become a matter of life and death because of the birth of a premature baby. The baby needed 24-hour observation due to a respiratory problem. This requirement rendered the couple's regular routines obsolete and, in fact, dangerous to the life of the baby. The mental and physical health of the mother and of the marriage were also at stake.

The husband and wife considered themselves to be a modern, liberated couple. Married five years, they looked like the ideal, white, upper-middle-class, all-American pair—tall, blonde, and beautiful; well-educated and successful; committed to their relationship; intelligent and insightful.

For the past five months, Terry, the wife, had been dividing her time between a high-paying job and the crisis unit at the hospital where the baby was on the critical list. By the time the couple came for therapy, the baby had improved and was to be sent home in three weeks. Terry's panic at the thought of continuing to bear the major responsibility for running the home, taking care of a three-year-old, and keeping the new baby alive prompted the call to our institute.

In the first session, Terry stated that there was very little physical or emotional partnership in handling the stress. Her major concern was with

Arthur's lack of initiative. Arthur "spaced out" when he came home, the very time when she needed him most. She was left to get dinner, put their three-year-old child to bed, straighten the house, pick up clothes, and so on. She responded to this situation in the stereotypical way, first by nagging, then by doing everything herself and feeling resentful.

Arthur responded to Terry's complaints by saying, "As a couple we suffer from traditional differences of roles and expectations as to how the household should be run and who should do what. I think I probably don't do a lot of the things one would do in a truly evolved relationship, although I've come a long way." He credited most of his wife's complaints to her "overreacting" and being "temperamentally different" from him. He stated that he needed more "space and privacy" than his wife. They had different ideas about how the household should be run. He was not as particular as his wife and believed in letting certain things "just slide." In response, Terry said that if she let things "just slide," they would never get done. Since the beginning of their marriage, she had been dissatisfied with the inequality in their domestic arrangement. She had been willing to pay the price for the sake of keeping peace in what she considered to be an otherwise very good marriage.

Now, she was no longer willing to pay that price since the well-being of their child was involved. She believed it was imperative for Arthur to become more "aware and more engaged." Although he had agreed to share in the caretaking of the baby once it came home from the hospital, Terry did not trust Arthur to be "alert and observant."

In my consultation with Evan, we agreed that whatever other problems might exist in this couple's relationship, the current crisis centered on the "second shift." But this was not simply a case of dividing the caretaking tasks more equally. What needed to be challenged and changed first was the couple's belief system concerning the roles of men and women. Arthur believed that the problem lay in "temperamental differences" and that it was natural for him to "space out" because he needed more "privacy and space" than his wife. Terry believed she must pay the price of doing double duty to preserve an otherwise good marriage. She kept assuming responsibility for an unfair portion of the burden. Since these people prided themselves on being sophisticated and intellectually up-to-date, we decided to begin challenging their beliefs by connecting their struggle to the wider cultural revolution taking place today. We did so by asking them to read a recently published book by Arlie Hochschild, *The Second Shift*. The book carefully documents the inequality in hours and responsibility that exists in two-career couples and presents statistics showing that women have changed their role drastically over the past few years while men have changed theirs very little. Hochschild interviews and observes husbands and wives over an eight-year period and carefully records their behavior, thoughts, and feelings as they struggle with the dilemma of the second shift. The couples' stories are personal and poignant, and the book provides many insights into the beliefs, myths, and attitudes about gender that get activated in the domestic scene.

We used the book as a third party in the therapy. It served as a base from which to examine the couple's own myths and beliefs, and the way these became activated in their marriage. It also gave us, as therapists, a way of sidestepping the possibility of Arthur's feeling that he was being ganged up on by three women. The book provided an objective outside voice that avoided a personal indictment.

Terry and Arthur were asked to read the book separately and to write down their thoughts about which couples they identified with, which experiences were most familiar to them, what they liked or did not like about the various ways the couples coped with their situation, and in what specific ways they would like their own marriage to be the same or different from the couples in the book. Hochschild divides marriages into three different categories: the traditional, the transitional, and the egalitarian. I asked Terry and Arthur to decide which category best described their relationship and which category they wished were most descriptive of it.

DEVELOPING AWARENESS

Terry and Arthur each had an intense but different reaction to the book. Arthur came with it under his arm and stated, "I thought it was an amazing book." He saw in it a "summation of our attempts over the past five years to reconcile these differences. We could have been in this book. I saw myself in a lot of the men and it was very disturbing. Most men perform badly in the second shift. It represented my worst nightmare about myself and the way I perform in this marriage."

His worst nightmare was that he would be a "traditional" husband and would not carry his share of the burden. In exploring this nightmare further, I asked what messages he had received from his parents about how men and women should perform in a marriage. He said he had grown up in a traditional household. He saw his father as being "autocratic" and his mother as being "sweet, accommodating, and conciliatory." He tried hard not to be the kind of old-fashioned husband his father was, but he saw himself behaving like his father at times. He placed their marriage in the "transitional" category.

Terry described her reaction to the book in a different way. She stated, "It was the most depressing book I have ever read because of the state of our culture and the part men play in it. I found even more depressing the tricks women play on themselves and the myths they use to rationalize and justify all this junk in their lives in order to keep the status quo." She had started thinking about the myths she grew up with. Like her husband, she had grown up in a traditional household with her father believing that men should work and that women should stay home and take care of the children. Her mother did not share this belief but acted in accordance with it because she had "no choice."

As she described her life, Terry kept repeating phrases having to do with "choices." She saw her father as having all the "choices" in life. He was "strong-willed, competitive, and aggressive." She became a successful business executive and tried to model herself after her father, but when she became a wife and mother, she felt she had "no choice" but to perform more like her mother. She saw herself as following in her mother's footsteps, and she saw her marriage as being "traditional."

DIFFERENT CHOICES

As a result of the book, Arthur and Terry started thinking about some of the ideas and behavior they were carrying over from their parents' generation. Neither wanted a relationship built on the model of their parents' marriages. Although they had disagreed on the kind of marriage they themselves now had—Arthur putting it in the category of "transitional" and Terry insisting it was "traditional"—both agreed they wanted a more "egalitarian" relationship.

We discussed ways they could begin to make different choices from those their parents had made and different choices from the ones they were now making. In order to help them to bridge the gap between their ideal and their reality, I asked them to observe and write down which choices they were making in their daily lives that they considered "traditional," which they considered "transitional," and which they considered "egalitarian." I asked them not to discuss this listing with each other but to bring their ideas to the next session. We would then compare them and see if they were each making the same or different choices in different areas.

CHOICES BY DEFAULT

True to form, Arthur did not get around to making a list, while Terry made a very long one. She discovered it was filled with "traditional details" which she carried out not by "choice" but by "default." Besides caring for the children and running the home, the list included making out Christmas cards, writing thank you notes, shopping for gifts, writing school applications, grocery shopping, planning vacations, arranging their social calendar, and doing the laundry. She conceded that Arthur had been taking on more responsibility, but she was still carrying an unfair share of the burden.

At this point, Arthur's sense of fairness had reached its somewhat short limit, and the threat of further change compelled him to escape into intellectualization. He was willing to agree that Terry's list consisted of "traditional tasks," but he wanted to make it clear that he did not think that he had a "traditional outlook on marriage." Indeed, he said that he considered his wife to be his "equal" in making all the "big decisions" in life such as decisions about retirement, vacations, career moves, childrearing, and the family's general values.

Terry pointed out that while he considered their relationship to be "equal," she was doing all the "traditional" tasks. Arthur then impatiently agreed to take on more of these tasks but belittled them by saying, "After all, in terms of the cosmos, the laundry is no big deal." He then complained that the fun had gone out of their marriage. He realized that he needed to do these things in order for them to "evolve" to this "higher level" they were striving for; however, he hoped that when they reached this higher level, Terry would "lighten up." She was no fun anymore.

Terry said that she was aware of this change and that it bothered her also. Although she would like to do something about it, she did not know what to do. I suggested that she choose three of the tasks on her "default" list, ask Arthur to take them over, and see if she "lightened up" and was more fun. If so, their problem would be solved; if not, we would look elsewhere for a solution.

In changing beliefs, it is important to work on the action level as well as the conceptual level. Unless some new form of action is taken in relation to beliefs, examining them can become little more than an intellectual exercise. Yet, if action tasks are given too early in therapy without any understanding of the beliefs that sustain the problem, the results will tend to be superficial. A set of beliefs is best changed by working on both the cognitive and behavioral levels of the relationship.

LAUNDRY – A COSMIC ISSUE

One of the tasks Arthur agreed to take over was the laundry. Since there were no machines in their apartment, he took it to his office where there was a laundromat. He created quite a stir at the office as he dragged the laundry bags, soap, and bleach into his office. The doorman seemed to be the most upset by this overthrow of traditional values, saying, "Mr. B., a man in your position should not be doing laundry!" This incident aroused his revolutionary spirit, and Arthur began proselytizing about equal rights for women. The office became the public sphere he needed for presenting his new image of himself as a liberated husband.

Terry did indeed "lighten up." She tried to explain to Arthur that her better mood was not only the result of his becoming more involved but was also a result of her feeling validated and listened to. After all, Arthur had cared enough about their relationship to do something about it. But at the same time, she was beginning to become aware of her difficulties in letting go and allowing Arthur to take over and do things his way. She was always looking over her shoulder to see whether he was doing things "right." She worked this way at her office, but there it served her well. She stated, "I have begun to realize that one of my myths is that I want it all to be egalitarian, but I want it to be egalitarian in my way. When Arthur does something, I want him to do it the way I would do it."

She came to realize that in order to have an egalitarian relationship that would enable her to have "choices," she would have to give up the choice of supervising Arthur's housework.

By the time the baby came home, Terry and Arthur were working cooperatively as a team. Their ability to make new and different choices sustained them through some nerve-wracking emergencies and the long ordeal of the baby's recovery. Arthur became more "intuitive" about the baby's needs, a change which allowed Terry to trust him enough so that she could relax and tolerate his doing things his way.

WRITING THEIR OWN CHAPTER

After several sessions of their reporting that things were going well, Evan and I decided that their own ideas were better than any we could offer at this point. I suggested a two-month vacation from therapy with the stipulation that they reserve the time of the therapy hour to hold their own session. They should use the time to talk about how they would present themselves if they were a couple in the book, *The Second Shift*. How would they describe the process through which they changed their ideas and behavior? What were the most difficult problems to overcome? How did they deal with them? What had they learned that they would like to pass on to other couples? This idea gave them a sense of being pioneers and connected them with a new generation that was changing the ideas of previous generations.

At the time of this writing, we are looking forward to our follow-up meeting.

SUMMARY

This case focused on changing the beliefs and behavior of a couple whose presenting crisis centered around the inequities in the "second shift." The therapists clarified the nature of the couple's crisis and placed it at a cultural level through the recommended reading of a book, *The Second Shift*. The book became a third party in the therapy and was used to facilitate an examination of the individual beliefs of each spouse and the way these beliefs were being enacted in their relationship. A historical perspective was provided by connecting their beliefs to intergenerational themes.

During the course of the therapy, the couple was able to change the marriage from "traditional" to "transitional" to "approaching egalitarian." At the end of the therapy, we asked our clients to write their own chapter about themselves. This task gave them a sense of themselves as part of a great modern revolution taking place in our time. It also implied that they might have something of value to teach others because they had learned from others themselves. Finally, it placed the therapists in a position of observer/researcher rather than guide/expert.

REFERENCE

Hochschild, A. C., with Machang, A. (1989). *The second shift: Working parents and the revolution at home*. New York: Viking.

21 🍎

RONALD TAFFEL

"Why Is Daddy So Grumpy?"

SEVEN-YEAR-OLD JENNIFER sat across from me on the floor and asked, "I know my daddy loves us, but why is he so grumpy all the time? Why does he get so mad at Mommy and me? How come he doesn't like to play?"

Jennifer's confusion did not surprise me, nor did it seem to be simply a product of her age. Our own psychological literature (and our everyday language) have long described men as obsessional (preoccupied and distant), compulsive (rigid and controlling), narcissistic (self-absorbed and fragile), and schizoid (remote, absent and unfeeling). These words are not only pejorative, but they confuse and obscure the underlying depression that many men experience—and that many women feel they must take care of.

Jennifer's parents fit this description. Her mother, Joan, was the classic caretaker. Although Joan worked full time, Jennifer's eating disorder, her obesity, her out-of-control, aggressive behavior, and her fears about death were believed by all members of the family to be the result of *Joan's* deficiencies in parenting. "There is a problem between Jennifer and me. I'm disappointed in her. I'm impatient with her. I'm abnormally involved with her," is how she thought of it. "What about Peter?" I asked. "What part does he play in her symptoms?" "Peter? He's not really the problem. Sure, he gets frustrated easily and is irritable a lot; it's often like walking on eggshells around him—but *that's the way men are*. You expect it. Let's face it, the real difficulty is with me." What did Peter have to say? "Let's face it, the real difficulty is with Joan."

However, as I saw it, the problem was that no one, except Jennifer in her childlike way, understood that Peter was more than irritable. No one recognized the existence of his depression, because his behavior had been normalized by their gendered expectations. He was simply being "a difficult man."

When I use the term depression here, I do not mean it in its formal, clinical sense, which implies loss of job and social performance, disturbances in sleep and appetite, lack of motivation, inability to concentrate, and fluctuations in mood (APA, 1980, p. 210). The combination of economic responsibilities, being looked after by other family members (usually women), and socially sanctioned, mood-regulatory behaviors such as drinking and violence keep most men from having to experience outright depressive episodes.

If we suspend formal diagnostic criteria for a moment, however, the distinction between depression and the everyday state of many men is not so clear-cut. What should we call someone who does not feel very much, who has no real friendships, who has few interests other than work, and who cannot relate to the people close at hand? How should we think of someone who is chronically agitated, angry, critical, restless, and explosive, or at the other end of the continuum, chronically passive, silent, worried, withdrawn, and morose?

Most of the time, both in our private and professional lives, we gather these qualities under the umbrella of the "difficult" man. Over the years, I have come to a different conclusion. I now take such descriptions as red flags signaling that a man may be depressed, and that this depression is hidden by gendered expectations of the way men are supposed to be.

If the description of Peter is recognizable, Joan's role as caretaker is just as familiar. Like most women, she had been socialized, from an early age, to look after other people before herself—to adapt her behavior to the needs of those around her. Therefore, when Peter's mood gets out of hand, she feels responsible and blames herself. She has not protected him adequately from the children's demands, thus leaving him feeling overwhelmed and exhausted. She has said the wrong thing, thus precipitating a bout of moroseness on his part which can last hours or, perhaps, days. She has erred in her scheduling of events, thus producing a logistical gridlock around the house, a bunching up of chores and responsibilities so "bad" that he just wants to leave and get away from things.

Just as Peter's irritable moodiness was labeled as normal by the family, Joan's nagging, resentful, and sometimes mocking efforts to regulate his moods were also considered normal by Peter, consistent with familial and cultural expectations of the way women are supposed to be. Neither Peter nor Joan saw anything unusual in this "battle of the sexes," yet neither was happy with this state of affairs. Peter blamed Joan (and the kids) for his continued internal dissatisfaction. No matter how well he did in the out-side world, he still felt a sense of inadequacy; he still had not quite mea-sured up to what his hopes about life had been. Joan, for her part, found the very qualities that attracted her to Peter—his decisiveness, his drive to succeed, his character as a man of "action, not words,"—had slowly worn away to reveal just another difficult man. After a decade of marriage, she found herself responsible for regulating his "moods," this task on top of looking after her children, her parents, her younger sister, and, to some degree, his parents.

From my perspective, the therapeutic task was to help Joan establish greater power by seeing Peter's depression and her caretaking role clearly, and to help Peter accept greater responsibility for the regulation of his own troubled moods.

REDEFINING THE PROBLEM

The first step was to take Jennifer's and Joan's reports about Peter as accurate descriptions that had been incorrectly interpreted. Jennifer be-lieved that Peter's irritability was her fault—that she was a "bad girl." Joan believed it was because he was simply being a man, and also because she was not doing her job as wife and mother well enough. Peter himself believed that he was irritable because of *them*, because of their demands on his time and patience. *Nobody* believed Peter's moodiness to be central to Jennifer's symptoms.

To redefine the presenting problem, I always begin by using the family's "difficult man" adjectives as a starting point for a detailed developmental history. I found that Peter had been irritable even as a young boy. In fact, as I got him to describe his life, it became clear that he had always been an agitated person—easily riled, a worrier, ever on the move. "There have been very few mornings when I wake up," Peter told us, "that I don't have a feeling of dread about what could happen that day." Over the space of several sessions, the couple was able to see Peter's irritability as something much more formidable—a depressive "angst" that pre-dated Joan, the chil-dren, and his business.

FAMILY-OF-ORIGIN INQUIRY

I next turned to their families of origin. I asked Joan, "Besides Peter's expectations, why do you think it's your responsibility to regulate his moods? Who else have you seen do this in your family?" Not surprisingly, her genogram revealed three generations of mothers/wives who all (with varying degrees of resentment, rage, submission, and contempt) had taken care of "difficult" men.

Upon closer examination, each of these men were, in fact, much more than just difficult. Their moods were erratic enough to create an undertow in the home. Whether they made the foundations of the house shake with their restless, possessive, critical, demanding moodiness, or whether they disappeared into the woodwork with their passive, flat, inhibited, worrying moods, these men pulled down the mood of everyone around them. In addition, they *all* looked to their wives and children to make them feel better.

Peter's genogram also revealed the shadow of depressed men. As is so often the case, generations of agitated, depressed men alternated with generations of passive, depressed men. Peter's father was a worrier who was dominated by his wife. His grandfather ruled like a despot.

CHALLENGING THE EXTERNALIZATION
OF RESPONSIBILITY

When the depressive/caretaker dynamic had been understood by the couple and anchored in a three-generational context, I began to challenge it. I asked Peter, "What would you need to do to be the first man in your family to take care of your own condition without your wife doing it for you?" Since Peter was 60 pounds overweight, with a history of unmonitored high blood pressure, and had not had a physical exam in almost 10 years, making a doctor's appointment seemed a good place to start. Joan's task was to try to let Peter do it—to not become impatient or badger him or make the appointment herself.

As one would expect, the task took many sessions to accomplish, with each falling into familiar roles. Peter kept forgetting. Joan kept reminding. Finally, they announced that an appointment had been made. As a testament to their depressive/caretaker enmeshment, they scheduled themselves to see the doctor for a joint physical exam.

Scaled down though this "victory" was, it was a turning point. Peter's blood pressure turned out to be seriously high, and his cholesterol was over 300. The doctor said he was a "coiled spring, a heart attack waiting to happen." This news further shifted the focus away from Jennifer as the sick or bad child, and from Joan as the overinvolved, problem-creating mother. It reframed Peter as being in the thick of the family's problems—a man in trouble. Once again, of course, the central question was whether Joan would take care of Peter or whether he would be responsible for his own vulnerable state.

As older daughters often do, Jennifer helped with this dilemma. While Joan held herself back from assuming total responsibility for Peter's health, Jennifer stepped into the void. She was so excited that Peter might go on a diet that she offered to begin "eating healthy" along with him. It was striking to see how relieved Jennifer was by her father's efforts at self-nurturance. They fixed meals together and went food shopping every week. Peter's newfound candor about his situation set an example. Jennifer announced to her classmates and her parents' friends that she needed help from everyone to eat healthier. Could they include fruit and vegetables at parties, not just cake and candies?

This change had systemic reverberations. The less responsible for Peter's condition Joan felt, the better she was able to respond to Jennifer. She set limits on Jennifer's aggressive behavior without feeling so guilt-ridden. Interestingly, as she saw Peter in more realistic ways, she gave up her idealized picture of who Jennifer ought to be. Many of the family's complaints started to diminish.

POWER REALIGNMENT

Within six months, Jennifer's tantrums had almost entirely disappeared, along with her secret binge-eating. Peter had lost 40 pounds. His cholesterol and blood pressure levels were down to high-normal. Peter still wakes up with dread on many mornings, but he no longer blames his wife for these feelings. He still wishes that she could make things better, but he does not *demand* that she do so.

The difference between Peter's wishing and his demanding is a big one for Joan. Caretakers, of course, always neglect themselves, and Joan was no exception. Joan decided to take over the family's finances, something she had wanted to do for years in order to remove herself from Peter's impatient scrutiny. In a related self-nurturing move, Joan began struggling with a 20-year, two-pack-a-day, cigarette habit. Jennifer's fears of her parents' dying had already disappeared, but she was further encouraged by her mother's commitment to self-care. Now that she is less focused on the family, she is busy with the usual concerns for her age such as dressing right and refining her expertise in tasteless movies.

Finally, in an empowering move for herself, Joan has started learning how to drive, a project that she had wanted to do for some time but had put off. Peter wonders how useless he will feel if Joan does not need him to drive her around anymore. "Don't worry," Joan laughs, seeing the edges of a bad mood start to form around Peter's eyes. "Maybe I'll only drive during the Super Bowl and the World Series. You'll be better off for it."

They both know that she is joking and that she is serious about wanting to drive. But, for an instant, the power of the depressive/caretaker relationship is once again painfully apparent in the room.

REFERENCE

American Psychiatric Association. (1980). *Diagnostic and statistical manual of mental disorders* (3rd ed.). Washington, DC: Author.

22

MARIANNE WALTERS

"The Horse Isn't Dead Yet!"

"SHE'S CRAZY. You can always count on her to start something unpleasant. We all know it. She's, she's, well, she's like, well, not normal; she's, well, hyper. Always aggravated. The best you can do is to figure out how to get out of the way of her barbs, her zingers. We all know she's like that. If you say white, she says black. She's mean. She's crazy. So there's no way Christmas will be fun. She just chews on everything. And nothing satisfies her; nothing is ever right. Oh, I know, I know. Everyone blames their mothers. And all the psycho books . . . it's all about mother problems. And, well, I've been in therapy before, and you're led to believe, well, and all the articles. It's mother this and mother that. It's like beating a dead horse, except, in my case, well, I think the horse isn't dead yet!"

This is the voice of Allison preparing herself to go home for Christmas. She is a 26-year-old graduate student in urban planning, mildly bulimic, gay, stunningly good-looking, articulate, funny, and deeply self-involved. She is in therapy because she is having difficulty with intimate relationships, she often gets depressed, she wants to manage her eating disorder better, and she wants to find ways to deal with her family about her sexual preference. I am doing a consultation with one of my supervisees who has been seeing her through 10 months of successful therapy. She has been successful in helping Allison to be more self-directed and to feel more in charge of her life. School is going well, and she is in a satisfying relationship that has been helping her to gain control over her destructive eating patterns. But Allison keeps getting stuck in feelings of alienation and anger in relation to her parents, especially her mother. The consultation occurred shortly before Christmas, when Allison was becoming increasingly agitated and anxious about her impending visit home for the holidays.

Allison describes her mother as an angry, vindictive person who is always finding fault and who cannot be trusted. Both parents are hard-working; her mother is a homemaker, and her father is a foreman in the automotive industry. Allison is the middle of three children; she has an older brother and a younger sister, all of whom have been helped to obtain a college education. Her mother seems to "always be working," picking up, taking care, worrying. When her children were young, she made all their clothes, always prepared a hot breakfast, and walked them to school. Allison's father was the "good times" parent—the one who took them out for ice cream. Her mother was the one who was always worrying about money, about the bills, about college, about possessions. She "never lets up."

MW   So, how are holidays celebrated in your family? ALLISON   My mother does it all. She always does. She never lets anyone help her, so we don't try. Then she'll bitch about it and try to make everyone feel guilty. Ah, yes, all those warm memories of family togetherness.

MW   So, if you made a favorite dish for the holiday dinner, she'd . . .

ALLISON   She'd hate it. It wouldn't be done right. It wouldn't fit in with her plans. If she had to, she would get up early in the morning to do all the shopping so no one could help.

MW   You've tried?

ALLISON   Yeah, and all she did was complain, criticize. Her whole life is work, work, work—keep moving.

MW   How does she relax?

ALLISON   She doesn't.

MW   How do you help her to relax? What happens when you try to help her? Does she fight you?

ALLISON   Well, hmmmm, geez, I don't think I've ever really tried. I didn't, I don't really trust her.

MW   Allison, it feels so grim. So tell me, what makes your Mom laugh? How do you get your Mom to laugh?

ALLISON   What makes her laugh? (*long pause*) What makes my Mom laugh? Well, I don't think I've ever thought about that. I don't know. I guess she appreciates a good joke—not one at her expense, but a good joke.

MW   You mean like something ironic?

ALLISON   Well, no, she's not that bright. Not that she's dumb, mind you, but you know, she's spent her whole life in small towns, didn't go to college.

MW   You know your mother well. You know her. Daughters often don't really know their mothers. That's nice. So what sort of joke makes her laugh? What does she enjoy?

ALLISON   Well, let's see. I think a good wise-ass remark. Yeah, like a put on, something spontaneous, like a funny comment on something that's going on. Yeah, that really does get her.

MW   Like what, Allison. Give me an example. I know you can be sort of a wise-ass sometimes.

Creating an experience of power in therapy is often about helping a client to move from a "victim position" to a place where she can begin to know herself as effective and significant in shaping her experience with others, particularly with those others who have seemed to be emotionally inaccessible. The task for the therapist, then, is to change the terms of the discourse. When someone is used to thinking and talking about what "hurts" and what is "wrong," exploring this misery can, in fact, exacerbate the helplessness and sense of powerlessness. To offer a different context in which to construct a new vision, we use whatever personal resources of the client are most available—in this instance, Allison's ever-ready sense of humor—to open areas of possibility for change. Of course, it is essential to validate the lived experience of the client, but it is equally important not to be held hostage to it.

For a person to be able to make a difference in the life of another, to know that one matters, that one can affect the way in which an event will play itself out—these are experiences of power as surely as setting limits, defining a "bottom line," or controlling one's space. To know what we do and how we do it is significant knowledge, that is, to be able to put into words for oneself the particular ways one uses to connect with others. Finding the power to take charge of one's life is dependent on the capacity to own one's need of another. These were some of the concepts guiding our work with Allison and her relationship with her mother. The poignancy of her struggle was revealed when we talked of gift giving.

MW   So, what sort of thing have you given your mother in the past that she has enjoyed receiving?

ALLISON   Well, not much. Well, actually, I've made her tapes of music that I know she likes.

MW   And how has she let you know she likes it?

ALLISON   Well, she'll say, "I really like this."

MW   And what do you say?

ALLISON   I say, "I'm glad you like it."

MW   And then what happens?

ALLISON   Well, nothing. I guess we just change the subject.

MW   And if you told her that it makes you feel good, that it makes you happy when she likes something you do for her?

ALLISON   Oh, God, I couldn't say that. Why couldn't I say that? (*starting to cry*) It sounds so simple. Why is it so hard, so hard? I don't think I could say that. Why is it so hard?

It is indeed hard to build a sense of one's personal power when it involves acknowledging one's need to matter to another, and so people, especially parents and children, often fall into behaviors with each other that deny their mutual need to make each other feel good. Changing the terms of the discourse with Allison in ongoing therapy meant building and maintaining her belief that, rather than just reacting to experiences, she has resources that could be used to transform them.

23

DANIEL J. WIENER

"You Wanna Play?"

ROSE AND ALAN, who had been married seven years and who were
both 41, came in for their fifth couples therapy session battling again.
As in our previous sessions, Rose accused Alan of not keeping his promise
to find steady employment, a charge that Alan took in impassively at first.
As Rose broadened her criticisms, Alan began to interrupt her, explaining
to me the reasonableness of his inaction. Rose countered by ridiculing his
explanation, whereupon Alan, with visible affect for the first time in the
session, complained that she was "hitting below the belt." Rose turned to
me, saying, in a dignified manner, that she could not respect Alan anymore. Over the next few minutes, Alan tried to enlist me in labeling Rose
"unreasonable." When I declined, he derided therapy as a waste of money
and stated that Rose had provoked his inaction by her punitive attitude.
Rose's dignified composure vanished as she mounted another angry attack
on Alan's selfishness and lack of responsibility. We were back to where
we started.

My inner reaction to their quarreling was surprisingly strong; I felt
sadness and concern, even anxiety. As a young, only child, I had witnessed
many such scenes between my "grasshopper" father and my "ant" mother.

My approach in this case example is guided by my training in and experience with improvisa-
tional theater (improv), particularly the approach of Keith Johnstone (1979). From the start, I
wish to acknowledge the contribution of my wife, Gloria Maddox, who has been my teacher,
co-presenter, and consultant in applying improv to family therapy over the past five years.

I remembered that I had been ineffectual in deflecting my parents from their tense, angry clashes until I would begin to cry, whereupon they would be distracted in attending to my distress. Thus, in my own experience, a shift in the prevailing emotional climate had worked. I first asked Rose and Alan if they wished to alter this quarreling; both of them agreed that they did. I told them that it was painful to see them go on in this way (although another part of me noticed that *they* were none too dismayed at what had happened), that it was evident that they cared a great deal about one another, and yet, that each was unable to let go of making the other wrong. I asked if they were willing to try some exercises to escape this frustrating quarreling. Warily, they agreed.

A construct of great importance in improv and of considerable value to family therapists is "status." Status here does not refer to "social standing" or "occupational prestige" but to behavior that creates a position of worthiness in relation to others. For example, traditionally socialized women frequently assume a low-status position around men; that is, they defer to men in their use of space, body posture, eye contact, vocal inflection, allowance of interruption, and use of qualifiers, as noted by numerous social scientists. Status, then, is a way of signaling dominance and submission in all social interaction; we are all constantly adjusting status in relation to others and to our surroundings. As there are no truly "status-neutral" transactions, much human interaction can be viewed as the struggle to avoid the devaluing consequences of having one's status involuntarily lowered.

In the way they quarreled, Rose and Alan seemed equivalent in their ability to denigrate one another. It might be concluded, therefore, that they were status equals. However, there is a crucial distinction between *playing* status and *having* status, a distinction typically overlooked in marital therapy. Often, wives play high status to their husbands in front of the therapist without having the power to elevate their real-life status outside of therapy. Rose and Alan presented with a typical belief system that located the power to solve the problem in the husband. Rose, though she lowered Alan's status, did not have high status herself and was at a disadvantage in relation to the *status quo*. Alan, though affected by Rose's criticism, was perceived by both as having the power to change or not, while Rose could only withhold or grant approval for Alan's choice.

Although I did not analyze the status transactions in any detail during the actual session, I was aware of the high-low status shifts that had occurred, and I knew from experience that this was a favorable sign of

Rose and Alan's flexibility. Couples who invariably assign the same status position to each spouse are far more difficult to shift out of these patterns. Though confident, I did not proceed with any highly developed plan because I knew that their reactions to the first exercise would guide further interventions.

After saying that I wished to explore the importance of winning and losing with them, I had Rose and Alan stand about six feet apart, facing one another and maintaining silence. I told them that there was a rope on the floor between them and that they were to have a "tug-of-war" on my signal. Both picked up the imaginary rope. At my signal, Rose began miming, pulling with great effort. Alan remained in position, neither pulling nor being pulled. Rose started getting angry.

I explained that the purpose of this exercise was to explore each one's commitment to winning/losing and that the stage reality did not allow a rubber rope. When one was hauling in rope, the other had to be pulled by it. After reminding them to attend closely to their partner, I signaled another round. This time, both mimed great effort, holding their positions static. After perhaps 15 seconds of this enactment, I called it off, asking each to describe the experience. Both reported feeling unwilling to yield to the other, and Rose added that she did not think Alan would ever let her win. I instructed them to experience taking turns yielding, but, nonetheless, to make the struggle real. When they did so (Alan "falling" theatrically), the atmosphere changed dramatically, with both of them laughing and chatting about the experience. I punned that they now seemed able to fall for one another, and we ended the session.

Improv is a method of acting that uses a minimum of prearranged structures such as plots, scripts, or props. The basic principles are: spontaneity, accepting offers, advancing action, supporting others to look good, and breaking routines. The context of improv is playful exploration. Friedman, writing about theater and therapy, notes:

So often in therapy, we attempt to alter the course of the family drama. Typically, however, the more serious the family is about the drama, the harder it is to induce the possibility of change. It is in an atmosphere of play, rather than intense seriousness, that such shifts are likely to take place. (1984, p. 26)

The therapeutic aim of using improv enactments is to guide family members to a heightened sense of intimacy within a context of playfulness, spontaneity, cooperation, and mutuality. Unlike conventional role-playing, neither the realism of roles nor the usual, assumed rules of social

interaction need apply. Applied to couples therapy, improv status enactments, in particular, are a useful way to explore status equality or reversal
without evoking hostility or fear. A more complete description of improv
and its value for family therapy is given in Wiener and Maddox (1988).

At the next session, Alan reported that he had spent considerable time
looking for a better-paying job, but that Rose had not been appreciative of
his efforts. Rose stated that she was aware of the improvement in Alan's
behavior, but that she did not want him to become complacent. The
atmosphere was significantly less hostile than during the previous session,
although each complained about the other's attitude.

After securing their consent to another exercise, I seated Rose on a
chair in the middle of the room and had Alan stand near a side wall. I
explained that Rose was to be a mistress and Alan her servant, and that
she was to summon him and give orders, and he was to comply with her
orders. Rose summoned Alan in a haughty tone and ordered him to
bring her tea at once. Alan complied behaviorally, but the scene lacked
authenticity. I stopped them and explained that, as her servant, Alan
needed to elevate Rose's status by deferring to her. When they redid the
scene, Alan was so obsequious that the effect was very comic. I then asked
Rose whether her character was satisfied by Alan's Servant. She replied
that she felt mocked rather than well served. I had them repeat the scene
again with Alan instructed to see to it that his mistress felt important and
well-cared for. This time, the undertone of mutual resentment was replaced by a sense of tenderness. Rose reported that, even though this was
make-believe, Alan had treated her in a way reminiscent of their courtship.
I congratulated them on having created such a satisfying scene together.

Status transactions, when directed by a therapist, become part of an "as
if" context where it is safer to explore alternatives to usual patterns. When
I had them reverse roles, Alan, as Master, found it awkward to give direct
orders at first; he reported that he felt apprehensive that Rose would
become angry with him in real life. I thought his apprehension well-
founded, given their oft-repeated sequence of Alan (calmly) lowering
Rose's status and Rose (angrily) lowering Alan's status. Then, we all discussed how they were not responsible for what their characters did with
my instructions, even though the feelings and reactions brought out during
this exercise were real. Alan made two more attempts; with minimal
coaching he enacted a benign master, elevating his own status without
devaluing Rose's servant.

It was significant to me that Alan had made the choice to explore this alternative when replaying the scene; he might instead have lowered Rose's status from an overtly domineering position. Each had now experienced being high-status without lowering the other, and had experienced supporting the other's high status without being lowered by it. It occurred to me afterwards that in both cases I had accomplished this shift by working directly only with Alan. In retrospect, I think it likely that I found it more expedient to work within the framework, noted above, of Alan's having the power to change.

Two sessions later, Rose came in happily reporting that Alan's part-time employer had offered him a full-time job. Alan looked uncomfortable. He stated that he still wished to find different work but that he would take the job in order to satisfy Rose. I suggested they discuss this decision and noticed that in their discourse they were being considerate of one another's feelings. Even so, I sensed an underlying tension. Alan appeared apprehensive that by turning down this steady job he would risk incurring Rose's wrath, while Rose seemed intent on not offering Alan any pretext to turn the job down.

I next had them repeat the Master/Servant exercise, but with the altered premise that the Servant was to find some pretext for not carrying out the order from the Master/Mistress without appearing insubordinate. Rose's Servant was tense and indignant to Alan's bemused, in-control Master:

MASTER   Where's the sugar for the tea?
SERVANT   (*tightly*) Sorry, it got used up yesterday.
MASTER   (*easily*) Well, then, go next door to borrow some.
SERVANT   (*upset*) But it's raining, and the sugar would get wet.

Throughout the brief scene, Rose looked miserable while Alan appeared at ease, a total reversal from their same roles in the Complying Servant exercise two weeks earlier.

What I thought had happened here was that Rose was feeling vulnerable to Alan's potential censure for her noncompliance. This hunch was confirmed when she complained that the instructions forced her character to be in the wrong. Even though the Master had been nice to her, she said, he had had the right to be angry with her. Evidently, Rose had assumed the legitimacy (high-status) of the Master's requests and felt compelled to allow herself to be criticized (low-status). In real life, Rose viewed her expectations that Alan keep his agreements as justifiable, and she viewed anger as a justifiable response to noncompliance. Therefore, in the improv, she was being consistent with her real-life beliefs, though her character need not have held these same beliefs. In the same way, an improviser often has his or her character avoid something that seems dangerous in real life.

When the roles were reversed, however, what emerged was quite unexpected. In an antic, glib style, Alan's Servant offered farfetched excuses that defeated the legitimacy of Rose's Mistress' orders, yet he did so without devaluing her character. Rose broke character, laughing and good-naturedly complaining to me that she could not stay angry with him. I coached her to keep in character and to find a way to justify, as the Mistress, any reactions she was having. What emerged was a scene with sexual innuendo between an elderly Mistress, trying to conceal her fondness for her young, charming Servant, and a vain, clever Servant who enjoyed being a naughty boy.

I was surprised to see both Rose's inability to get angry and the seductive element in Alan's underresponsibility that had emerged from this exercise. They had not previously revealed this aspect of their relationship in our therapy. Because I guessed that a similar dynamic operated elsewhere in their marriage, I inquired about it. They told me that this was similar to their lovemaking and had been more present during their courtship, along with Alan's previously noted tenderness. I also observed that Alan's voluntary low-status behavior seemed to prevent Rose's anger while leaving Alan with most of the power.

As we began to analyze what had occurred, I asked Alan and Rose to notice and describe their present feelings and to recollect their feelings in the roles they had just enacted. Rose was feeling some anxiety and reported having felt quite helpless in role; she had been unable to call forth the distancing function of her anger in order to feel in control and to be obeyed. Alan was feeling a mix of satisfaction at having gotten close to Rose during the exercise and some anger at his own Servant character for "getting away with such laziness." Both readily confirmed parallels in these roles to patterns in their families of origin.

With the experiences of these exercises to guide us, our therapy focused on how their marital interaction had deteriorated from the days of their courtship. Both had enjoyed the tenderness and playfulness of the past, yet when Alan did not keep his agreements, he found that his charm was ineffectual in preventing Rose's anger at him. Because he thought that what she wanted of him was to be dignified and "grown-up," he had taken a posture of reasonableness, only to find her further angered. Although

Rose also missed their former playfulness and warmth, she most wanted him to make a fair contribution to the relationship. In the status struggle that ensued, each reacted to the perceived devaluation of self by other by attempting to raise self-status at the other's expense.

The status improv enactments had offered Rose and Alan a safe opportunity to explore different positions. In the two examples reported here, the play context had allowed them to experience self and other in character in ways that would have been too threatening in reality. The enactments also made their status struggles transparent to them, something that verbal explanation alone would have been unlikely to achieve. With the struggle unmasked and alternatives rehearsed, they were able to establish quickly a partnership of mutual esteem as well as of playful intimacy. Alan agreed to take the full-time job for six months, while concurrently looking for a better one; he found a better job within that time. Therapy tapered off three sessions after their last enactment. At last report, Rose and Alan are enjoying their marriage.

REFERENCES

Friedman, E. (1984). The play's the thing. *The Family Therapy Networker, 8* (1), 26.

Johnstone, K. (1979). *IMPRO: Improvisation and the theatre.* New York: Theatre Arts Books.

Wiener, D. J., & Maddox, G. J. (1988). *Using theatre improvisation in family therapy practice and training.* Unpublished manuscript.

24

DONALD S. WILLIAMSON

If Not This Way, Then That

IT IS MY CONVICTION THAT male therapists are generally ineffective and inappropriate as consultants to women who are dealing with issues of "women and power." There may be rare exceptions to that general observation, but this writer is not one of them. The situation is perhaps analogous to a white person's seeking to instruct and enlighten a black person about the character and meaning of "the black experience." What I can do as a male therapist, and what I have come to do frequently over the years, is offer consultation to couples in situations where the woman is on the disadvantaged end of an unequal marital interaction, and the husband is locked into a dominating position in an intransigent and inaccessible fashion. Such couples are frequently referred to me because I have developed a way of working with these situations and with these men which, in many cases, is reasonably effective. It is not a method that is necessarily applicable or useful elsewhere.

I believe that direct and transparent conversation should always be the first choice in all human relationships, including professional psychotherapy relationships. However, there are a few situations—especially those that are convoluted and conflicted around power and control issues—where that does not seem to bring relief. It is that particular situation that I am addressing here, and it is that premise which underlies and qualifies everything that follows. The stance to be described is usually accepted well by men because I make it clear that no husband can present with any "shenanigans" that I cannot easily identify with, so in addressing him, I am addressing myself.

It is now generally accepted that an unequal marriage should be encouraged to move as closely as possible to an equal distribution of power. In my experience, the person in the less powerful position, at least as far as all the outward signs are concerned, is most often the woman. This circumstance explains the predisposition behind this clinical note which is organized around "women and power."

There are at least three different contexts in which, in a variety of ways, I address the issue of "women and power" in my everyday practice of family psychotherapy: couples therapy, women's support groups and family-of-origin mixed-gender groups. I usually work with aggressively dominant males who have already proved themselves highly resistant to change.

COUPLES THERAPY

Five strategies have proved useful to me in using therapeutic intervention to redress an imbalance of power in marital relationships.

1. The first is to de-scapegoat the "scapegoat," as in the case where the wife is expressing the symptoms for a dysfunctional marriage. This shift can be done either by focusing on or exaggerating the "pathology" of the husband. An alternative is to reframe the wife's symptoms in some benign fashion. The following dialogue illustrates the point that a playful and not fully rational intervention can sometimes soften the rigidity inherent in an interaction.

HUSBAND   I hate coming here when she just sits there depressed and won't talk.
THERAPIST   Why do you need her this way?
HUSBAND   I don't need this. I hate this.
THERAPIST   Then why do you pretend to your wife that you need this?
HUSBAND   I don't pretend I need this. Nobody needs this!
THERAPIST   Then why do you not let your wife know that you're not pretending to still need it? Which of course doesn't necessarily mean that you do need it?
HUSBAND   What?
THERAPIST   Why are you letting it continue to appear that you are still pretending to be pretending to need it?
HUSBAND   You're confusing me.

THERAPIST   Is that a lot better than being depressed?

HUSBAND   I can get depressed too.

THERAPIST   Yes, but not as good as your wife does it.

HUSBAND   I maybe could be!

THERAPIST   So maybe your wife is trying to help you out with that? Like . . . so you don't have to do it?

HUSBAND   (*irritated*) I know I don't have to.

THERAPIST   Yes, but what if you might have had to or will have to have to?

WIFE   (*chuckling*) This is getting very, very silly.

THERAPIST   (*to husband*) Now see what you've done to her.

At this moment, the marriage is poised, if temporarily, in a new and uncharted moment. Both parties are suddenly freed from the usual commitments to the same lines and, therefore, to the same actions. Because these "realities" are constructed in the head, playing with the head often seems to help.

2. One can intervene simply by reassigning or relocating the power with the wife rather than with the husband. This shift is readily done by explaining that when the husband is behaving very "help-fully" towards his wife, who is acting in unduly needy or dependent ways, he may simply be doing so at the covert and subtle dictates of his spouse. Furthermore, if the husband had been available to a more rational and good-natured approach to negotiating the relationship, obviously she would have preferred that approach and would not have been pressed to this one. Additionally, this description can bring the collusive character of the interaction a little closer to awareness.

Alternatively, one can describe the wife's symptomatic behavior as expressing very successful and imaginative power moves which have proved effective in achieving important (if still unidentified) goals. Further, these moves may reveal a problem-solving intelligence of which not even she has been fully conscious. In his deeper if unaware wisdom, the husband first chose her, in part, because of these skills.

As another option, one can explain that the wife's "problem behaviors" constitute a loving sacrifice intended to protect her husband from personal upset and distraction because he needs to go off early and work long and hard every day. Meeting the double demands of home and work comes naturally to women, but men, as a class, are relatively unskilled at dealing with emotional issues—both for social and biological reasons.

3. One can take a time-out and visit with the wife separately, if very briefly, during the course of a conjoint interview. One can use this brief conversation as a coaching session. The intent of this conversation is to boost the wife by offering suggestions for alternative things she can say and new behaviors she can adopt in the interactions with her husband. These uncharacteristic actions on her part are often destabilizing to the husband's power position. Again the goal is for her to achieve a more equal position in the relational transactions with her mate.

4. A male therapist can ask a female colleague to regularly visit alone with the wife, concurrently with the couples therapy. Over time, the female therapist can model empowered behavior which the wife can try out, practice, and, if comfortable, incorporate. This change on her part may result in the chagrin of her husband who may now need and benefit from some direct support from the male therapist.

5. If the situation is intractable enough, and sometimes it is, then sustained male-female co-therapy may be called for. The two therapists can thus have the support of each other and the strength and power of their relationship to combat the virulent destructiveness of the marital process they are confronted with. Where things are not quite this bad, the male therapist can seek episodic consultation from a female therapist. The latter can consult on power and control issues in both the therapeutic relationship and the marital relationship.

WOMEN'S SUPPORT GROUPS

As another context for intervention, I use small groups of four to six members, composed entirely of women, all of whom are engaged in family-of-origin work in general and the renegotiation of family politics in particular. This work necessarily includes the issue of women and power. This is a situation where having a female colleague is mandatory for sustained, effective results. In this case, the female consultant can act as a guarantor for and give credibility to the comments of the male therapist. The male therapist can play an Inspector Clouseau kind of figure. This playful stance encourages group members to "get it" more clearly and more quickly themselves and to help others "get it."

FAMILY-OF-ORIGIN MIXED-GENDER GROUPS

As a third context, I commonly use small gender-mixed, family-of-origin therapy groups of individuals aged between 30 and 45 years. All of these people are working on redistributing power and control across the inter-generational boundary between themselves and aging parents. Thus, the women in the group have an opportunity to work on power issues by working on the goal of redistributing power between the self and parents. Each one has an opportunity to review her personal style of relationship to her parents, and to develop more skill in dealing with power issues by dealing with *power politics at the source*. Beginning with the relationship between adult children and their parents has turned out to be a most effective method of helping both women and men empower themselves in the most important relationships in their social lives, including their mar-riage (Williamson, 1981, 1982a, 1982b).

Renegotiating and redefining the love relationship with father frees a woman to renegotiate the power and the politics of the relationship with her husband and all other men. Giving up father as the *number one love* in a woman's life is a crucial preparatory step. She humanizes father by seeing this aging man—who used to be Daddy—looking back on his life with mixed feelings of success and failure and looking forward to his own death with a mixture of hope and fear. Frequently, this perspective creates a context for an experience of shared humanity and mortality. Sharing at that level results in a mutuality of forgiveness that goes not simply back a generation in time, but forward into the next generation as well. In this way, intergenerational intimidation moves towards resolution. To forgive a parent is to offer oneself more compassion as parent. This process is an excellent preparation for equality and celebration in marriage.

If some of the ideas described above seem devious, we can remind ourselves that the conscious can never match the unconscious. Clients can always defeat the therapy if they stay committed to doing so, and they can continue to sabotage their own lives. In the particular pattern of chronic marital unhappiness being described here, if a man and a woman can move beyond the complementary roles of overacting patient and bogus therapist, then the marriage may have a genuine chance of healing both partners and again being the great natural therapy in our culture. The therapist will then have served a good purpose as consultant to the natural healing in the marriage.

REFERENCES

Williamson, D. S. (1981). Personal authority via termination of the intergenerational hierarchical boundary: A "new" stage in the family life cycle. *Journal of Marital and Family Therapy, 7*, 441–452.

Williamson, D. S. (1982a). Personal authority via termination of the intergenerational hierarchical boundary: Part II—The consultation process and the therapeutic method. *Journal of Marital and Family Therapy, 8*, 25–37.

Williamson, D. S. (1982b). Personal authority in family experience via termination of the intergenerational hierarchical boundary: Part III—Personal authority defined and the power of play in the change process. *Journal of Marital and Family Therapy, 8*, 309–323.

Index

NAMES

SUBJECT INDEX